BATTLE LINES
YPRES

NIEUWPOORT TO PLOEGSTEERT

The Ijzer Tower at Diksmuide.

BATTLE LINES YPRES

NIEUWPOORT TO PLOEGSTEERT

*The Western Front
by Car, by Bike and on Foot*

Jon Cooksey
and Jerry Murland

Pen & Sword
MILITARY

First published in Great Britain in 2012 by
PEN & SWORD MILITARY
an imprint of
Pen & Sword Books Ltd
47 Church Street
Barnsley
South Yorkshire
S70 2AS

ISBN 978 1 84884 793 4

A CIP catalogue record for this book is
available from the British Library.

Typeset in Palatino and Optima by
CHIC GRAPHICS

Printed and bound in India by
Replika Press Pvt. Ltd.

Pen & Sword Books Ltd incorporates the imprints of
Pen & Sword Aviation, Pen & Sword Maritime, Pen & Sword Military,
Wharncliffe Local History, Pen & Sword Select, Pen & Sword
Military Classics, Leo Cooper, Remember When,
Seaforth Publishing and Frontline Publishing

For a complete list of Pen & Sword titles please contact
PEN & SWORD BOOKS LTD
47 Church Street, Barnsley, South Yorkshire, S70 2AS, England
E-mail: enquiries@pen-and-sword.co.uk
Website: www.pen-and-sword.co.uk

CONTENTS

INTRODUCTION AND ACKNOWLEDGEMENTS

There are twenty-five detailed routes in this guide as well as several suggestions for additional excursions where information can be obtained from tourist information offices. The routes we have selected cover many of the more renowned locations and, hopefully, some of the less well-known spots along the front line. They have been designed to cater not only for those wishing to see the area by car but also for walkers and cyclists. Toilets can be found in most cafes and bars but we have also noted those that are to be found en route.

The guidebook focuses on what the battlefields look like today, hence we have used very few contemporary Great War photographs. We have been careful when designing routes to ensure vehicles are not left at isolated points, however please take the usual sensible precautions when leaving a vehicle unattended by not putting valuables on display but by locking them securely in the boot. Coordinates are provided for the start of each route. On the majority of routes it is possible to cycle and walk, but on some of them cycling is either prohibited or not possible because of the terrain. As in Britain, cycling on footpaths is not allowed. Where possible we have directed the battlefield tourist onto quiet and little-used minor roads as well as local pathways and cycle tracks but be aware that even on the quietest of rural roads there is always the likelihood of meeting farm machinery.

The car tours are designed to take in as much of the area as possible but they should only be regarded as a framework which can be expanded to take in other sites of interest as required. The car tours do use some of the more major roads which can be very busy and unpleasant to cycle along, particularly if there is no marked or dedicated cycle path. With this in mind, we suggest the car tours in the guide are unsuitable for the occasional cyclist. Those of you who are dedicated and hardbitten *veloists* should have no difficulty completing the car tours on two wheels.

The depth of historical information devoted to each route has, by necessity, been limited by available space but we hope we have provided you with an outline around which to develop your understanding of what took place and why. There has been a vast amount written about the Great War and it is sometimes difficult to know where to start when seeking further information and to this end we have made a number of suggestions for your consideration. One series of very readable and affordable books that focuses on specific areas of the battlefield is the *Battleground Europe* series of guides published by Pen and Sword Books. These are slim paperback volumes which can be carried easily in a pocket or rucksack and in our opinion serve a very useful function in filling the gaps in detail that guide books inevitably omit. There are currently some nine titles that are relevant to the front line covered in this guide which we refer to in the Further Reading section. We also point you in the direction of other useful guidebooks that cover part or all of the Western Front in Belgium.

What is often confusing to the first-time battlefield tourist is the terminology used in describing the organization of the Allied armies of the Great War. The basic formation begins with the infantry platoon. Commanded by a second lieutenant or lieutenant and assisted by a platoon sergeant, it comprised about fifty men who were organized into four sections, each commanded by a corporal or lance corporal. There were generally four platoons in a company, all of which answered to a company commander, usually a captain or major. Four companies and a headquarters company made up a battalion, commanded by a lieutenant colonel. Within the headquarters company was the second-in-command, the battalion adjutant – the colonel's right-hand man, the regimental sergeant major and the battalion quartermaster. Usually the battalion medical officer was part of this group. The next unit of command was the brigade; this was initially made up of four battalions but later in the war was reduced to three and in overall command was a brigadier general. A division consisted of at least three brigades and was commanded by a major general. Beyond that, divisions were organized into Corps usually commanded by lieutenant generals and Armies (generals) and the whole lot was under the direction of the Commander-in-Chief.

Cavalry were organized in a similar fashion except they had troops, squadrons and regiments which were organized into cavalry brigades and divisions. Artillery units had batteries of guns that became brigades when grouped together and the Royal Engineers used the term sections and companies to describe their basic formations. The Royal Flying Corps organized their aircraft into flights and squadrons and later grouped squadrons into brigades.

We also considered it useful to provide a list of the principal museum and open-air sites in the area, together with a star rating of each facility which, *we must emphasize*, is a purely personal grading. This should assist you in taking full advantage of what the area has to offer. The opening times and admission prices were accurate at the time of writing but it is advisable to check these before setting out. Those of you who are curious about the whereabouts of winners of the **Victoria Cross** can find them by referring to the guide we have provided in Appendix 2.

Whilst most of the photographs we have used in the guide are from our own personal collections, we must thank Pierre Vandervelt, Aurel Sercu and Rudy Laforce for permission to use their photographs. Special thanks must go to Joris Ryckeboer and Sabine Declercq Couwet for their help with taking the additional photographs we needed. Thanks must also go to the Belgian IGN for permission to reproduce map extracts. Without the help of Paul Webster, David Rowland, Bill Dobbs, Rob Howard and Tom Waterer of the Heart of England Western Front Association the preparation of the guide would have been a much harder task. These sturdy individuals walked and biked many of the routes with us and were always on hand to bring us both back to earth on the occasions we allowed our enthusiasm to run amok! We must also thank Dave O'Mara for reading the Belgian Ijzer material and offering valuable advice based on his extensive knowledge of the area.

HISTORICAL CONTEXT

After the British Expeditionary Force's (BEF) historic 200-mile retreat following the Battle of Mons on 23 August 1914, the Allies finally turned the tables on the rampaging German Armies the following September at the Battle of the Marne. What followed was a drive north; first to the River Aisne and then beyond as both sides attempted to outflank the other in a series of huge sidesteps which has often been referred to as 'The Race to the Sea'. It was a race that neither side really wanted to win as victory – reaching the coast in this case – would have signalled a failure to outflank the enemy and thus an inability to secure a strategic victory.

What is often overlooked is the crucial part played by the Belgian Army in flooding the polder lands north of Diksmuide which brought the German advance to a dead stop. Although the polders remained inundated until the end of the war, fighting on this front continued. Now, with the route to the Channel ports to the north effectively blocked, the German Fourth Army redirected its efforts towards Ypres in an attempt to force another way through to the coast, cut the BEF's vital supply lines and isolate the French. This forced the ancient and architecturally rich town of Ypres to centre stage and it became the focal point of the final throw of the dice in a war of movement that had already slowed dramatically on the Aisne.

In October 1914 the German juggernaut collided with the BEF just north of Langemark which marked the opening shots of the First Battle of Ypres. Throughout the rest of October and November 1914, try as they might, the German Armies failed to break the Allied line and take the town of Ypres, the Allies surviving the relentless battering by the skin of their teeth. A line was held just beyond Ypres and both sides dug in. Trench deadlock ensued eventually forming a continuous line of opposing defences from the North Sea coast down to the Swiss border.

April 1915 witnessed a second German attempt to break through, on this occasion marked by the use of poison gas – chlorine – for the first time in history. Although the line marking the boundary of what had become known as the Ypres Salient was significantly reduced by late May 1915, once again the Allies clung on in the face of overwhelming odds and barred the way once more to the Channel.

The line now remained relatively stable until 7 June 1917 when the British launched the curtain raiser to the Third Battle of Ypres by blowing the top off the Messines Ridge with the aid of nineteen offensive mines. Seven weeks later, on 31 July 1917, the British launched their huge offensive in Flanders with the aim of seizing Bruges and denying the German U-boats access to the North Sea.

The battle coincided with a period of unseasonal wet weather which, together with strong German defences, slowed the British advance dramatically. The final stages of the battle – often referred to as 'Passchendaele' – were fought in the most appalling conditions in a morass of almost liquid mud and the battle ground to a halt on 10 November 1917.

It was the Germans who went on the offensive again in April 1918 and once more tried to force the gates of Ypres as they launched 'Operation Georgette' as part of the Battle of the Lys. Although they came within spitting distance of the town before they were halted – pink granite demarcation stones today reveal just how close they came to breaking down the door – they succeeded in taking Mont Kemmel before the offensive finally lost impetus towards the end of April. 'Georgette' was one of a series of German offensives in 1918 in which the Germans tried and failed to force a result and to win the war.

With the failure of the German offensives and Allied recovery during the summer of 1918, the Allies built their strength for a final Advance to Victory which began on 8 August 1918. In the Ypres sector the Allies started their advance in late September and finally pushed their way out of the 'Immortal' Ypres Salient which they had held so doggedly for four years.

VISITING THE WESTERN FRONT IN BELGIUM

During our preparation and research for this volume of *Battle Lines* we based ourselves in two main centres, Diksmuide for the northerly Belgian sector and Ieper for the Salient and points south. The Belgian Yser front, north of Boezinge, is well worth spending time exploring and although we have only included two routes in that area which you can walk or cycle, there are countless other pathways and cycle tracks waiting to be explored along the whole length and depth of the front line. Details of these routes can be obtained from the tourist office at Diksmuide where you can purchase walking and cycling maps of the area. Diksmuide, like Ieper, was completely rebuilt after the Great War and, similarly, owes its origins to the medieval cloth industry. There is a reasonably good selection of both hotel and bed and breakfast accommodation which can be booked online. The four-star **Best Western Hotel Pax** is popular, as is the three-star **Hotel Sint-Jan** and the two-star **Bladelijn Farm Hotel** at Lampernisse. Bed and breakfast accommodation can be found in and around the town. **Huize Caesekin**, located near the Ijzer Tower, is of good quality, as is **De Groot Waere** near Vladslo. Restaurants are mainly to be found in the town centre and the Marina, which is by the Ijzer Tower. The town has a long and interesting history, much of which is featured in the 3km walk around the town that includes all the Great War sites; details and a map can be obtained from the tourist information office in the Grote Markt. Cycles can be hired from the **Fietsen Catrysse** on Kaaskerkestraat, near to the Ijzer Tower and from **Fietsen Versyck** on Koning Albertstraat. Monday is market day in Diksmuide and it is worth bearing this in mind when planning your visit.

Ieper is the iconic symbol of resistance in Belgium and its shattered remains which were enclosed within the 'Immortal Salient' were in Allied hands throughout the Great War. Ieper boasts a good choice of hotels and bed and breakfasts and plenty of restaurants and bars particularly around the Grote Markt. Accommodation can easily be searched for and booked online but we would advise booking several months ahead, particularly for the summer months and around the period of the commemoration of Armistice Day on 11 November and Remembrance Sunday. There are a number of good-quality three- and four-star hotels such as the **Ariane**, **Novotel** and the **Flanders Lodge**, together with some acceptable two-star establishments such as the **Regina** and **Ambrosia** hotels. Ieper abounds with bed and breakfast accommodation of which the **Hortensia** near the Lille Gate is very good. For those who prefer to be outside the town **Varlet Farm** near Passendale is an ideal location. If you prefer camping there is a municipal campsite near the sports centre. The town has several bookshops where books and Great War memorabilia can be purchased and of course there are the chocolate shops. Probably one of the most well-known war memorials in Flanders is the Menin Gate which stands on the site of one of the old town gates. Here the Last Post ceremony is held each night of the year at 8.00pm and for many is a highpoint of their visit to Ieper. It's also worth remembering that Saturday is market day in Ieper which brings additional congestion to the centre of town.

If you are not using your own cycles they can be hired at the **Sports Centre** but it's worth checking to see if your accommodation also has cycles for hire. The **Hotel Ambrosia** on D'Hondtstraat has eight cycles for hire to residents and non-residents. They also have a number of electric cycles. The tourist information centre is on the ground floor of the Cloth Hall – the Lakenhalle, in the Grote Markt. Here you can buy maps of the region and obtain details of the host of other walking and cycling routes around the Salient.

Regular visitors to the battlefields will be familiar with the collections of old shells and other explosive material that is often placed by the roadside by farmers. This lethal harvest is uncovered each year as farmers plough the land and the Belgian Army undertakes regular collections to dispose of this material at their centre at Houthulst. Incredibly there are still occasions when British customs find such 'souvenirs' hidden away in car boots by enthusiastic battlefield tourists who have no idea of the danger they are placing themselves and others in! By all means look but please do not touch.

It goes without saying that walkers and cyclists should come to

Belgium properly equipped to enjoy their activity. The weather is often unpredictable and it is always advisable to walk in a decent pair of boots and carry a set of waterproofs with you.

Using this Guidebook

Unless stated otherwise, all directions to the start point of each route are from Ieper. As a general rule we have used the modern Flemish spelling of place names but where appropriate in describing the contemporary action at locations we have used the 1914–18 spelling; thus we refer to 'Ieper' but use 'Ypres' when describing the Battles of Ypres. Similarly we use 'Passchendaele' when describing events that took place during the war years but the modern spelling, 'Passendale', when we refer to the village today. Although this can be a little confusing we felt it was important to recognize and give due deference to the Flemish language. There is also a more practical element to this decision in that all road-traffic signposts and modern maps are in Flemish and it makes for easier navigation. Occasionally we use flemish words, such as 'beek', meaning stream.

Whilst we have provided simple route maps for walkers and cyclists, we have not drawn maps for the four car tours. These tours tend to cover large areas of the front and are best supported by the Belgian NGI 1:50 000 Series maps which can be purchased at most good tourist offices and online from www.mapsworldwide.com. For the walker and cyclist, the larger scale 1:20 000 Series maps can also be bought in Belgium or online. We do recommend that you use the relevant NGI map when out walking or cycling to supplement the maps provided in the guide. Distances are in kilometres – the first figure in the table – and miles. You will find the alpha/numeric references in the text of each route correspond directly with those on the relevant map.

To assist you in your choice of route is a summary of all twenty-five routes in the guidebook together with an indication as to their suitability for walkers, cyclists or car tourists. Although we have purposefully kept the majority of the walking and cycling routes comparatively short, there are plenty of opportunities to extend your exploration of the area by linking nearby routes together, giving you the choice of determining the distance you feel able to manage comfortably. We have indicated at the beginning of each route description where this is possible and which routes can be linked

Route No.	Route	Distance	🚶	🚲	🚗
1	Ijzer Front Tour	52km/32.5			✓
2	Oud-Stuiveskenskerke an Trenches of Death	9.5km/59.9	✓	✓	
3	Houthulst Forest	4.3km/2.7	✓		
4	Langemark Area Car Tour	14.9km/9.3			✓
5	Langemark Central	5.6km/3.5	✓	✓	
6	Pilkem Ridge	10.6km/6.6	✓	✓	
7	Kitchener's Wood	4.1km/2.5	✓	✓	
8	Frezenberg Ridge	6.1km/3.8	✓	✓	
9	Polygon Wood	3.8km/2.4	✓		
10	Passendale	12.3km/7.7	✓	✓	
11	Geluveld and Zandvoorde	8km/5.0	✓	✓	
12	Bellewaarde Ridge and Hooge	4.8km/3.0	✓		
13	Sanctuary Wood and Hill 62	3.2km/2.0	✓	✓	
14	Zillebeke and the Aristocrats' Cemetery	6.4km/4.0	✓	✓	
15	Caterpillar Crater and the Bluff	6.7km/4.2	✓		
16	Ieper South	12.8km/8.0	✓	✓	
17	Ieper Town and Ramparts	3.2km/2.0	✓		
18	A Day in the Salient Car Tour	49.8km/30			✓
19	Messines Ridge – Wijtschate	5.9km/3.7	✓	✓	
20	Messines Ridge – Craters and Mines	9.9km/6.2	✓	✓	
21	Messines Ridge – The Peace Park	2.7km/1.7	✓		
22	Kemmel Area Car Tour	22.5km/14			✓
23	Kemmelberg	4.1km/2.6	✓		
24	Loker	4.5km/2.8	✓	✓	
25	Ploegsteert Wood and Hill 63	8.5km/5.3	✓		

together. Thus it is quite possible, for example, to begin a walk at Hooge Crater Museum and explore the Bellewaarde Ridge, Sanctuary Wood, Hill 60 and the Bluff and return to your vehicle via Zillebeke and Observatory Ridge. But whatever your choice of route, we hope you enjoy exploring the Western Front in Belgium with us and take home some lasting memories of a period of history long gone but always remembered.

Route 1

Ijzer Front Car Tour

Suitable for 🚕
Circular route starting at: Grote Markt in Diksmuide.
Coordinates: 51°01 51.55 – 2°51 53.21 E.
Distance: 52km/32.5 miles.
Maps: NGI 1:50 000 11–12 and 19–20.

General description and context: This is the most northerly sector of the Western Front which runs south from Nieuwpoort to Diksmuide and although it has been designed for the car tourist, it can be cycled. Not only is this an area largely overlooked by battlefield tourists but was also one that was vital to the whole course of the war. The front line was established during the Battle of the Yser in 1914 and remained static for almost the entire duration of the war. To avoid a German breakthrough along the Ijzer (Yser) River, the Belgians were forced to open the sea defences at Nieuwpoort and flood the polders between the Ijzer and the Nieuwpoort–Diksmuide railway line. For this they relied upon the local expertise of **Hendrik Geeraert,** who together with **Karel Cogge**, managed to open the sluice gates in the Gazenpoot (Goose's Foot) and begin the flooding of the Ijzer plain. Unaware of this, the Germans continued their offensive attributing the initial flooding to the bad weather and on 30 October they took Ramskapelle on the west bank just 8km/5 miles from the coast, threatening a breakthrough before the polders could be completely flooded. The Belgian Army, with help from the French, managed to retake Ramskapelle in a 'backs to the wall' battle that pushed the Germans back beyond the Ijzer where they were held by the, now rapidly rising, floodwaters. The **inundations**, as they were called, flooded the whole area between the railway line – known as Line 74 – and the Ijzer River to a depth of about waist height, effectively preventing any further advance by the German Army. Where 'islands' of higher ground remained above the floodwater, each side competed for occupancy in order to fortify them as strongpoints.

Directions to start: From Ieper take the N369 north to Diksmuide. On arriving at the junction with the N34 at Diksmuide, follow signs for the Centre and the Grote Markt, which is straight ahead. Park in the square where you will find the tourist information office and opportunities for refreshments.

Route description: From the Grote Markt take the N35 to Esen. Follow the road out of town in an easterly direction and take the left-hand turning to Vladslo just before the church at Esen. Continue to Vladslo village where you can park opposite the church on your left. In the churchyard and visible from the road is a memorial to the **XII Manitoba Dragoons**, a Canadian armoured regiment, which fought in the area in 1944 during the liberation of Belgium and the Low Countries. The crypt-like building to the left of the memorial is the Vladslo memorial to the Great War dead of the village. Continue through Vladslo bearing left round a number of bends until you see a signpost for the cemetery on your right, you are now only a short distance from the junction with the N363. At the junction go straight across and **Vladslo German Military Cemetery** is in the wooded area ahead of you. Park in the lay-by on the left. The cemetery is similar to other German cemeteries in that it contains large numbers of dead who were buried in mass graves. In total 136,314 German soldiers who were killed in the Great War are buried in Belgium and at Vladslo there are 25,644 soldiers commemorated on headstones each inscribed with twenty names. Amongst these is 17-year-old **Musketier Peter Kollwitz** who was killed on 23 October 1914. Deeply affected by her son's death, **Käthe Kollwitz** began work on the sculpture of the Grieving Parents which stands in the cemetery today. The sculpture was originally displayed at the Esen-Roggeveld military cemetery but was moved to its present site in 1957. Käthe Kollwitz was a well-known Berlin expressionist painter but her work was removed from public display by the Nazi regime as it was considered to be 'perverted art'. At nearby Koekelare you can view some of her work in the renovated brewery building. Her grandson was killed on the Eastern Front in 1942. Three casualties of German Airship LZ37 – **Karl Mahr**,

The Grieving Parents of Vladslo.

Gustav Ruske and **Otto Schwarz** – are buried in the centre of Plot 5 in the right-hand corner. The airship was shot down by **Lieutenant Rex Warneford** on 7 June 1915 for which he was awarded the Victoria Cross. As you leave, please remember to sign the visitor's book.

After leaving the cemetery look for the timber-framed house in the woods on the right. This building, erected in 1915, was once a German officers' mess or *Offizierskasino*. Continue past the first turning on the left until you see a large private house, turn left here along the minor road – Ramboutstraat – to reach the junction with the N369. At the junction take the road on your right – Keiemdorpstraat – leading to Keiem village. Drive through the village until you see the **Keiem Belgian Military Cemetery** on the right. Stop here. If the visitor's book is an accurate indication of the number of visitors to this cemetery, then sadly there have been only a handful of visitors in the last few years. Most of the 590 soldiers buried here belonged to the 8th and 13th Infantry Regiments who fell during the unsuccessful attempt to recapture Keiem in October 1914. Tragically, more than half of the graves are of unknown soldiers, many of whom died in the retreat back to the Ijzer River. There are two Belgian pilots buried here. **Sergent Jan Adolf Pauli** (450) was shot down and killed on 30 April 1917 during his seventh air operation and **Lieutenant Armand Gilbery** (494) who was shot down and killed on 8 April 1917 by the German air ace Walter Göttsch. Adding your name to the visitor's book would recognize the bravery of these Belgian soldiers and airmen. Leave the cemetery and almost immediately turn left onto the N369 and look out for the turning on the right signposted Pervijze. Turn right here onto Tervatesstraat which will take you to the lifting bridge at **Tervate**. In late October 1914 **Major Count Hendrick d'Oultremont** commanded the troops of 1st Regiment of Grenadiers which attempted, unsuccessfully, to force the Germans back across the Ijzer. As you cross the modern-day bridge – which is only metres from the original site – turn right to the **Grenadiers Memorial** which you will see ahead of you on the left. For the remaining four years of the war the Germans occupied most of the left bank of the Ijzer from here down to the Trenches of Death northwest of Diksmuide.

Continuing in the direction of Nieuwpoort, drive along the river until you reach the bridge at **Schoorbakke**. Here the N302 crosses the river in front of you. Your route is going to take you straight across the road to continue alongside the river on the other side. Cross with care and park. On the bridge are two memorial plaques that commemorate the 3rd, 22nd and 23rd Infantry Regiments which took part in the fighting of October 1914. Despite the efforts of the Belgians the Germans did manage to establish another bridgehead here.

Continue to the next junction and take the left turning – signposted Ramskapelle. You are now crossing the flooded area of the inundations. In just under a mile you will see a farm on your right, this is the rebuilt **Grote Hemme Farm** which was a German-held strongpoint situated on an island of high ground, although in 1914 it was located on the other side of the road. Across to your left you can see **Kleine Hemme Farm** which was also held by the Germans. Continue along the road and cross the bridge over the Grote Beverdijkvaat which was the approximate position of the Belgian front line in this sector. Just before you enter the village of Ramskapelle and cross over the Nieuwpoort–Diksmuide cycle track, you will come to the site of the

old station on your left which was used as an artillery observation post. Close by is an **Albertina Marker** commemorating the 1914 Battle of the Yser. Continue into the square and park. By the churchyard you will find a memorial commemorating the French 16th Chasseurs and the Belgian 6th Infantry Regiment which fought to retake the village from the Germans at the end of October 1914. There is also a very convenient bar on the corner of Molenstraat.

On leaving the square follow the signs for *Belgische Militaire Begraafplaats*, **Ramskapelle Belgian Military Cemetery** is a short distance ahead on the right where there is ample parking in the lay-by. The majority of the 634 men buried here fell in the battles around Ramskapelle and over 400 are unknown. These Belgian cemeteries are a stark reminder of the fighting that took place on this front. Had the Belgians not been successful in preventing the German advance to the Channel ports then the history of twentieth-century Europe might well have been very different. As with the other Belgian cemeteries, the visitor's book is in the small wooden sentry box.

After leaving the cemetery drive under the E40 motorway bridge to a T-junction with the N367. As you turn left **Ramscappelle Road Military Cemetery** is immediately to your left. Park in the lay-by.

There are 841 Commonwealth casualties of the Great War buried or commemorated here, 312 of which are unidentified. Two special memorials commemorate two soldiers known or believed to be buried here and a further twenty-six special memorials commemorate casualties originally buried at Nieuwpoort and Nieuwpoort-Bad whose graves were destroyed by shellfire. **Lieutenant Edward Selby Wise RN** (IV.A.3) was killed aboard the Humber class Monitor HMS *Severn* on 20 October 1914. His ship was involved in the bombardment of German positions during the Battle of the Yser. Selby would have been on board when the ship survived a torpedo attack by the submarine U-8 on 10 October. Tragically his younger brother, **Lieutenant Stacey Wise**, was drowned two days later on 22 October 1914 when his ship, HMS *Cressy*, was sunk by U-9 off the Belgian coast. **Lieutenant Colonel George Everard Hope** (VI.A.1) went to war with 1/Grenadier Guards and was one of the few officers of the battalion who survived the First Battle of Ypres during which he was badly wounded near Gheluvelt. Promoted shortly afterwards to captain, he was awarded the MC in 1915 before he was eventually given command of 1/8 Lancashire Fusiliers and was killed on 10 October 1917. Nearby is 40-year-old **Lieutenant Colonel Ernest Alfred Brooke** (II.B.21) who was commanding 10/Duke of Cornwall's Light Infantry when he was killed by a shell on 11 August 1917. Royal Naval Air Service pilot 21-year-old **Captain Harold Mellings** (VI.E.29) was decorated with the Distinguished Service Cross and bar to which he later added the Distinguished Flying Cross. With sixteen victories to his credit, his last flight was with 210 Squadron on 22 July 1918 when he was shot down south of Ostend. A young man with only two weeks' service at the front was **Flight Sub Lieutenant Maurice Baron** (VI.D.4). The 18-year-old Baron was flying his first

Captain Harold Mellings.

operational flight in a Sopwith Camel of 9 Royal Naval Air Service Squadron when he was shot down and killed during a clash with *Jasta* 17. Another pilot, **Second Lieutenant Horace Smith** (II.C.36), can be found next to his observer, **Lieutenant Eric Budd** (II.C.35). Both were killed on 11 September 1917 when they were shot down during an artillery observation flight flying an RE8 from their 52 Squadron airfield at Bray Dunes. Amongst the unidentified are a large number of men from 17/Highland Light Infantry all killed in the fighting of June and July 1917. One of the few identified HLI soldiers is 31-year-old **Private George Kerr** (IV.B.20). George was married with two children and before the war was a junior partner in the family building firm. He initially joined the Royal Scots Fusiliers but was transferred to the machine-gun section of 17/HLI. He was killed on 27 June 1917.

Some 250m further down the road is **Nieuwpoort Communal Cemetery**. The majority of the men buried in the cemetery are casualties of the July 1917 fighting. Twenty-three years later in May 1940, the British Expeditionary Force was involved in the later stages of the defence of Belgium following the German invasion, suffering numerous casualties in covering the withdrawal to Dunkirk. There are

Ramskapelle Belgian Cemetery.

The Albert Memorial at Nieuwpoort.

three distinct plots of Commonwealth graves here; the first is on the right-hand side about half-way down the centre pathway. Of the nineteen headstones in this plot thirteen are men of 2/Manchesters killed in the July 1917 fighting. The second plot is at the far end on the right marked by the Cross of Sacrifice and the third is in the far left-hand corner. This plot consists of the Second World War burials where there is a casualty of the 1942 Dieppe Raid. 20-year-old **Private George McClean** (III.31) was killed on 19 August 1942 fighting with the Royal Regiment of Canada. Also of note is the Belgian memorial to **Hendrik Geeraert** which can be found on the right-hand wall of the cemetery.

Leave the cemetery continuing towards Nieuwpoort and in about 800m you will cross the Noordvaart over the easily missed **White Bridge**. On the left here is a demarcation stone. At the junction turn right and continue bearing left over four bridges, the lock gates of the **Gazenpoot** are on your left. As the road bends round to the left you will see the three lions of the **British Memorial to the Missing**. Turn in here and park below the steps of the **Albert Memorial**. Before you visit the memorial take the opportunity to stretch your legs and walk back in the direction you have just come to the French **Memorial to the 81st Territorial Division** set back off the road. If you walk through the park towards the sluice gates you will get a fine view of the Gazenpoot sluices and the Albert Memorial. Three shipping canals and three drainage canals linking Nieuwport to Ostende, Brugge, Ieper and Dunkirk converge at the Gazenpoot and these once played a vital role in the region's economy. Further round you will find the Belgian memorial to the Yser battles which was unveiled in 1930 and the private memorial to **Lieutenant Leopold Calberg** who was killed here on 16 October 1917. Nearby is an **Albertina Marker** with the inscription 'Inundation, October 29 1914'.

Retrace your steps to the Albert Memorial and take the opportunity to enjoy the panorama from the top. The memorial was dedicated in 1938 and designed by Julien de Ridder and the striking sculpture of Albert on horseback is by the well-known Belgian artist Karel Aubroeck. The opening times are: 8.45am–12.00 noon and 1.15pm–6.00pm. From the top you will get a superb view of the Ijzer estuary and the Ijzer plain. The German lines were on the east of the estuary and before the German **Strandfest** offensive in July 1917, the British also had a foothold on the east bank which they accessed via a number of foot bridges named after London bridges. Closest to the Gazenpoot was *Vauxhall* with *Putney* and *Barnes* further downstream. At the far end of the estuary at Nieuwpoort-Bad were *Mortlake*, *Kew* and *Richmond*. It was when these bridges were destroyed by shellfire on 12 July 1917 that so many British soldiers were left isolated in the sand dunes which covered this part of the coast. The red and white lighthouse that can be seen marks the most northerly point of the whole Allied line prior to July 1917. Those in the bridgehead were overrun, killed, captured or escaped by swimming the river if they could. As a result the bridgehead was lost and never recovered. By September the British had returned this part of the line to the Belgians.

Rejoin your vehicle and turn left. You are going to go over the road bridge you can see to your left. Cross the carriageway and drive over the bridge to the roundabout, take the first exit – signposted Koksijde N34. Keeping the river on your right, continue to the next roundabout and take the third exit signposted N39 and E40. At the next crossroads – traffic lights – turn right onto the N396. After 300m you will cross the bridge over the Oude Veurnevaart which was known on trench maps as the **Bridge of Sighs**. Continue along the N396 until **Triangle Wood** with its collection of concrete bunkers appears on your right. Parking is difficult along here and we recommend that you either park near Triangle Wood and take the opportunity to stretch your legs again or continue to the junction with the N355 and turn right to find a suitable parking place. Situated on the junction itself is **Square Wood** where a number of Great War bunkers can be seen from the road. As you walk back towards Triangle Wood you will pass a cluster of Second World War bunkers which was the site of a coastal flak battery. Across the road on your right there is another large bunker and in the wood, hidden from view, is the site of a Great War communication post. Triangle Wood was used extensively by artillery units during the Great War and is a remarkably preserved site, probably due to the use of the bunkers by local farmers.

Depending on where you have parked your vehicle, at the junction with the N355 – traffic lights – either turn left or go straight across in the direction of Pervijze, crossing over the Nieuwpoort–Duinkerke Canal and the E40 motorway. Soon the road will begin to run parallel with the old railway line. Slow down here as on the left you will catch a glimpse of some of the Belgian bunkers and shelters that were built into the side of the embankment. Should you wish to visit them take the minor road on the left to Schoorbakke and park by the railway line. The bunkers are a short walk back up the line.

Mairi Chisholm (right) and Elizabeth Knocker.

Rejoin your vehicle and continue into **Pervijze.** During the Great War the village was occupied by Belgian forces which also held outposts along the road up to the Schildersbrug, whilst Stuivekenskerke and the heavily fortified Vicogne Farm were in German hands. Pervijze was also home to the 'Angels of Pervijze', the name given to two British nurses, **Elizabeth Knocker** and **Mairi Chisholm**, who established an aid station in the village. Both women were decorated by King Albert after the war. On entering the village stop and park in the obvious car park by the church to visit **Flying Officer James Robertson** of 412 Squadron who was shot down and killed flying a Spitfire IX on 29 November 1943. His headstone is the only CWGC burial in the churchyard and can be found to the left of the church. Before leaving the village it is well worthwhile visiting the **Observation Tower** which is situated only a short distance down the N35 – Pervijzestraat – directly opposite the car park. To find the tower take the second turning on the right into Brouwerijstraat. After rejoining your vehicle leave the village and, keeping the church on your left, turn right along the N302. After 400m you will cross the Nieuwpoort–Diksmuide cycle

Bunker at Triangle Wood.

Oud-Stuiveskenskerke.

track where you can still see the **old railway station** – now a private house. After crossing over the Schildersbrug take the first turning on the right to Stuivekenskerke.

At **Stuivekenskerke** bear right and continue south until you reach a minor road on the left, signposted O.L. Vrouwhoekje – Our Lady's Corner. This narrow road takes you to the tiny hamlet of **Oud-Stuiveskenskerke** which was a fortified Belgian outpost in the midst of the inundations. The church tower, the remains of which you can see standing next to the chapel of remembrance, formed an important Belgian artillery observation post and was commanded by **Captain Martial Lekeux**, a Franciscan father, who is remembered with his own memorial plaque. Climb to the top where there is a useful orientation table and a view over the surrounding polders. Around the exterior of the chapel of remembrance are memorial stones to the units of the Belgian Army which served here. The demarcation stone bears the standard inscription, 'here the invader was brought to a standstill'.

Retrace your route to the road junction and turn left. At the T-junction turn left again – signposted Dodengang – passing **Hoevre Poort Farm** on your left. The farm was just inside Belgian lines which ran from the farm along the road you are now following down to the **Trenches of Death** and along the west bank of the Ijzer to Diksmuide. Continue to the Trenches of Death and park. This reconstructed network of trenches and dugouts was one of the most dangerous Belgian positions on the Western Front and under constant fire from snipers and machine guns from the German positions located at the Petroleum Tanks and from the **Minoterie** – flour mill – position to the south at Diksmuide. An **Albertina Marker** had been placed on the site of the Petroleum Tanks. You will also find a demarcation stone at the far end of the trenches. With the German positions just metres away, the casualty rate was exceptionally high and one casualty commemorated here with a plaque is **Major Felix Bastin**, a Belgian medical officer who was serving with 8th Regiment of Artillery when he was killed on 4 November 1917. Entrance to the site is free and from the top of the museum building there is a good view down the river towards

Memorial plaque to Felix Bastin.

A section of a German trench map depicting the position of the modern Ijzer Tower and the site of the Minoterie.

Diksmuide with the tower of Sint-Niklaas Church on the left and the Ijzer Tower (Ijzertoren) dominating the skyline on the right.

Continue along the river to Diksmuide to reach the junction with the N35. Opposite you, on the other side of the road, is the **Ijzer Tower** where you can park by the side of the river. Before you visit the tower and museum look across the river to the **Sint-Jan Hotel** on the opposite bank. This was the site of the infamous **Minoterie**, the German-held strongpoint that had its machine guns and mortars ranged on the Trenches of Death. On the German trench map of the Belgian and German trenches at Diksmuide above, the position of the Ijzer Tower is marked with a black arrow. You can see just how close the two front lines were at this point! The Belgian front line ran along the bank of the river where you are now standing, continuing up to the Trenches of Death before it swung to the west joining the railway embankment of Line 74. South of Diksmuide, the front line followed the Ijzer towards Ieper. The German front line was directly opposite and ran along the bank of the river. Diksmuide was defended doggedly in 1914 by the **Belgian Meiser Brigade** and 6,000 French marines, commanded by **Admiral Pierre-Alexis Ronarc'h**. On 10 November the town of Diksmuide was finally taken by the Germans which, by the time of the Allied offensive of 1918, had been reduced to rubble.

The first Ijzer Tower was built in the 1930s as a memorial to the Flemish soldiers who died whilst serving at the front and was destroyed by opponents of Flemish nationalism in an explosion in 1946. Rebuilt by 1965, the 84m-high tower is now listed as an international peace centre and has come to represent Flemish nationalism which has been an unresolved issue in Belgium since the eighteenth century. The letters AVV – VVK, visible on the very top of the tower, stands for 'All for Flanders – Flanders for Christ'. In August 1914 French was the dominant language in Belgium and whilst the majority of Belgian Army officers were French speaking, the rank and file were largely Flemish speaking. Flemish nationalism was championed during the war years by individuals such as **Joe English**, who became well known for his war art and the design for the special headstones for the Flemish war dead. He died at the age of 36 on 31 August 1918. He was initially buried in the Belgian military cemetery at Steenkerke before his remains were placed in the crypt of the tower. The large gate in front of the tower was built using material from the original structure and today the museum tells the story of Flemish nationalism and its links with the Great War. The museum is well worth visiting and from the top of the tower there are superb views over the battlefield. After leaving the tower turn right over the bridge and head back to the Grote Markt.

Route 2

Oud-Stuiveskenskerke and Trenches of Death

Suitable for 🚲 👤
Circular route starting at: the Ijzer Tower.
Coordinates: 51°01 56.53 N – 2°51 15.08 E.
Distance: 9.5km/5.9 miles.
Grade: Easy.
Toilets: Trenches of Death Visitor's Centre.
Maps: NGI 1:20 000 Lo-Reninge–Langemark 20/1–2.

General description and context: This route uses part of the Belgian front line along the old Diksmuide–Nieuwpoort railway line and visits the Belgian Army artillery outpost at **Oud-Stuiveskenskerke** before crossing the polders to the Ijzer River where it joins the **Trenches of Death.** Using little-frequented tracks and minor roads you will quickly find yourself amidst a landscape hosting a profusion of wildlife as you traverse an area that was almost completely inundated with floodwaters in 1914.

Directions to start: From the centre of Diksmuide head west along the N35 in the direction of Pervijze. As you cross the road bridge turn left and park near the Ijzer Tower, the cycle path is another 250m further down the road on the right.

Route description: Once on the cycle path ❶, with the Ijzer Tower on your right, you will find yourself on the line of trenches known as *Boyau du Rail* which was an integral part of the heavily fortified Belgian front line in this sector. Either side of the path were belts of barbed wire and communication trenches connecting other parts of the line.

The Ijzer Tower.

The Trenches of Death.

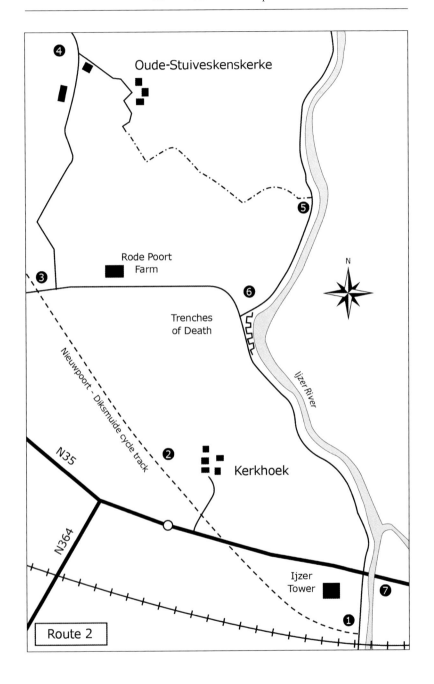

Oude-Stuiveskenskerke

Rode Poort Farm

Trenches of Death

N

Nieuwpoort - Diksmuide cycle track

IJzer River

N35

N364

Kerkhoek

Ijzer Tower

Route 2

With the German front line just metres away across the river this area was of great strategic importance. Continue along the track crossing the N35 with care until you are clear of the town at ❷ where you should be able to see the brick viewing platform and museum building of the Trenches of Death over to your right. At the obvious junction with a minor road ❸ you will find an **Albertina Marker** on the right commemorating the Battle of the Yser. The cycle track continues ahead to Nieuwpoort but we are now going to turn right and then almost immediately take a left turn for Stuivekenskerke. On your right is **Rode Poort Farm** which was a Belgian fortified strongpoint connected to the Trenches of Death by a series of communication trenches and raised walkways.

Soon the hamlet of **Oud-Stuiveskenskerke** will come into view on your right marked by the flagstaff and Belgian flag flying above the old observation post. This is our next port of call. Just past a large farm on the left is a minor road on the right ❹ marked O.L.Vrouwhoekje – Our Lady's Corner – take this road which will lead directly to Oud-Stuiveskenskerke. With the Ijzer Tower in the distance, go over the bridge where you will find an information board. There are further information boards in the hamlet and a description of this Belgian outpost in Route 1. Just past the **Demarcation Stone,** and opposite the bus stop, you will find a small wooden bridge on the right. Go across and onto the gravel pathway which will take you across the polders. After numerous twists and turns your will arrive at a T-junction with the road ❺ running alongside the Ijzer, turn right here. At this point along the river the German lines were on the west bank and you will soon pass the former site of the German observation post at the Petroleum Tanks and the northern end of the Belgian trenches. At the road junction by the **Trenches of Death** ❻ turn left to the main building and entrance. There are toilets here and racks where you can leave your cycle. The trenches are described in more detail in Route 1 and there is an excellent photographic display inside the main building which is well worth visiting, as is the balcony from where there is a marvellous view. After leaving the trenches, Diksmuide is only a short distance along the Ijzerdijk back to your vehicle, but take care along the road as it is frequented by tour buses.

Route 3
Houthulst Forest

Suitable for **♦**
Circular route starting at: Church of Sint-Jan Baptist, Houthulst.
Coordinates: 50°58 36.97 N – 2°57 04.49 .
Distance: 4.3km/2.7 miles.
Grade: Easy.
Maps: NGI 1:20 000 Staden–Roeselare 20/7–8.

General description and context: A delightful forest walk in a little-known and rarely visited part of the Western Front. The fighting of 1917 during the Third Battle of Ypres saw French and Commonwealth troops occupying the southern edges of the forest but during the German spring offensives of 1918 these lines were quickly overrun as the Allies were pushed back to within a mile of the gates of Ieper itself. It is hard to believe that the forest was the scene of another bloody and savage battle in September 1918 when the area was re-taken by the Belgian Army in the final offensive. In 1914 Houthulst Forest, or Vrijbos

The Houthulst Forest in 1918.

The Houthulst Forest.

Houthulst Belgian Cemetery.

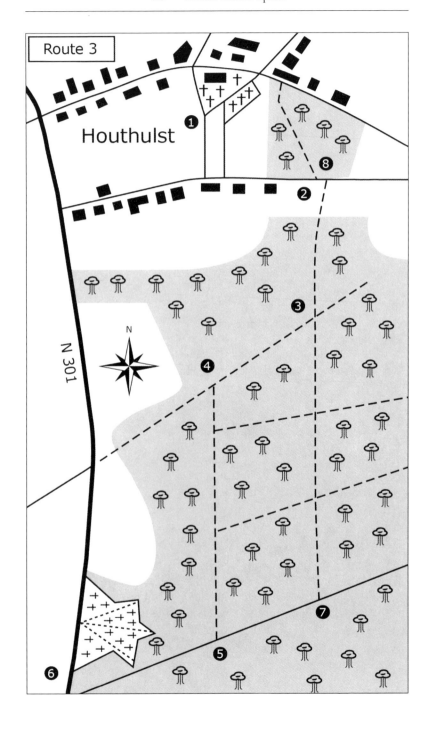

as it is known locally, covered some 20 square kilometres and was divided in two by the Houthulst–Poelkapelle road. Today it is a fraction of that size with a large proportion of it now the domain of the Belgian Army unit with responsibility for the disposal of the endless haul of explosives that come to light each year on the former battlefields. In October 1914 the forest was taken without a fight and turned into a veritable fortress by the Germans, the forest canopy concealing a light railway, artillery batteries, ammunition dumps and command centres. The forest was also the site of the infamous 'Ypres Express', a large-calibre German gun which regularly shelled Ieper As the war ground on several military cemeteries were established in the forest by various German Field Lazarettes (field hospitals). Today nothing remains but a few scattered shell holes and the area has been returned to its former beauty with a network of forest footpaths and cycle tracks.

Directions to start: From Ieper take the N313 through Sint-Juliaan to Poelkapelle where you turn left onto the N301. Continue into Houthulst and turn right to reach the church. From Diksmuide take the N35 towards Esen turning right onto the N301 in the direction of Klerken. Continue through Klerken to Houthulst where you take a left turn to the church.

Route description: Next to the church is a rectangular recreational area surrounded by spaces for parking. Park here ❶ and with the church behind you walk to the end of the road and turn left. Ahead is a straight road with woods on the left. Go past the path on the left leading to the Lourdes Grot and look for a path ❷ on the right – signposted Vrijbos – leading into the forest. Turn right here into the forest and continue down the tree-lined avenue to the barrier ahead. Go straight across and at the next junction ❸ turn right down the wide tree-lined forest ride. Although the forest has re-grown, the old trench lines can still be made out in the undergrowth.

Just before the next barrier turn left ❹ and continue until you reach a junction with a metalled road ❺. Ahead of you is a fence that marks the Belgian Army domain. Turn right at the junction and walk along this road, you will soon catch sight of the cemetery through the trees ahead of you on the right. Go to the end of the road, through the gate and turn right. On the small green in front of you is an **Albertina**

Marker commemorating the Belgian Offensive of 1918 during which the forest was regained.

On your right, set into the wall of the cemetery, is a small metal gate which is extremely difficult to open. This takes you into **Houthulst Belgian Military Cemetery** without having to walk along the main road. The cemetery ❻ is one of ten Belgian cemeteries in West Flanders for Great War casualties and Houthulst contains almost 2,000 men who were killed in the 1918 fighting here. The cemetery is arranged in an interesting star shape and at the rear of the cemetery you will find a number of Italian graves, these men were prisoners of war who died in captivity. The visitor's book can be found in the wooden sentry box together with a list of all those who are buried here.

Retrace your steps to the side gate and turn left back through the gate and into the forest. Continue along the road, ignoring the first turning on the left to take the second turning left. This path ❼ will take you straight back to the main road.

On reaching the main road again turn left and then immediately right – signposted Lourdes Grot – ❽ to enter the wooded area ahead of you. On your right you will see the Lourdes Grotto situated in a forest clearing. Continue straight ahead, turning left at the road to reach the church. **Houthulst Churchyard Cemetery** contains seven Second World War graves, four aircrew who died when their Hampden bomber crashed locally in 1941, and three soldiers killed during the BEF's retreat to Dunkirk in 1940. The aircrew were all members of 83 Squadron who were returning from a raid on Cologne on 21 April 1941. To find them enter the churchyard by the main entrance and as you reach the main door turn left and follow the narrow path. The war graves are on the right-hand side of the path. War graves of Second World War British aircrew are scattered all over Belgium and can very often be found tucked away in obscure corners of village churchyards like this one.

Route 4
Langemark Area Car Tour

Suitable for

A circular tour beginning at: the church at Langemark.

Coordinates: 50°54 49.04 N – 2°55 08.10 E.

Distance: 14.9km/9.3 miles.

Toilets: Langemark German Cemetery.

Maps: NGI 1:50 000 Roeselare 19–20 and Ieper 27–28–36.

General description and context: The tour covers part of the ground that saw some of the early engagements in October and November 1914 during the First Battle of Ypres. It also includes ground that was taken by the Germans during the April 1915 German gas attack (officially the Battle of Gravenstafel Ridge) and subsequently re-taken by Allied forces during the Third Battle of Ypres in 1917. During the Third Battle of Ypres Langemark was back in Allied hands only to be lost again in the March 1918 German offensive. The town was finally liberated by the Belgians in the final months of 1918.

Directions to start: From Ieper take the N313 towards Sint-Jan. Continue through Sint-Juliaan until you reach Vancouver Corner and the Canadian Monument. Turn left here and drive straight into Langemark. Park by the church.

Route description: With the church on your left continue east along the Korte Ieperstraat until you reach the the traffic lights. Turn sharp right here along Boezingestraat and in a little over 600m you will find the **Memorial to the 20th Light Division** on your right. The memorial commemorates the advance of the 20th Division

The 20th Light Division Memorial.

across the Steenbeek by temporary bridges on 16 August 1917. The artillery barrage began at 4.45am and the infantry attacked under the cover of a creeping barrage. The division captured a German strongpoint known as *Au Bon Gite*, and although the condition of the ground was little more than a swamp they successfully advanced into Langemark. During the action, **Private Wilfred Edwards** of 7/King's Own Yorkshire Light Infantry and **Sergeant Edward Cooper** of 12/King's Royal Rifle Corps both won the Victoria Cross. Just 200m further on by the Steenbeek is a Belgian **Albertina Marker** commemorating the final Belgian offensive in September 1918.

Continue along the Boezingestraat for a short distance until you reach **Cement House Cemetery** on your left. Stop here. The cemetery was named after a fortified farm building that once stood close by and was begun in August 1917 during the Third Battle of Ypres. It is still used for the burial of remains which continue to be discovered in the vicinity, and a number of plots have been extended to accommodate these graves. In the years immediately following the Armistice most of Plots II–XV were added when Commonwealth graves were brought in from the battlefields and small burial grounds around Langemark and Poelkapelle. Buried here is **Captain the Honourable Patrick Ogilvy** MC of 1/ Irish Guards (XIII.D.3.), the 21-year-old son of the 10th Earl of Airlie. He initially enlisted as a private soldier in the Fife & Forfar Yeomanry in August 1914 and was commissioned into the Irish Guards in June 1915. He was awarded the Military Cross for gallantry at Lesboeufs on the Somme on 25 September 1916. On 9 October 1917 he was commanding Number 1 Company in an attack from Ruisseau Farm during which he was killed in action. Several burials date from the early battles of 1914. Sixteen officers and men buried at Masnières near Mons in 1914 were transferred here, including **Captain Jonathan Knowles** (VIIA.D.9.) of 4/Middlesex who was one of the first British officers to lose his life in the Great War. Also reinterred here are several men of 1/Battalion Cheshire Regiment who were killed at Audregnies, near Mons, on 24 August 1914. Killed on 18 February 1915 near Blauwepoort Farm south of Ieper was **Sergeant Edward Ashton** (XVI.B.50) who was serving with 1/Suffolks. His battalion lost heavily that day supporting the front line against a determined German attack. An interesting inscription can be found on **Second Lieutenant Duncan Cunningham-Reid's** headstone (VIIA.D.8.) which reads

'Sent 60 miles to protect another he fought in the air for half an hour surrounded by the enemy enabling reconnaissance machine to return safely'. Flying as observer with **Second Lieutenant Norman Gordon-Smith** (VII.D.9.), their BE2c was escorting a reconnaissance aircraft when they were engaged by enemy aircraft and shot down over Oostcamp on 19 December 1915. There is a plaque dedicated to Cunningham-Reid in Holy Trinity Church, Stratford-upon-Avon.

After leaving the cemetery continue for 450m to the next crossroads. This is the **Hagebos or Iron Cross crossroads** and marks the site of a regimental aid post where the Welsh poet **Private Ellis Humphrey Evans** died on 31 July 1917 during the 38th Division attack on Pilkem Ridge. We visit this site again in Route 6. Evans, known in Wales by his Bardic peusdonym **Hedd Wyn**, fought with 15/ Welsh Fusiliers (London Welsh). A more recent memorial of Welsh slate has been placed on the wall of the Cafe Hagebos on your left. He is buried in the nearby **Artillery Wood Cemetery** along with the Irish poet **Francis Ledwidge**.

Turn right at the crossroads taking the Groenstraat for 2.5km to the Kortekeer crossroads. Stop here but take care as the road is a busy one. In 1914 there was an inn at the crossroads known as the **Kortekeer Cabaret**. On 22 October 1914 the crossroads was held by 1/ Cameron Highlanders. Late in the afternoon the British positions at the crossroads were overwhelmed by German forces of the 45th Reserve Division attacking from the north. The next day, under the command of **Brigadier General Edward Bulfin**, the Kortekeer position was retaken by two battalions, 1/Loyal North Lancashire and 1/ Queen's Royal West Surrey. The Kortekeer position, which was of no great strategic value, was abandoned by the British later in the day when the front line was re-established further south. However, the strength of the British counter-attack at Kortekeer did help in convincing the German Fourth Army command that there was little hope of breaking through in this sector in 1914. On 31 July 1917 the crossroads formed the boundary line between the advancing French troops on the left and the British on the right. Earlier that morning the French captured Bixschoote and the German trench system south and west of the village, whilst the British Guards Division got to within metres of the Steenbeek.

At the crossroads go straight ahead to take the next turning on the right – Pottestraat – towards Sint-Janskap. Cross the Broenbeek stream

The Steenbeek Albertina Memorial.

The Canadian 'Brooding Soldier' memorial at Vancouver Corner.

The Fred Dancox Memorial at Namur Crossing.

The German Cemetery at Langemark.

and at the next crossroads turn right along Beekstraat. You are now driving along the line of the approximate Allied positions of October 1914 which were on the opposite side of the Broenbeek to your left. On your right situated in a field you will see the rectangular shaped memorial to **André Malliavin** and **Emilien Girault**, the brigadier and adjutant of the 2nd *Chasseurs d'Afrique* who were killed here on 19 October 1917. In 350m you will see the **34th Division Memorial** on your left. Park here. This memorial commemorates the men of the 34th Divisional Artillery and Royal Engineers units and has been erected on land captured in 1917. Behind is a German bunker which was part of a 1917 defensive line.

At the T-junction ahead turn left and continue for just over 800m until you reach the second turning on the right – Galgestraat. Turn right here and after a sharp bend you will find the **Dancox Memorial**. You are now standing at **Namur Crossing**, close to the spot where 38-year-old **Private Fred Dancox**, fighting with 4/Worcestershire Regiment, won the Victoria Cross on 9 October 1917 when he single-handedly captured a German machine gun in a bunker situated some 150m to the east of the memorial along with some forty prisoners. The bunker was part of a German defensive position that included the bunker you have just visited and those you will find in the German Cemetery. Dancox was killed near Cambrai on 30 November 1917 and is commemorated on the Cambrai Memorial to the Missing at Louverval.

Turn your vehicle around and rejoin the main road, turning left towards Langemark. Continue for just over 1km to the car park at **Langemark German Cemetery** visitor's centre on the right. You can park here. Before you visit the cemetery walk back along the road to the point the road crosses over the Broenbeek. You are now standing at the point where **Captain Robert Rising** and three platoons of 1/Gloucestershire Regiment were dug in across the Koekuit road on the morning of 23 October 1914. To their left were the Coldstream Guards and on the right the 1/Welsh Regiment. The brunt of the German attack came down the road and here Rising and his men held off a large force of German infantry advancing from Koekuit. Rising was subsequently awarded the DSO for his part in the action but was killed on 7 November 1914 and is buried at Zillebeke Churchyard Cemetery (see Route 14).

Return to the cemetery. As one of only four Great War German military cemeteries in Flanders, visiting Langemark makes for an interesting contrast with nearby Tyne Cot and if you have visited Vladslo German Cemetery you will notice a remarkable similarity. In 1940 **Adolf Hitler** visited the cemetery as part of his tour of Belgium and France. Langemark German Cemetery is the only one in the area bounded by the Ypres Salient and contains over 44,000 burials, concentrated from many smaller cemeteries in the area. At the rear of the cemetery is a sculpture by **Professor Emil Krieger** of four mourning figures seen in shadow from the front of the cemetery. Flat stones mark

Erwin Böhme.

burial plots. Along the north wall are the remains of three German bunkers. The names of the individuals known to be buried here are recorded on bronze panels beyond the entrance. To the left is a plaque commemorating two British soldiers who are buried here, Privates **Albert Carlill** and **Leonard Lockley** who were killed in 1918. *Leutnant* **Erwin Böhme** is one of the two German Air Service *Pour le Mérite* holders who are buried here. With twenty-four victories to his credit, Böhme was shot down and killed on 29 November 1917, just five days after he had been invested with the award. Also known as the *Blue Max*, the medal was the greatest honour that could be awarded to German servicemen during the Great War. After being shot down over Zonnebeke, he was buried by the British at Kerselaarhoek German cemetery some 700m east of the present-day Tyne Cot until 1955, when his remains were moved to Langemark. Records confirm he was reburied in the mass grave of the *Kameradengräb*, although his name is not commemorated on any of the bronze memorial panels. *Leutnant* **Werner Voss** scored the first of his forty-eight victories on 27 November 1916 and was awarded the *Pour le Mérite* on 8 April 1917. On 23 September 1917, flying a

Werner Voss.

Fokker Triplane, he was engaged by six aircraft of 56 Squadron which included the British air aces **James McCudden** and **Arthur Rhys-David**. In a rather one-sided air battle, Voss fought off the enemy aircraft with a demonstration of combat flying that won the admiration of his adversaries. He was finally downed by Rhys-David and crashed near Plum Farm, north of Frezenberg. Voss was only 20 years old and his name is commemorated on panel 63. After leaving the cemetery continue into Langemark and park by the church. The church of Sint-Paulus was totally destroyed during the course of the Great War. Close to the entrance is the memorial to the civilian victims who died at Langemark. In July 1917 there was enough of the church tower left for the Prince of Wales who was serving with the Grenadier Guards to have a close brush with death when the church was shelled by German artillery. The car tour ends here but you may wish to continue to explore the area on foot or by bike by taking advantage of Route 5 which also begins at this point.

Whilst you are in the Langemark area, find a moment to return to the **Canadian Memorial** at Vancouver Corner which you would have passed on your way to Langemark on the N313. The statue of the 'Brooding Soldier' with his head bowed and arms reversed commemorates the 18,000 Canadian soldiers who fought in the gas attack of 1915. Unveiled in 1925, the statue is surrounded by a park outside which there is ample parking. The 'Brooding Soldier', designed by Frederick Chapman Clemesha, who originally envisaged it would be worked entirely in concrete, was runner up in the search for a national monument to the Canadian dead of the Great War which was to stand on Vimy Ridge. Many felt that the imposing column which now stands at Vancouver Corner, 'something of bigness, vigour and untrammelled youth' according to Clemesha's original vision, was a greater reflection of the national grief than the design eventually chosen for Vimy.

Route 5

Langemark Central

Suitable for 🚲 🚶

Circular route starting at: Sint-Paulus Church, Langemark.
Coordinates: 50° 54 49.04 N – 2°55 08.10 E.
Distance: 5.6km/3.5 miles.
Grade: Easy.
Maps: NGI 1:20 000 Lo-Reninge–Langemark 20/5–6.

General description and context: This is a short tour that is suitable for walkers and cyclists. The tour looks in more detail at the centre of Langemark and visits the ground to the west of the town that saw the 38th Welsh and the Guards Divisions attack of 31 July 1917 at the opening of the Third Battle of Ypres. Apart from a short section along the Pilkem road, the route uses minor roads and the old railway line, now a cycle and pedestrian pathway.

Route description: The tour begins at Sint-Paulus Church ❶ in the centre of Langemark. The town had been largely destroyed by May 1915, and the information board outside the church shows several pictures of Langemark and the church in ruins. Today the rebuilt town still has some cobbled streets in evidence but the grand chateau in grounds that once occupied the centre of the town was never rebuilt. During the German occupation of the town after the 1915 gas attack, a light railway system was installed by German engineers which ran along Poelkapellestraat and Boezingestraat connecting the first and second line trench systems with the supply areas further to the rear.

From the church walk west along Statiestraat until you see the municipal park ❷ and the ornamental lake on the right. This is all that remains of the large chateau that occupied this ground before it was destroyed by shellfire. A comparison of the two map segments opposite will give you a clearer idea of what the chateau and its grounds looked

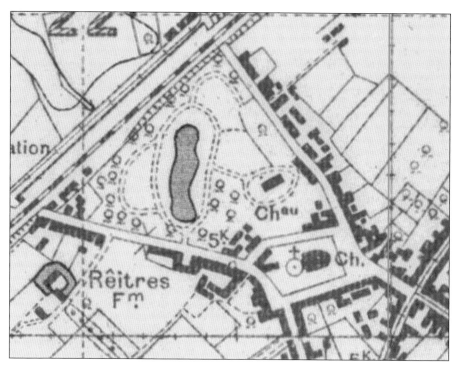

Trench map detail from 1916.

Langemark as it is today.

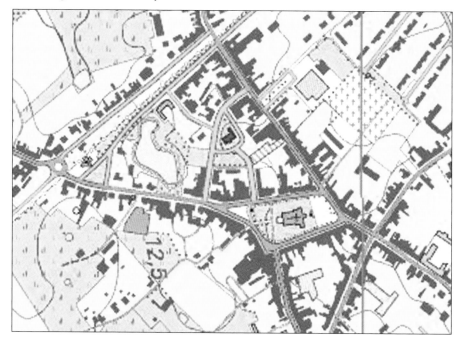

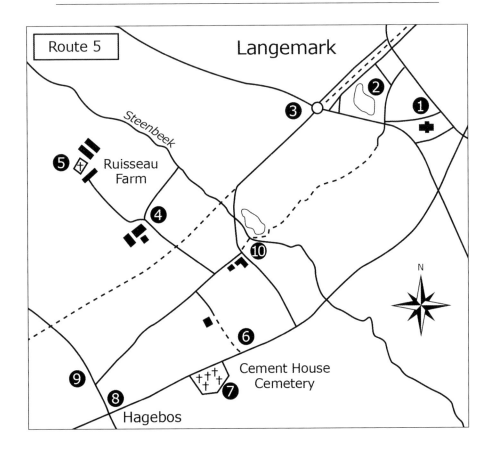

like in 1914. Walk through the park to join the cycle and pedestrian track. Turn left and continue past the large roundabout, there is now an open space on your left as the cycle track ❸ takes you out of the town. After crossing the Steenbeek take the next road on your right which soon leads to a T-junction ❹ with large farm buildings on your left. Bear left to **Ruisseau Farm** and walk through the farmyard to find the cemetery ❺ ahead of you. Ruisseau Farm was taken by Number 1 Company, 2/Grenadier Guards on 31 July, and thirty enemy soldiers and a number of officers were taken prisoner here. The same company, led by **Captain J.N. Buchanan**, also took the nearby **Signal Farm** before crossing the Steenbeek and digging in on the far side. The cemetery was begun when the fighting was over. Buried here is **Captain Robert Wilmot** (C.1.) of 10/ Sherwood

Foresters who was killed on 29 October 1917. Robert, aged 31, was the eldest of the three sons of the Revd Francis Wilmot of Chaddeston, Derby. His younger brothers were both killed before him, Henry in July 1917 and Thomas, aged 20, in August 1916. Killed on the same day and serving in the same battalion was 21-year-old **Lieutenant Clarence Cox** (D.4.). Cox had been awarded the Military Cross for gallantry during a trench raid which was not announced until January 1918. Also buried here is 19-year-old **Second Lieutenant Ralph Babington** (C.45.) of 3/Coldstream Guards from Coulsdon, Surrey. A Sandhurst graduate, he was killed on 9 October 1917 along with a number of his platoon, six of whom lie close by. Another Coldstream officer, **Second Lieutenant John Brenchley** (D.12.) was killed near the Veldhoek crossroads on 12 October. A South African from Port Elizabeth, he had been serving with 4/Coldstream Guards since August 1916. His award of the MC was announced in September 1917. **Driver Harry Saffell** (B.2.) initially enlisted in the Royal Horse Artillery but later transferred to the Royal Field Artillery. Serving in B Battery, 159 Brigade, he was killed in action on 24 October 1917. On either side of him lie three other members of his battery, all killed in the same incident.

After retracing your steps to the cycle track, continue straight ahead in a southeasterly direction along Melkerijstraat across fields. You are now walking towards the busy main Langemark–Pilkem road. Continue until you reach the next T-junction. Turn right here and then left down the track to pass through the farm. The farm is on the site of a fortified stronghold known as **Cardiff Castle** to the men of the 38th Welsh Division who attacked across this ground on 31 July 1917. The farm track will take you to ❻ the main road. **Cement House Cemetery ❼** is on the opposite side of the road to your right. You can find details about the cemetery in the Route 4 guidance. From the cemetery continue to the Hagebos crossroads ❽. Take care here, the road is a busy one. This was the site of a regimental aid post where the Welsh poet **Private Ellis Humphrey Evans** died on 31 July 1917. Details of the memorial plaque can be found in the Route 4 guidance. At the crossroads turn right. The road you are now walking along is the approximate position of the Green Line which was the third objective allocated to the Guards Division on 31 July 1917 and ran parallel with the road you are on about 100m over to the right. The old

Ruisseau Farm Cemetery.

THE LAST FIGHTING TOMMY
Pte. HENRY JOHN PATCH (HARRY)
C COMPANY 7TH D.C.L.I.

17TH JUNE 1898 - 25TH JULY 2009
AGE 111
Fought in the battle of Passchendaele
During the 1914 - 1918 war
Freeman of the City of Wells
also representing all the brave young men
lost in The Great War

The inscription on the memorial to Harry Patch at Wells Museum in Somerset. Harry's funeral took place at Wells Cathedral in 2009.

Ypres–Staden railway line formed the divisional boundary between the 38th Division and the Guards Division which was attacking towards Langemark north of the railway. Continue along the Groenstraat for 130m to take the next turning on the right, the Donkerweg **❾**.

> *Should you wish to join **Route 6**, the Pilkem Ridge route, you can do so by continuing for another 300m to turn left down the cycle track. Follow instructions for Route 6 from **⓬**.*

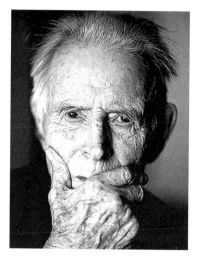

Harry Patch.

You are now parallel to the main road which you can see on your right and are heading in the direction of the attack of 31 July. On that day the ground would have been pitted with shell holes with groups of men from the Welsh Division moving from shell hole to shell hole towards the Steenbeek, which was the limit of the advance made on that day. Continue straight ahead, past the Ruisseau Farm turning, to cross a minor road – care here as you cross over – which will take you to the Harry Patch Memorial on the banks of the Steenbeek.**⓪** This is the spot where **Henry John 'Harry' Patch** crossed the Steenbeek in September 1917 during the Third Battle of Ypres. At his death in 2009 he was 111 years and 38 days old and the third oldest man in the world. Harry was conscripted into 7/ Duke of Cornwall's Light Infantry in 1916 and later related his wartime experiences in his autobiography *The Last Fighting Tommy*, in which he famously wrote 'if any man tells you he went over the top and wasn't scared, he's a damn liar'. The bridge you can see over the Steenbeek was marked on 1917 trench maps and was known then as **Reitres Bridge**. At one time it supported a branch of a German light railway network. Cross the bridge and return across the fields to Langemark along the narrow pathway that will bring you back to the church.

Route 6

Pilkem Ridge

Suitable for 🚲 🚶

Circular route starting at: Artillery Wood Cemetery.

Coordinates: 50° 53 58.72 N – 2°52 21.25 E.

Distance: 10.6km/6.6 miles.

Grade: Easy.

Maps: NGI 1:20 000 Poperinge–Ieper 28/1–2.

Link this with: Route 5 – Langemark Central.

General description and context: The route for the most part follows the attack of the 38th (Welsh) Division and the 51st (Highland) Division of 31 July 1917 on the first day of the Battle of Pilkem Ridge. Although hardly a ridge, the height difference between the bridge at Boezinge (9m above sea level) and Pilkem (25m above sea level) is a mere 16m, it was still strategically important high ground in a largely flat landscape. This period also saw the first use of mustard-gas shells by the Germans. The 38th Division attack was contained by the Ypres–Staden railway line to the northwest and a line running from the Vijfwegen crossroads northwest to the Steenbeek. On its right was the 51st Division which was attacking on a 1,300m-wide frontage. The enemy defences included the heavily fortified **Stutzpunkt Line** which lay some 700m from the start line and included numerous concrete bunkers and fortified farms and ran roughly from Pilkem, skirting Kitchener's Wood to the south towards Frezenberg. The objective for both divisions on 31 July was the Steenbeek – the Green Line – and in that they were successful. The route visits four small cemeteries which probably receive very few visitors and the larger Artillery Wood Cemetery using relatively quiet minor roads and tracks.

Directions to start: Artillery Wood is best approached using the N369 from Ieper turning right towards Pilkem and Langemark at Boezinge.

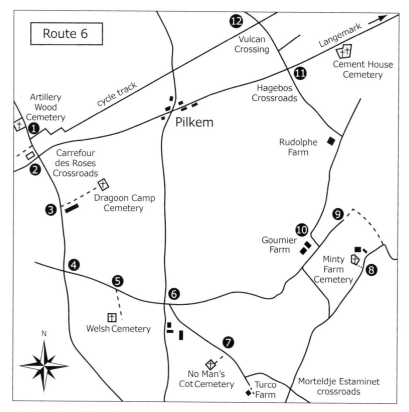

At the Carrefour des Roses crossroads turn left and park outside the cemetery.

Route description: We suggest you visit the cemetery on your return. ❶ Head south towards the wind turbines and the main Pilkem road. After 200m you will come to the **Francis Ledwidge Memorial** – set back from the road on the right – which marks the spot where the Irish poet was killed on 31 July 1917. Ledwidge was a lance corporal in 1/Royal Inniskilling Fusiliers and is buried in Artillery Wood Cemetery. Continue to the **Carrefour des Roses crossroads** ❷ and the **Breton Memorial**. Here you will find the memorial to the French 87th and the Algerian 45th Divisions which were in the front line when the German gas attack was launched on 22 April 1915. Continue across the road into Klein Poezelstraat – known to the British as Huddlestone Road – following the CWGC signposts for Dragoon Camp, Welsh Cemetery

The Francis Ledwidge Memorial near the Carrefour des Roses crossroads.

(Caesar's Nose) and Colne Valley Cemetery. Just before a long, low factory building on the left you will find a track ❸ leading to **Dragoon Camp Cemetery**. The site was taken on the 31 July 1917 and was known then as the Villa Gretchen Cemetery after a fortified stronghold nearby. Dragoon Camp Cemetery contains sixty-six burials, ten of them unidentified. This site was behind German lines until taken by the Welsh and first used by 13/Royal Welsh Fusiliers; you will find thirty-six of the identified burials are from this battalion. There are eight casualties most probably from the costly raid carried out by

15/Royal Welsh Fusiliers on 27 July 1917. The most senior officer who died as a result of the raid was **Major Evan Davies** (B.1.) from Newport, who died of his wounds the next day. Another casualty of that raid was 30-year-old **Private Alfred Horne** (B.33.). He lived in the Carmarthenshire village of Pwll with his wife, Mary Jane. On the right as you enter is a line of gunners all killed in August 1917, testament to the very effective counter-battery fire that the German gunners managed to maintain despite their loss of territory. **Air Mechanic E.T. Rose** (A.3.), aged 19, from 9 Squadron RFC was probably killed whilst attached to the field artillery operating ground to air communications with pilots from his squadron.

Retrace your route to the main road and turn left. Some 300m further on is where the German first-line trenches crossed the road from left to right in front of you; these were captured by 113 Brigade early on 31 July. When you reach the junction ❹ and turn left into Moortelweg, you will be crossing what was no-man's-land for a short distance until you reach the farm track on the right leading to **Welsh Cemetery (Caesar's Nose)**. This track was the point where the German trenches crossed the road in front of you to form a small salient on the right called **Caesar's Nose**. After stopping at the information board ❺ follow the grass track on the right of the private drive to the cemetery. Welsh Cemetery is another small isolated site that was begun after the attack and takes its name from the nearby German 'Caesar's Nose' trench system. There are sixty-eight burials here, nine of which are unidentified. There are four more possible casualties of the 27 July raid here, **Lance Corporal F. Sheldrick** (I.B.8.), **Private Charles Kyffin** (I.B.12.), **Private A.R. Davies** (I.B.6.) and **Private Edwin Griffiths** (I.A.6.). Buried on his own and to the left of the Cross of Sacrifice you will find 20-year-old **Private Cecil James** from Hayle in Cornwall who was killed on 2 September 1917 serving with 13/Welsh Regiment. **Captain Percy Lloyd Humphreys** (I.A.1.) was a bank clerk at Llandeilo prior to the war and one of the original officers of 15/Welsh Regiment. After landing in France on 4 December 1915 the battalion held nearly every section of the British line from Givenchy on the La Bassée Canal to Laventie. At

Percy Lloyd Humphries.

the end of May 1916 the 38th Division moved to the Somme and was involved in the fighting for Mametz Wood. Having survived that, 35-year-old Percy was killed on 31 July 1917 on the opening day of Third Ypres attacking the German first-line trenches just metres from this spot. The inscription on his headstone reads, 'Absent from the body, present with the Lord'. **Private Owen Roberts** (I.A.3.) was another 15/Welsh Regiment soldier. Born on Anglesey, he was killed a week before the start of the battle on 25 July, probably from shellfire. The inscription on his headstone is from a Welsh hymn and reads: 'O Frynia caersalem ceir cweled holl dath yr anialwch i cyd'.

Retrace your steps to the road and turn right. Continue to the ❻ Vijfwegen crossroads, an inn on this junction was known as 5 Chemins Estaminet and was the divisional boundary between the Welsh Division on the left and the Highlanders on the right. To your right is **Koln Farm** which was part of the fortified German first-line defences. Cross straight over and follow the road – Moortelweg – round to the right. After some 400m you will pass a house on the right, you are now leaving the German first line and walking back into no-man's-land. Ahead is **No Man's Cot Cemetery**. Follow the grass path ❼ to the cemetery entrance.

No Man's Cot was named after a building that was sited on the opposite side of the road to the northeast, so named because of its position in no-man's-land. Of the seventy-nine men buried here fifty were killed on the first day of the attack and half of the graves are of officers and men of the 51st Division. **Private Arthur Ewen** (B.10) was one of six brothers from Seven Kings in Essex who all served. Enlisting initially into the Pay Corps in 1915, Arthur transferred to 10/Welsh Regiment in May 1917. **Second Lieutenant William Rae** (A.38.) was 32 years old when he was killed serving with 6/Black Watch on 31 July. The Black Watch suffered heavy casualties in the 30 minutes before the attack began and during the course of the day they lost 9 officers and 292 other ranks. Rae was probably killed before the attack began along with **CSM J. Wallace** (A.9.) who, at 22 years old, had already won a Military Medal. **Second Lieutenant Joseph Avery** (B.4.) returned home from Argentina to serve with 10/Welsh Regiment. Originally from Newport in South Wales, the 20-year-old was killed whilst his platoon was attacking a German machine-gun position.

After leaving the cemetery return to the road and turn right and continue to the junction. Straight in front of you is **Turco Farm** – or Klokhof Farm as it is today – which was inside British lines and, for a time, the divisional HQ of the 51st Division. On 19 November 1915 **Corporal Samuel Meekosha**, 1/6 Yorkshire Regiment, won the Victoria Cross for digging out dead and wounded comrades under murderous shell and machine-gun fire near British positions known as **Knaresboro Castle** and **The Pump Room** which were about halfway down the farm road and 150m to the left. Meekosha was promoted to captain and survived the war and was commissioned in the Second World War, finally being discharged in 1948, due to a name change, as Major Ingham! Bear left here onto the continuation of Moortelweg to reach the crossroads and stop. This is the Morteldje Estaminet crossroads. Straight ahead, running down to Wieltje, is **Admiral's Road**. The road is said to be named after **Lieutenant Cyril Aldin-Smith** DSO, a 39-year-old naval reservist who avoided capture and internment at Antwerp and somehow finished up attached to the 6th Division HQ staff where he remained until he was reported missing on 10 June 1916. However, whether the road was actually named after Lieutenant Smith or not will probably never be known for sure. Smith is commemorated on the Menin Gate, Panel 57.

At the crossroads turn left onto Briekesstraat and in approximately 150m, where a farm road branches off to the right, you will cross the German front line again, running left to right in front of you. The road you are on now runs along the divisional boundary with the 39th Division which was attacking towards the northeast on the right of the road. Ignore the next road on the left and continue to the junction where there is a large red-brick house. Bear right here along Bruin Broekstraat and just before you reach Minty Farm cast your eyes over to the left to catch a glimpse of the German bunker at '**Gournier Farm'**, which is how it was marked on British trench maps of spring 1917. The entrance to **Minty Farm Cemetery** is on the left ❸ just before the farm house. The farm was taken by 6/Gordon Highlanders on 31 July 1917 and here they established their company HQ. The cemetery is the final resting place of 187 identified casualties including several Royal Navy reservists who fought as infantrymen in the 63rd Royal Naval Division. The division was composed largely of surplus reserves of the Royal Navy who were not required at sea. Battalions were named after famous British naval commanders. There are a

Minty Farm Cemetery.

The Gournier – or Goumier – Farm bunker.

number of gunners buried here who probably met their deaths from German counter-battery fire when the artillery was brought up to this point to begin bombarding the German Steenbeek defences.

Leave the cemetery and turn left. Where the road bends sharply to the right, take the narrow farm track on the left which runs alongside a field boundary, continue and make a sharp turn left to rejoin the road by a private house. You are now on Wijngaardstraat **9**, and right in the middle of the heavily fortified Stutzpunkt Line which ran along the line of the track you have just followed. Continue to the next junction and turn right. Where the road bends to the right stop **10**. Across to the left is **Gournier Farm** with its bunker. On 31 July 1917 it was taken by

Henry Maxwell-Stuart's headstone.

men of 6/Black Watch who captured the garrison and took twenty prisoners by working round the flanks of the bunker from shell hole to shell hole. Current opinion suggests the original spelling of '*Gournier*' as it appeared on the trench maps is a misreading of the French word '*Goumier*', which probably has its origins from the French cavalry's tenure of the position in 1915. '*Goumier*' more properly described North African tribal auxiliaries or irregular soldiers attached to the French Army. Here also the Stutzpunkt Line carried on towards Pilkem, for the purposes of the attack of 31 July this was called the Black Line which was the second objective of the attack of 31 July and taken by about 7.45am. It was somewhere near Goumier Farm that **Second Lieutenant William Maitland**, advancing with C Company 5/Gordon Highlanders, won the DSO for attacking a machine-gun position, killing the gun crew and capturing the weapon. Shortly afterwards he was badly wounded but survived the war.

Continue along Briekestraat until just after the large farm then take the left turning into Groenstraat. This was the site of **Rudolphe Farm**, another fortified stronghold where there was a bunker of similar proportions to Goumier Farm. This stronghold was taken by a platoon from 15/Welsh Regiment. The church you can see in the distance is Sint-Paulus at Langemark. In 600m you will arrive at **Hagebos crossroads ⓫**, sometimes referred to as the Iron Cross crossroads. The enemy positions here were taken by 14/Welsh Regiment and to the left you will find the plaque commemorating the Welsh poet **Private Ellis Humphrey Evans** on the roadside building. This

Francis Ledwidge.

was the site of a regimental aid post where Evans, serving with 15/Welsh Regiment, died on 31 July. Details of the memorial plaque can be found in the Langemark Area Car Tour. Cross straight over – signposted Ruisseau Farm Cemetery – and continue to the first road on the right. This is the Donkerweg and you now have a choice of route.

To join the Langemark Central route and visit Langemark, Ruisseau Farm and Cement House Cemetery, turn right and follow directions for Route 5 from ❾.

Route 6 continues straight ahead and in another 300m you will meet the cycle and pedestrian path, this is **Vulcan Crossing ⓬** and was cleared by 3/Grenadiers at about 8.00am on 31 July. Turn left along the track, it is a little over 2km to **Artillery Wood Cemetery**. There are now 1,307 Great War casualties buried or commemorated in this cemetery. Sadly, just under half of the burials are unidentified but special memorials commemorate twelve casualties known or believed to be buried amongst them. Buried here are **Ellis Humphrey Evans** (II.F.11) and **Lance Corporal Francis Edward Ledwidge** (II.B.5.) who was serving with 5/Royal Inniskilling Fusiliers. The 29-year-old Irish poet was killed on 31 July 1917, the same day as Evans, and it is probable they died within a few hundred metres of each other. You will have already passed by the separate **Ledwidge Memorial**. Spare a moment for 21-year-old **Private John 'Jack' Lynham** (X.C.18) who served first with the Leinster Regiment but deserted from Portlaosie Barracks and enlisted in the Irish Guards with his cousin John

Redmond. John Lynham was killed on 3 August 1917 crossing no-man's-land. His cousin survived. Pause for a moment by **Second Lieutenant Henry Maxwell-Stuart** (VIII.E.1.) of 3/Coldstream Guards who was one of four brothers killed in the war. All educated at Stonyhurst College, Henry's brothers were **Alfred**, aged 20, killed on 24 August 1918, **Edmund**, who served in the RE and was killed on 24 April 1916, and the youngest, **Joseph**, aged 19, who was killed on 2 March 1916.

Joseph Maxwell-Stuart.

Alfred Maxwell-Stuart.

Edmund Maxwell-Stuart.

Route 7
Kitchener's Wood

Suitable for 🚲 🚶

Circular route starting at: St Julian Dressing Station Cemetery.

Coordinates: 50°53 16.07 N – 2°56 08.54 E.

Distance: 4.1km/2.5 miles.

Grade: Easy.

Maps: NGI 1:20 000 Poperinge–Ieper 28/1–2.

Link this with: Route 8 – Frezenberg Ridge.

General description and context: The first German gas attack was launched at 5.00pm on 22 April 1915, the effect of the cloud of chlorine gas on the French 87th and Algerian 45th Divisions was cataclysmic and an 8km gap was opened up in the Allied line. Fortunately it was the rapid response of the Canadians and Belgians that prevented complete disaster. At Kitchener's Wood units of the 1st Canadian Division counter-attacked at midnight in bright moonlight, but after an initial success were forced to retire back on Mousetrap Farm. On 23/24 April the Allied lines were reinforced and the next day further gas attacks took place along the northern rim of the Ypres Salient and Sint-Juliaan was captured. There was a further attempt on 26 April by the Indian Lahore Division and 149 Northumbrian Brigade to take Mauser Ridge and Kitchener's Wood. Both units barely got beyond their jumping off positions and suffered horrendous casualties. Sint-Juliaan was not retaken until 1917 and temporarily lost again during the German 1918 offensive to be captured finally by the Belgian Army six months later in September.

Directions to start: From Ieper take the N369 north towards Boezinge and after passing Duhallow ADS Cemetery on the right, turn right onto the N38 in the direction of Sint-Juliaan. St Julian Dressing Station Cemetery is on the right as you enter the village.

Route description: We suggest you visit the cemetery after completing the route. With the cemetery ❶ on your right, proceed up to the main road, turn right onto the N313 and cross over. Take the next road on the left – Peperstraat. Just after turning left you will see a calvary on the left, half concealed by ivy, immediately after is a narrow pathway ❷ between two private houses that is easily missed. This is the path that takes you past Juliet Farm and along which you will later re-enter the village. Continue towards the large factory buildings ahead taking care not to miss the concrete bunker on the right-hand side of the road. This bunker was called **Hackney Villa** by the British and used as a command post and field hospital and should not be confused with the **Alberta Bunker** which was demolished a few years ago. Continue past the factory buildings to reach a crossroads – known as **Regina Cross** ❸ on trench maps. This crossroads was the scene of bitter fighting on 31 July 1917 after 116 Infantry Brigade had recaptured Sint-Juliaan and units of 117 Brigade overcame the three concrete bunkers at Regina Cross with only rifle grenades and mortars.

Turn left at the crossroads into Broekstraat passing a private road on the right. This road marked the approximate divisional boundary between the German 51st and 52nd Reserve Infantry Divisions prior to the attack of 22 April 1915. You will soon come to another track, this time on your left, which in 1915 formed the edge of **Kitchener's Wood** ❹ or, as it was prior to the war, the Bois des Cuisiniers, the translation of which gave rise to the name Kitchener's Wood and not, as is often supposed, the Secretary of State for War, Lord Kitchener. The wood bordered the road for some 150m after it met the line of the track where you are now standing. Although nothing remains of the wood today, it extended some 300m from the road towards Juliet Farm. A walk down the track will give you an

The Kitchener's Wood Memorial.

indication of its extent in 1915. Continue down the road alongside what was the edge of the wood to a T-junction. Turn left here into Wijngaardstraat and shortly afterwards you will see a private house on the left, here ❺ you will find the **Kitchener's Wood Memorial**. Designed by **Jozef Dekeyser**, the memorial was erected in 1997 by the school children of the Vrije Basisschool in Sint-Juliaan. The memorial depicts the oak trees of the wood topped by clouds of gas. After leaving the memorial continue to the small crossroads ❻ and stop. To your right is **Oblong Farm**, known by the Germans as **Hof Soetaert**. On the night of 22 April 1915 there was a German machine gun here which was responsible for a large number of casualties in the ranks of the attacking Canadian 10/Battalion heading towards Kitchener's Wood. To your left is the track leading down past Juliet Farm. This was the position of the front line at midnight on 22 April, running from Oblong Farm across to Juliet Farm and thence to Sint-Juliaan. You now have a choice of route.

> *To join **Route 8** you will need to continue straight ahead. Before you do so, however, go down the track past Juliet Farm to visit the bunkers and stand on the spot where the Canadians began their attack on the wood.*

To return to Sint-Juliaan turn left down the path towards Juliet Farm which in 1915 was on the other side of the track. The ground on your right is where the 10th (Alberta) and 16th (Canadian Scottish) Battalions of the Canadian 1st Division formed up after leaving **Mousetrap Farm** prior to their counter-attack on Kitchener's Wood. The farm was previously called Shelltrap Farm, the name change considered to be less ominous! This attack was the first by a Canadian Army on foreign soil and carried out by men who had no battle experience. To your left would have been the wood that had been captured earlier that day by 51st and 52nd German Reserve Infantry Divisions after the launch of the gas attack. Ponder for a moment on the scene south of Juliet Farm on the night of 22 April. Some 1,800 Canadian troops were moving forward to assault the wood which would have been a dark patch some 300m ahead on the skyline. Even before they got to the wood the fusillade of German rifle and machine-gun fire cut down hundreds of the young

Canadians but they took most of the wood and some even penetrated beyond it. The cost in human life was enormous. Of the 2 battalions only 10 officers and 449 men were still capable of fighting, the wounded included the CO of 10/Battalion, **Lieutenant Colonel Russell Boyle**, who died of his wounds two days later. Tall and courageous, Boyle was an imposing figure and a popular commander. As you go past the farm keep a look out for the four bunkers in the farm grounds, these were captured during the British advance in 1917. The track continues past the farm and brings you to back to Sint-Juliaan at its junction with Peperstraat.❷ Turn right and cross the N313 with care back to your vehicle at the cemetery.

Lieutenant Colonel Russell Boyle.

St Julian Dressing Station Cemetery was begun in September 1917 and was badly damaged during the 1918 battle. After the Armistice, when bodies from the battlefields surrounding Sint-Juliaan were brought in, the cemetery was expanded to its present-day capacity. There are 420 men buried or commemorated here, 180 of the burials are unidentified, but there are special memorials to 11 casualties known or believed to be buried amongst them. In the left-hand corner, beneath two beech trees, lie eight **Royal Marines** of 150 (RN) Field Ambulance, six of whom were killed on 30 October 1917. **Lieutenant Cecil Dutton Darlington** (I.F.1.) was flying a Sopwith Camel of 204 Squadron when he was shot down and killed on 15 August 1918. His aircraft was one of four lost by the squadron that morning. In the far left-hand corner is the solitary grave of **Robert Dyott Willmot** (III.C.1.), a 19-year-old second lieutenant in 2/King's Royal Rifle Corps killed on 17 February 1918. Two years earlier, his brother **Second Lieutenant John Dyott Willmot**, who was also 19 years old, was killed on 3 July 1915 serving with the Worcestershire Regiment. It was a double tragedy for the boys' parents who lived at Coleshill in

A total of 413 pilots died flying the Sopwith Camel in combat after it came into service in May 1917.

Warwickshire and one that prompted their father, George Dyott Willmot, chairman of the Coleshill Finance Committee, to instigate the funding and building of the Coleshill War Memorial in 1919. One of the numerous Royal Naval Division infantrymen in the cemetery is 36-year-old **Able Seaman Henry Colgrave** (I.D.1.), a former furnace labourer from Kettering. Serving with the Nelson Battalion, Henry was conscripted in 1916 and wounded in April 1917. After rejoining his unit on 19 May 1917 he was killed in action six months later. He left a widow and a daughter, Ellen. **Second Lieutenant Lawrence S.B. Brown** (II.K.36.) went straight from the George Heriot's School in Edinburgh into the Army in 1915 as a private soldier but was soon commissioned, initially into the Royal Scots before transferring to the Machine-Gun Corps. He won his MC on 17 September 1917. He was killed by shellfire on 27 November 1917.

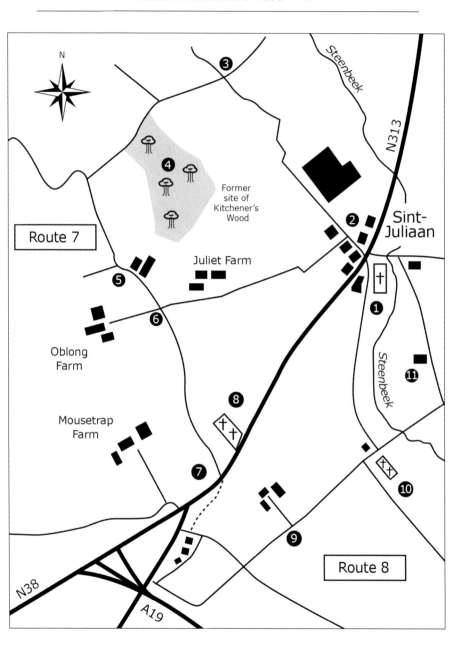

Route 8

Frezenberg Ridge

Suitable for 🚲 🚶

Circular route starting at: St Julian Dressing Station Cemetery.
Coordinates: 50°53 16.07 N – 2°56 08.54 E.
Distance: 6.1km/3.8 miles.
Grade: Easy.
Maps: NGI 1:20 000 Poperinge–Ypres 28/1–2.

General description and context: After the German gas attack of April 1915 the Salient around Ieper was reduced in area by a third and a new defensive line prepared on the forward slopes of the gentle ridges in the north and centre of the Salient. On 8 May the Germans launched another attack on Ieper over the Frezenberg Ridge. Supported again by gas and a furious bombardment, it succeeded in pushing the British off the high ground in some of the bitterest fighting then experienced in the Salient. Our route passes across the northern end of the ridge where the front line, held by the 28th Division, ran approximately along the line of the present-day A19 motorway to Wieljte and then across to Mousetrap Farm. It was on these slopes that infantry battalions such as 2/Cheshires and 1/Monmouths were practically annihilated as they stood firm against overwhelming odds. You may find it useful to read the Route 7 context.

Directions to start: From Ieper take the N369 north towards Boezinge and after passing Duhallow ADS Cemetery on the right, turn right onto the N38 in the direction of Sint-Juliaan. **St Julian Dressing Station Cemetery** is on the right as you enter the village.

Route description: This route starts as per that for Kitchener's Wood and crosses the start line from where the Canadian battalions began their attack on Kitchener's Wood on 22 April 1915. You will find the general description and context for the Kitchener's Wood route useful as you walk across to Juliet Farm. From the cemetery ❶ on your right, walk up to the main road, turn right onto the N313 and cross over. Take the next road on the left – Peperstraat. Just after turning left you will see a calvary on the left, half concealed by ivy. Immediately after is a narrow pathway ❷ between two private houses that is easily missed. Turn left along the pathway. This path is a little to the south of the front line as it was on 22 April 1915 and across to your right is where 51st and 52nd German Reserve Infantry Divisions attacked following the gas attack. Continue along the path until **Juliet Farm** comes into view on the right. Just before the farm are four German bunkers. Continue to the crossroads and stop. Directly opposite you is **Oblong Farm** and 220m to the right ❺ is the **Kitchener's Wood Memorial** (see Route 7).

Turn left and continue towards the N313. The farm you can see across to the right is **Mousetrap Farm –** where the Canadian division had its HQ and from where the attacking Canadian battalions moved up to Juliet Farm to begin their counter-attack. At the junction with the main road ❼ turn left to find the **Seaforth Cemetery, Cheddar Villa.** Cheddar Villa ❽ was the name given to the farm on the west side of the road from Wieltje to Sint-Juliaan. On 25 and 26 April 1915, during the **Battle of St Julien**, severe fighting took place in this area when Allied forces counter-attacked in an attempt to regain ground lost during the German gas attack. The dead were buried on the spot. At the time the cemetery was called Cheddar Villa Cemetery, but at the request of the Officer Commanding 2/Seaforth Highlanders, its name was changed in 1922. The names of twenty-three officers and men of the Seaforths who fell here on 25/26 April 1915, but are known to be buried in the cemetery, are recorded on a tablet. These casualties are officially commemorated by name on the **Menin Gate Memorial** and are in addition to the ninety-nine Seaforth Highlanders who also fell in the same action. Buried here is **Major Kenneth Wyndham Arbuthnot** (A.5.), aged 40, who was the Brigade Major of the Gordon Infantry Brigade. He was commissioned into the Seaforths in 1893 and fought at the Battle of Omdurman and in the Second Boer War. Twelve years his junior is **Lance Corporal Kenneth MacKenzie** (A.29.) from Ullapool who at 18 years old is the youngest known casualty in the cemetery. Along the right-hand wall are eighteen men of the Northumberland Fusiliers who were all killed on 26 April 1915 during the

Seaforth Cemetery, Cheddar Villa.

The Cambrai Bunkers.

The Monmouthshire Regiment Memorial.

149 Northumberland Brigade assault on Sint-Juliaan. Another tragically young second lieutenant is 19-year-old **Granville John Fielden** (A.3.) whose father commanded 2/Seaforth Highlanders during the Boer War and was awarded the DSO in 1902. Granville Fielden was commissioned into the regiment in August 1914 and killed on 25 April 1915. You will find the **Cheddar Villa Bunker** to the right of the cemetery amongst the farm buildings.

Retrace your steps to the T-junction with the N313 and cross over the road with care to the marked cycle path on the opposite side. Turn right along the tree-lined track, turning left into Tentestraat and then almost immediately right onto Kattestraat. In about 100m you should be able to see the **Pickelhaube House Bunker** in a field across to your left. Continue past a row of residential houses and turn left at the junction with Roeselaarsestraat. Follow the road round the left-hand bend. Just before the next crossroads in a field on your right you will see the three **Cambrai Bunkers**. You are now heading into part of the area which was fought over during the **Battle of Frezenberg Ridge** and if you look across to the right you can see the flat top of the Frezenberg Ridge before it drops away to Polygon Wood and the Menin Road further to the southeast. At the crossroads continue straight on for another 150m to **1st Battalion Monmouthshire Regiment Memorial ❾** on the right.

Bridge House Cemetery.

The British withdrawal in early May to shorten the line of the Salient left 84 Infantry Brigade on the forward slopes of the Frezenberg Ridge, where on the morning of 8 May they faced a devastating bombardment followed by an infantry attack. The day before the attack 1/Monmouths moved into the line close to where the monument is sited and found themselves defending a line consisting of rifle pits and breastwork emplacements. The next morning the German assault was fought off gallantly all along the line until 83 Brigade on the right was forced to retire, allowing enemy troops to exploit the gap in the line. A bitter hand-to-hand fight ensued and although the Welshmen were partly surrounded, they fought on until they were eventually forced to retire leaving two-thirds of the battalion dead or wounded behind them. **Second Lieutenant Henry Anthony Birrell-Anthony** was one of 13 officers and 382 other ranks who became casualties close to this spot. The memorial tablet reads: 'In memory of Lieut H A Birrell-Anthony and the officers of the 1st Battalion the Monmouthshire Regiment who fell at this spot in the Second Battle of Ypres on the 8th May 1915 and the NCOs and riflemen who fell at the same time'.

A little further on, sandwiched between farm buildings, is the tiny **Bridge House Military Cemetery ⑩**. Named after a farmhouse, the cemetery was begun by the 59th (North Midland) Division at the end of September 1917. There are forty-five burials here and all but one, **Rifleman Walter Baker** (C.1.) serving with 14/Royal Irish Rifles and killed on 16 August 1917, were killed in September 1917 at or near Polygon Wood.

After leaving the cemetery ignore the turning on the left – Peperstraat – and continue along the road to the next left-hand turning just before a large private house on the right. Turn left here onto Haezeweidestraat. When you get to the farm, about 400m ahead of you on the left, stop. This was the site of **Wine House ⑪**, a 1917 German strongpoint in a fortified line that ran all the way back to Juliet Farm over to your left and included **Pond Farm** across to the right. Just past the farm a German trench known as **Canvass Trench** ran across the road. Once past the farm you should be able to see the Cross of Sacrifice in the St Julian Dressing Station Cemetery ❶ ahead of you on the left. Cemetery details can be found in the Kitchener's Wood route description. Continue into Sint-Juliaan, turn left at the junction with the N313 and follow the road back to your vehicle.

Route 9
Polygon Wood

Suitable for 🚶

Circular route starting at: Passchendaele Memorial Museum or Polygon Wood Cemetery.

Coordinates: Polygon Wood Cemetery 50°51 25.53 N – 2°59 25.81 E.

Distance: 4km/2.5 miles (7.2km/4.4 miles if starting from Zonnebeke).

Grade: Easy.

Toilets: Passchendaele Memorial Museum.

Maps: NGI 1:20 000 Zonnebeke–Moorslede 28/3–4.

General description and context: Polygon Wood, like much of the Salient, was heavily fought over as the front line moved back and forth in the great battles that focused on Ypres. Prior to the war the wood was often referred to as Racecourse Wood and contained two recognizable landmarks: the Buttes, a large earthen mound that had been the backdrop to the Ypres rifle range, and the racecourse which was in the centre of the wood. Today only the Buttes remains, upon which stands the memorial to the Australian 5th Division in the Buttes New British Cemetery. In 1914 the wood was held by the British during the First Battle of Ypres until the German offensive of 1915 pushed Allied forces back towards Ypres. It was not until September 1917, during the Third Battle of Ypres, that it was retaken after some exceptionally bloody fighting by two Australian (4th and 5th) and five British divisions. If you approach Polygon Wood along Citernestraat from Zonnebeke you will be walking along the road that was the first objective of the 4th Australian Division which was attacking north of the wood on 26 September 1917. With this line taken they poured over the road to the Blue Line some 500m further to the east. Later that day the 5th Australian Division, having successfully cleared the wood, reached the Buttes and that afternoon went on to reach their final

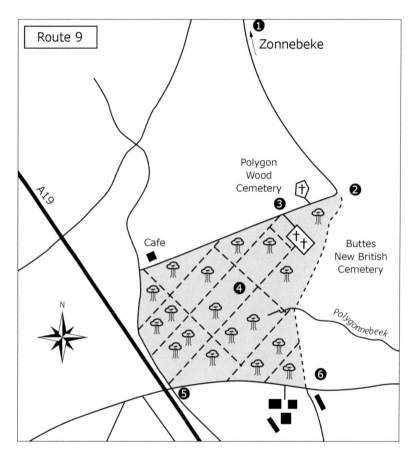

objective. In April 1918 the last German offensive of the war forced Allied troops back to within 1.5km of the gates of Ypres and for the final time the wood fell into German hands before it was retaken by the 9th (Scottish) Division on 28 September 1918.

Directions to start: Zonnebeke is best approached using the N332 from Ieper. In Zonnebeke turn right onto the Berten Pilstraat just before the museum. There is ample parking in the large car parks of the Memorial Museum and Library. There is a restaurant and bar next to the museum building.

Route description: This short walk takes us through Polygon Wood and along its southern and eastern edges visiting Polygon Wood Cemetery and the Buttes New British Cemetery. The wood can be approached on foot from Zonnebeke which is only 1.6km to the north and visitors may prefer to leave their vehicles at the **Passchendaele Memorial Museum** car park ❶ and include a visit to the museum in their itinerary. Should you decide to start your walk from Zonnebeke turn left into Berten Pilstraat after leaving the museum car park and then shortly afterwards turn right into Grote Molenstraat. At the crossroads turn left into Citernestraat. This small country road will take you directly to the northeastern corner of Polygon Wood ❷ where CWGC signs will direct you to the Polygon Wood Military Cemetery. The wood can be muddy at times and is popular at weekends with local walkers.

The present-day wood is much smaller in area than it was in 1914 and by September 1917 it had all but vanished in the muddy morass of the battlefield. We suggest you visit **Polygon Wood Cemetery** first and leave the larger **Buttes New British Cemetery** until you return. The entrance to Polygon Wood Cemetery from Lange Dreve leads to a circular area containing the Cross of Sacrifice, where, at an angle, steps lead down to the cemetery itself. There was at one time a German cemetery adjoining the British one, the old entrance can still be detected along the back wall of the cemetery by the section of newer stonework. The cemetery was begun between August 1917 and April 1918, and used again in September 1918. One unusual inscription at the base of his headstone is the postal address of **Private Arthur Samuel Holland** (H.7). Arthur was 19 years old when he died on 11 April 1918 during the German offensive. His parents, Clement and Anne Holland, lived at 45

Scott's Post.

Patterson Road, Norwich, where Clement worked as a postman. One can only imagine the sorrow at Patterson Road when news of their eldest son's death reached them. In the same row as Arthur Holland is buried **Lieutenant Eustace Keatinge** (H.2) of the Northumberland Fusiliers who was on attachment to the Durham Light Infantry. The 27-year-old Keatinge was killed on 13 April 1918, two days after he had joined the battalion. One of the most recent burials is that of **Private John Thomson** (D.2). John had been one of the missing until his body was discovered by a local gardener at Moleraarelst near Zonnebeke in 1998. Personal possessions found with the body and DNA confirmed his identity and he was buried here on 21 October 2004. Alongside him are the remains of two other soldiers found with him but who were unidentified.

From the cemetery gates ❸ turn right along Lange Dreve until you see a wide track on your left going into the wood. Turn left here and continue for another 45m until a narrow path is found on the left. This path is easy to miss but once you have spotted a red and white mark on a tree you have reached the path. A glance to your left through the trees will give you a glimpse of the Buttes Cemetery. Continue for another 100m and then turn right down a wide ride with the Buttes Cemetery now behind you. The area to your right was where the pre-war racecourse was located and during the German occupation of the wood a light railway ran down the track along which you are now walking. At the next crossroads continue for a short distance until you find a path on the right. Take this path which leads to Scott's Post ❹. This bunker along with several others was captured by the Australian 56/Battalion and named after their commanding officer, **Lieutenant Colonel Alan Humphrey Scott**, who was killed near the Buttes by a sniper's bullet on 1 October 1917.

Retrace your steps and turn right at the ride to reach the next crossroads where you turn left past the remains of a concrete bunker. Pass the obvious open area on the left and turn right at the T-junction. On reaching the wooden barrier ahead turn right again. Note the remains of another concrete bunker to your left. Follow the wooden fence on your left to a crossroads and turn left down the wide ride to reach the road. You are now at the Lotegatstraat/Oude Kortrijkstraat crossroads, known by the troops as **Black Watch Corner** ❺. The wooded area across the A19 motorway is Nonne Boschen Wood and gave its name to one of the most decisive confrontations of the First Battle of Ypres. In 1914 a small cottage and garden was located at the corner of the wood where you are now standing and was to become instrumental in defeating the attack by the elite Prussian Guard on 11 November. Commanded by **Lieutenant F. Anderson,** some forty men of 1/ Black Watch opened fire on the advancing German 3/Foot Guard Regiment from a trench inside the hedges of the cottage garden protected only by a few strands of barbed wire. Together with the combined shellfire from 51 and 16 Artillery Batteries, they forced the Germans into Nonne Boschen Wood where they were later cleared out by 2/Oxford and Buckinghamshire Light Infantry with a bayonet charge led by **Captain Henry Dillon.** Dillon was awarded the DSO for his part in the battle.

Black Watch Corner was also the start point for the charge of the 2/Worcestershire Regiment to Geluveld (Gheluvelt) Chateau on 31 October 1914. If you stand with your back to the gate at the corner of the wood and look along the motorway you can see the church spire at Geluveld. It was from this corner of the wood that **Major Edward Hankey** led his 370 men in their famous counter-attack to push back the Germans who had broken the British line at Geluveld. Hankey and his men used the church spire as a marker for their objective as they doubled across the kilometre of open ground before retaking the chateau grounds.

From Black Watch Corner turn left, away from the motorway along Oude Kortrijkstraat, passing a large farm on your right. After approximately 300m, turn left to follow a farm track alongside the eastern edge of the wood ❻. This is approximately the spot where **Lieutenant Colonel Philip Bent DSO**, commanding 9/Leicestershire Regiment, won a posthumous Victoria Cross leading a counter-attack on 1 October 1917. A little further to the northwest was the scene of another posthumous VC, awarded four days earlier to **Private Patrick Bugden**, a 20-year-old Australian hotel keeper from New South Wales, who was killed in action on 28 September fighting with 31/ Battalion.

Continue along the track with the

Private Patrick Bugden VC.

wood on your left until the Polygonebeek enters the wood at the point where the track bears slightly right. Stop here and look across to your right. Ahead of you to the left would have been the shell-torn remains of what was once **Jetty Wood** (although another wood has now grown up to the southeast of it), its few remaining tree stumps appearing as solitary sentinels amongst duckboard pathways and a maze of interlocking communication trenches. Now look behind you and imagine the same panorama stretching away to the west, add the noise of battle and the screams of the wounded and dying and you can begin to appreciate the scene that faced the Australian and British troops on the morning of 26 September 1917.

Continue along the track, ignoring the turning on your right (Spilstraat), until you come to a metalled road. Go straight ahead with the wood on your left to reach the northeastern corner ❷. Turn left to find the pedestrian path leading to **Buttes New British Cemetery** on your left. Almost entirely surrounded by trees, the cemetery is approached along a walled walkway which leads the visitor directly to

The Australian 5th Division Memorial at the Buttes Cemetery, Polygon Wood.

the imposing Australian Memorial to the 5th Division standing on the top of the Buttes. This is one of the most beautiful cemeteries in the Salient and is well worth the visit. There are 2,108 Commonwealth soldiers buried or commemorated here, sadly 1,677 of them remain unidentified. From the top of the Buttes the view over the cemetery is quite stunning, on the far side the New Zealand Memorial to the Missing commemorating 378 officers and men of the New Zealand Division who died in the Polygon Wood sector between September 1917 and May 1918 and who have no known grave. This is one of seven memorials in France and Belgium to those New Zealand soldiers who died on the Western Front and have no known grave. Amongst the Australian dead of the 5th Division

Lieutenant Colonel Alan Humphrey Scott.

is **Private Archibald Cameron** (XXX.A.10), 53/Battalion. Aged 21, from Bogan Gate, New South Wales, he was probably caught by the German barrage that opened on the rear areas after the initial Australian advance. Advised to go back to the regimental aid post after being wounded, he was never seen alive by his mates again.

New Zealander **Private Leo Gilbert Donohoe** was a gunner with 4/Trench Mortar Battery when he was killed on 3 December 1917. His death was a double blow to the Donohoe family in Papanui who had only been notified of the death of Leo's twin brother, 21-year-old Lawrence, six weeks previously. Leo was killed in action at the nearby Polderhoek Chateau and you can find his grave at II.B.14. Here also you will find 27-year-old **Lieutenant Colonel Alan Scott** (II.A.12) who had the distinction of being the longest serving commanding officer of 56/Battalion and, at the time, one of the youngest in the AIF. He took command of his battalion in February 1916 after the Allied withdrawal from Gallipoli having fought with distinction and won a DSO whilst serving with 4/Battalion. In his thirty-three months of service he had progressed from lieutenant to lieutenant colonel and was mentioned in despatches on three occasions.

On leaving the cemetery you can either return to Zonnebeke along Citernestraat or return to your vehicle via Polygon Wood Cemetery.

Route 10
Passendale

Suitable for 🚲 🚶

Circular route starting at: the Passchendaele Memorial Museum at Zonnebeke.

Coordinates: 50°52 13.91 N – 2°59 15.29 E.

Distance: 12.3km/7.7 miles.

Grade: Moderate.

Toilets: Memorial Museum and Tyne Cot Cemetery.

Maps: NGI 1:20 000 Zonnebeke–Moorslede 28/3–4.

General description and context: The Allies' objective in the Third Battle of Ypres was to break through the German defences, seize the high ground of the Passchendaele Ridge and from there capture the German-occupied Belgian Channel ports. These ports were important to the German strategy, as many of their deadly submarines operated from them. The battle has become known as 'Passchendaele' which in itself is misleading as the battle for the village (called Passendale today) only occupied a few weeks of the four-month-long campaign. Today, the imagery of acres of mud and water-filled shell holes is closely associated with that battle and is one that has been adopted by popular history as typical of the whole war. This is of course incorrect. The Third Battle of Ypres began in the warmth of a very dry July 1917 and even in September there was another exceptionally dry period when water shortages became an issue for the attacking troops. Our route is punctuated with numerous information panels, particularly along the old railway line, and starts at Zonnebeke. For the most part it follows the advance of the Canadian Corps to Passendale village on traffic-free pathways and minor roads. Superb views can be had across the battlefields from the Wieltje road before the route cuts across the Ravebeek valley to Tyne Cot Cemetery and returns via the old railway to Zonnebeke.

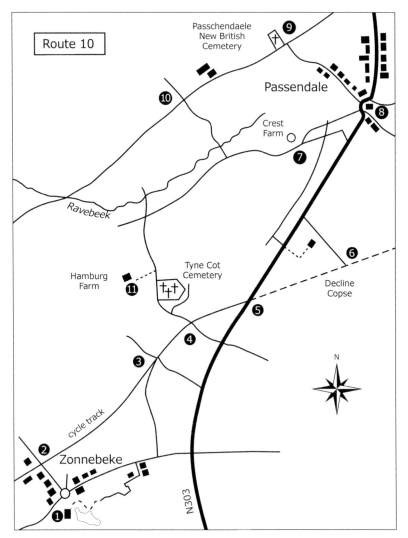

Directions to start: Zonnebeke is best approached using the N332 from Ieper. In Zonnebeke turn right before you reach the church on to the Berten Pilstraat. The museum is signposted on the right. There is ample parking in the large car parks of the museum.

Route description: From the car park ❶ return along Berten Pilstraat and turn right. At the roundabout turn left onto Ieperstraat. Continue straight ahead to meet the cycle and pedestrian path immediately after

The Thames Farm bunker alongside the line of the old Ypres–Roulers railway.

the old brick station building ❷ on the right. The station was built in 1898 and today only a small part of the original complex remains. Turn right along the cycle track. The high ground of the West Flanders Ridge soon comes into view after a short distance. It was this ground the Allied forces had to take in 1917. Continue along the cycle track, passing the **Thames Farm bunker** on the right, until it crosses a metalled road – Schipstraat. This is **Daring Crossing** ❸ where the Ypres–Roulers railway crossed the road. On British trench maps the level crossings in this area all began with the letter 'D'. Captured by the Australian 44th Battalion, the crossing was fortified at the time by three bunkers, each of which had to be overcome. On 4 October 1917 the Australians launched their attack which became known as the Battle of Broodseinde, and although casualties on both sides were very high it was a day that is regarded as the most successful of the entire Third Ypres campaign. The 4 ANZAC Divisions suffered more than 8,000 men killed wounded or missing. The Australian 10 Brigade alone lost 25 officers and almost 900 men in a battle that exacted a heavy price on both sides. Of the many German dead killed that day, one man – **Otto Bieber** – is buried in the original battlefield cemetery at Tyne Cot Cemetery just 500m away to the north, along with three other unidentified German soldiers. Here you would be pushing through the German front-line system which ran, left to right to your front, between you and the site of Dash Crossing up ahead.

Continue to the second crossing ❹ with Tynecotstraat. This was **Dash Crossing**, the point at which the railway sliced through the West Flanders Ridge in a deep cutting with steep banks on either side. That cutting is now directly ahead of you. There is an information board 150m further along the cycle track. Stop here. German dugouts, shelters and machine-gun positions were situated in the bank to your left, whilst the

Australian soldiers sheltering amongst the dead in the railway cutting north of Dash Crossing. Private Austin Henderson of the 38th Battalion AIF is on the extreme right.

German cemetery of Kerselaarhoek was on the elevated ground just beyond. In the 1950s the German soldiers buried there were moved into the large German concentration cemetery at Langemark. This spot marks the furthest point reached by the Australians of 44/Battalion on 4 October 1917.

The capture of the Broodseinde Ridge was not the end of the story; this section of railway witnessed some of the most vicious fighting of the entire campaign. On 9 October, 4 Territorial battalions of Lancashire Fusiliers of the 66th Division lost 307 dead of whom 247 were listed as missing. During excavations of the railway in 2005 the original rails and sleepers were uncovered along with the remains of one of those Lancashire Fusiliers – a young private of between 18 and 24 years of age who was found in a shell hole between two sleepers. A Bible had been placed on his splintered skull and he had been wrapped in a canvas groundsheet. Sadly it was impossible to identify him and he now lies in Tyne Cot Cemetery.

Continue on to where the track meets the Broodseinde–Passendale road. This was **Defy Crossing ❺** and if you look along the road to your left you will see Passendale church up the rise and the rather squat memorial to the 85th Canadian Infantry Battalion – vegetation permitting – standing alone on the skyline. Take care when crossing as this can be a busy road. Stay on the cycle track, which is now unmetalled. The going is good initially but the ground becomes uneven and in wet weather can be quite heavy going. Just before reaching the road you will pass through the former site of **Decline Copse** which straddled the railway line in 1917. The 3rd Australian Division attacked across this ground on 12 October during the First Battle of Passchendaele. It was here that the Australians were held up by machine-gun fire from a pill box just this side of the road ahead. **Captain Clarence Smith Jeffries**, who had already organized the capture of

Captain Clarence Jeffries VC.

two pill boxes north of Tyne Cot that day, planned another attack on the strongpoint holding the Australians up. The pill box was captured but he was killed in the attempt and Jeffries received a posthumous VC. Jeffries is buried in Tyne Cot Cemetery ironically very close to a pill box similar to the ones he attacked that day.

Confusion as to who had – or had not – cleared Decline Copse of enemy troops led to a German counter-attack a little over two weeks later on 28 October just as the Canadian 85/Battalion were relieving the hard-pressed 44/Battalion. It was here that **Private Lawrence** held off the attack on the eastern edge of the copse with a single Lewis Gun and two pans of ammunition to allow more men to come forward and re-establish the line.

At the junction with the road ahead, turn left ❻ on to Nieuwe-molenstraat and continue uphill towards the N303.

At the junction with the N303 – Passchendaelestraat – turn left to the access track which leads to the 85/Battalion memorial containing the names of the 13 officers and 113 other ranks that fell during their attack. After visiting the memorial, return to the main road and cross straight over into Rozestraat, following the road to the junction. Turn right and continue parallel to the N303 until you reach the junction with Martinegatstraat. Turn left to the Canadian Memorial at **Crest Farm** ❼ which was taken by the 72/Canadian Infantry Battalion on 29 October. The farm held a dominant position over the two spurs of ground that ran southwest from the main Passendale Ridge, if you stand next to the memorial and look around, you can get some idea of the fields of fire the defending Germans had over their attackers. Looking north over the Ravebeek valley you can see Passchendaele New British Cemetery on the Bellevue Ridge. The sheer determination of the Canadians in continuing their advance and keeping very close behind the artillery barrage still ranks as one of the finest infantry attacks by a single unit in the whole campaign. The survivors held the farm until they were relieved in the early hours of 2 November 1917. It was from here that the final assault on the village began four days later.

Retrace your route and take the first turn left on to Canadalaan. As the road bears right the church comes into view dead ahead. Continue uphill to the village centre. Although this road was not in existence in 1917, it was the route the 27/Battalion took when they entered the village on 6 November and it was somewhere in the vicinity of this road

The Crest Farm Memorial with Passendale church in the distance.

Passchendaele New British Cemetery.

that **Private James Robertson** of the 27th won his Victoria Cross by rushing a German machine-gun position. He is the only one of the nine Canadian VCs killed in the campaign who has a known grave. You will find him at Tyne Cot. It is difficult to believe that Passendale village was completely obliterated due to the intensity of the British shelling. What was in 1916 a village with houses, shops, roads and lanes shaded by avenues of trees had, by early November 1917, become a slough of closely overlapping shell craters filled with water. There were no identifying features and even the site of the church – a point of identification today – had to be marked by a board erected by the defending Germans.

Private James Robertson VC.

The church of Sint-Audomarus ❽ now dominates the village square and inside you will find the memorial window to the British 66th Division featuring the names of Lancashire towns with their coats of arms around the central figure of St George. Across the road on the front of the Stadhuis are several plaques commemorating Belgian regiments of both world wars and the Western Front Association Passchendaele Memorial, whilst in the square itself is a relief map by Australian sculptor Ross Bastiaan.

Leave the square with the Stadhuis on your left and continue up Vierde Regiment Karabinierstraat until you meet the main road. ❾

Opposite is **Passchendaele New British Cemetery** where you will find an Albertina Marker to the right of the entrance. Look over the back wall of the cemetery into the fields beyond. Even after the closure of the Third Ypres campaign on 10 November 1917 some very heavy fighting took place in the weeks that followed as the Allies tried to gain overall command of the ridge northeast of Passendale for the winter. At 1.55am on the bright moonlit night of 2 December 1917, 2/KOYLI launched an attack – part of the only large-scale night attack during the entire campaign – on the German trenches from positions some 500m off into the fields, moving diagonally away from you to the right. They had set off from Irish Farm almost seven hours earlier. The march of 8km along wooden duckboard tracks on a winter's night through what was by then a cratered, featureless wasteland of cloying mud can only be imagined. The men were seen as soon as they rose to the attack and were cut down by heavy machine-gun fire as they struggled forward, almost all officers and senior NCOs becoming casualties. The attack failed and losses were very heavy. A total of 6 officers and 23 men were killed with 120 men wounded and 41 missing. Later revisions put the total number of killed at 52. Amongst the missing was pre-war regular soldier **Private Albert Cooksey**, great uncle of one of the authors. Albert Cooksey has no known grave and is remembered at Tyne Cot on Panel 108 along with many of his comrades who went missing that night.

Passchendaele New British Cemetery was begun when graves were brought in from the battlefields of Passchendaele and Langemarck after the Armistice. Of the 2,101 burials most are from 1917, tragically 1,600 are unidentified. As you would expect there are a large number of Canadian troops buried here along with their ANZAC comrades. Amongst the identified Canadians are ten officers and men of the Princess Partricia's Canadian Light Infantry (PPCLI), probably all casualties from the 30 October fighting up the Ravebeek valley. **Lieutenant Harold Agar** (X.E.22) was originally from Hull before emigrating to teach in Canada. A former territorial soldier, he was killed on 30 October serving in A Company PPCLI. Another PPCLI officer was **Captain Rider Lancelot Haggard** (VII.A.19), who was the nephew of the author Sir Rider Haggard. He worked as a bank clerk in Ottowa before enlisting as a private in August 1914 and was commissioned a year later. He saw action at the Battle of Mount Sorrel and on the Somme before he was wounded in September 1916. After returning from leave in October 1917, he was killed by shellfire on 30 October 1917. He was 24 years old. **Private William Barclay** (VIII.B.17) was killed on 26 October serving with A Company of the Canadian 58/Battalion. William enlisted in February 1916 at Stratford, Ontario, where he was working as a labourer. Originally from Aberdeenshire, his death left his wife Mary a widow who remembered him with the inscription, 'A silent thought, a secret tear, keep his memory ever dear'. **Second Lieutenant Stanley Lorne Crowther** (VII.E.30) from Toronto was killed flying a Nieuport Scout with 29 Squadron on 20 September 1917. The inscription on his headstone reads, 'He died at his post of duty, a soldier of the air'. His brother William, serving as a major with the Canadian 3/Battalion, was killed on 3 May 1917 at Fresnoy. On the rear wall of the cemetery are seven special memorials, one of which commemorates the **Revd 4th Class Harry Dickinson** from Hall Green in Birmingham who was attached to the Artist's Rifles and killed on 30 September 1917. Five more of the Artist's Rifles lie in the cemetery. Before you leave say hello to **Rifleman Percy Milburn** (XII.B.5) of 16/King's Royal Rifle Corps who lies in a row with of ten of his comrades, of which only three are identified.

> *After leaving the cemetery turn right. This short section of road (0.89km) has no dedicated foot or cycle path and pedestrians should walk on the left facing towards the oncoming traffic. This section can be avoided altogether by retracing your steps to Crest Farm and following Canadalaan to the junction with Tynecotstraat.*

You are now heading down the West Flanders Ridge, known also as the Bellevue Ridge, in the direction of Ieper. As you begin to descend, the views over to the right open out and there are superb views over the 1917 battlefield towards Ieper. On a clear day you can see Kemmelberg in the distance. In 1917 British and Commonwealth forces slogged their way up the ground you see stretching out below you. It took them almost exactly 100 days to get from a line some 8km away down the slope up to Passendale village which you have just left. Across to your left is Crest Farm and if you follow the ridge round to its right, the Cross of Sacrifice at Tyne Cot Cemetery can be seen. This is our next port of call.

At the next crossroads **⑩**, named **Mallard crossroads** on trench maps, turn left into Bornstraat, the road now descends into the Ravebeek valley. The first farm you pass on the right is the approximate position of **Snipe Hall** and on the opposite side of the road about 200m to the east was **Duck Lodge**, now no longer in existence. The strongly defended Snipe Hall had held up the advance in this area since 26 October and was finally overcome by the PPCLI in a night attack. Overall progress was severely handicapped by the watery nature of the valley which had been made worse by shellfire from both sides destroying the banks of the beek with the result that the valley quickly became a quagmire and, in places, impassable for attacking troops. On 30 October the PPCLI were again attacking up the valley and were held up by machine-gun fire from Duck Lodge and from a bunker on the ridge just south of the present position of Passchendaele Cemetery. The subsequent action resulted in two Canadian VCs: **Sergeant George**

Lieutenant Hugh McKenzie VC.

Sergeant George Mullin VC.

Mullin, PPCLI, and **Lieutenant Hugh McKenzie**, Canadian Machine Gun Corps. George Mullin survived the war and died in 1963 but Hugh McKenzie was killed and is commemorated on the Menin Gate. The cost of progress had been high; that evening the battalion had been reduced to a mere 180 fighting men.

After crossing the beek turn right at the junction into Canadalaan, ignore the first turning on the left and continue to the crossroads with Tynecotstraat. This is the area known as **Waterfields**. Turn left at the crossroads and climb gently uphill, go past the first farm and just before you reach the cemetery stop by the farm track on the right which leads

Tyne Cot Cemetery at sunset.

down to farm buildings. This was known as Hamburg Farm ⓫ where there were two pill boxes, one of which still stands on private land behind the farm buildings obscured by the trees and the other – now gone – which stood just to the north of the drive in the field in front of you. Up ahead along the road to your left you can see the front wall and entrance of Tyne Cot Cemetery. It was from a position about 1,500m across the fields over to your left front that the men of the Australian 40/Battalion began their advance on the morning of 4 October 1917 at the start of the Battle of Broodseinde. Their objective

Sergeant Lewis McGee VC.

was to take the pill boxes and trenches of the German Flandern I positions around Tyne Cot but as the Tasmanians pushed through 39/Battalion onto the ridge, machine-gun fire from the Hamburg bunkers pinned them down. Under murderous fire **Captain William Ruddock** managed to work his company from shell hole to shell hole around the side of the pill box to lay down covering fire. **Sergeant Lewis McGee**, pistol in hand, jumped up and charged across 50m of open ground straight

Otto Bieber's grave in Tyne Cot Cemetery.

A profound epitaph for Second Lieutenant Arthur Young – IV.G.21.

Tyne Cot Cemetery – Grave XXX.VIII.24.

towards the pill box, shot the machine-gun crew and captured the rest of the garrison. The entire 'Hamburg' position was then stormed at a rush – imagine wild-eyed Tasmanians racing across the field towards you. Casualties included 22-year-old **Lieutenant Norman Meagher** who was killed at the head of the charge. All the final objectives, including the Tyne Cot system of five pill boxes which were part of the German Flandern I defences in this area – three of which you can still see today, including the one on which the Cross of Sacrifice was built – were taken. A fourth still lies beneath the surface at the end of the incomplete Row G in Plot 45 whilst the fifth no longer exists.

For his actions at Hamburg Farm, **Lewis McGee** was awarded the Victoria Cross. Eight days later he was killed attacking another pill box in similar daring fashion near a position named Augustus, just 700m to the northeast of the cemetery.

Walk on to the lower entrance gate where there is an information board. You can either enter the cemetery at this point or continue and turn left to find the visitor's centre and toilets. Cyclists will find bike racks in the car park. With regard to the cemetery's name, the generally accepted version is that 'cot' was derived from 'cottage', so called by 50th Northumbrian Division as the outline of German pill boxes of the Flandern 1 Stellung on the horizon reminded men of 'cottages beside the Tyne'. The name, however, appears on maps from mid-1916 – on earlier maps it is marked as 'cott' – before the arrival of 50th Division, and also in the immediate vicinity are other farmhouses named after French and English rivers: Marne, Seine, Thames. There is also a local legend that the name is an Anglicized corruption of the Flemish word for chicken coop – 't'hinnekot'. In truth the origins of the name will probably never be known for sure.

Tyne Cot contains nearly 12,000 graves, over 8,000 of which are unidentified Apart from being the largest British military cemetery in the world it is probably one of the most visited, attracting school parties and battlefield tours from far and wide. The rows and rows of Portland stone headstones are almost overwhelming, particularly when the setting sun casts a glorious pink hue over the stonework. What does become clear is that a single visit to this cemetery is not enough. If you stand at the Cross of Sacrifice and look southwest towards Ieper you can see how the high ground you are standing on – the Broodseinde Ridge – dominated the 3rd Australian Division's attack of October

1917. From here the spires of Ieper can be seen in the mid-distance and on a clear day you can see Kemmelberg in the distance. The cemetery is organized into sixty-seven plots which can be identified from the plan in the cemetery register which you can find in the entrance gatehouse. Remains were brought here after the Armistice from all over the battlefield, hence the size. There are three VC holders buried here: **Captain Clarence Jeffries** (XL.E.1), **Sergeant Lewis McGee** (XX.D.1) and **Private James Robertson** (LVIII.D.26). It is interesting to note that Lewis McGee won his VC, was killed and is buried all within an area not much larger than 500m^2. Three other VC holders have their names on the Tyne Cot Memorial which stands at the rear of the cemetery, **Lieutenant Colonel Phillip Bent** (Panel 50), **Lance Corporal Ernest Seaman** (Panel 70) and **Corporal William Clamp** (Panel 52). The register for the memorial is kept in the left-hand pavilion. The New Zealand Memorial is to be found in the central apse. Altogether there are some 35,000 names of the missing on the 150m-long memorial wall.

The most senior officer buried here is **Brigadier General James Riddell** (XXXIV.H.14) who was killed whilst in command of 149 Infantry Brigade on 26 April 1915, having arrived in Belgium only a few days previously. Riddell was a native of the Northumberland coastal village of Warkworth and is also commemorated on the village war memorial. On the same village memorial is **Second Lieutenant Robert Thompson**, a Military Cross holder who was killed on 26 October 1917 serving in 7/Northumberland Fusiliers. Thompson's name is commemorated on Panel 19. The memorial wall holds the names of at least ten pairs of brothers and one family of three boys who were all killed within a week of each other. **Privates Edwin** and **Leslie Newlove** (Panel 2) died whilst serving with 2/Canterbury Regiment on 12 October 1917, whilst their brother **Leonard Newlove (**Panel 1), serving with 3/Auckland Regiment, was killed eight days earlier. **Edward** (Panel 112) and **Robert Hannah** (Panel 138) from Barrow-in-Furness were both serving as second lieutenants and both killed on 16 August 1917. Robert with 7/Royal Irish Rifles and Edward, who had been awarded the Military Cross in May 1916, with 1/King's Shropshire Light Infantry. Father and son, **Lieutenant Colonel Harry Moorhouse** (Panel 108) and **Captain Ronald Moorhouse** (Panel 113) MC were serving together in the same unit of 4/King's Own Yorkshire Light Infantry when they were killed on 9 October in the Ravebeek valley. On Panel 10 is **Sergeant William Johnston** who was serving with 3/Coldstream Guards when he was killed on 9 October 1917. From Coldstream in Berwickshire, the 25-year-old was a Metropolitan policeman when he was called up in 1914.

Of the seventeen RFC aviators buried here **Captain Vivian Wadham** (LXII.C.5) is perhaps the most distinguished. A brilliant pilot, he was killed on 17 January 1916 flying a BE2c with 15 Squadron, while his observer, Sergeant N.V. Piper, was taken prisoner. The 24-year-old Wadham was one of the original aviators who flew to France in August 1914 and flew some of the first ever air reconnaissance patrols before the Battle of Mons. **Second Lieutenant Charles Moody** (LVIII.A.28) was only 18 years old when he was shot down near Houthulst flying a Nieuport Scout with 1 Squadron, he had been with the squadron for only ten days. Another 18-year-old pilot was **Second Lieutenant George Cowie** (I.AA.21) who was shot down on 22 October 1917 in his

Living history near Dash Crossing. Belgian schoolchildren follow in the footsteps of the Commonwealth soldier.

Sopwith Pup flying with 54 Squadron. **Lieutenant Guy Drummond** (LIX.B.28), serving with 13/ Canadian Infantry Battalion, was the son of the Montreal banker Sir George Drummond. He was killed on 22 April 1915 during the Second Battle of Ypres. You will find the gallant **Lieutenant Norman Meagher** (XVI.A.7) from Hobart, who took part in the charge on Hamburg Farm just a few hundred metres away, buried close to the Cross of Sacrifice.

Exit the cemetery via the gate at the rear which will take you to the visitor's centre and toilets. After leaving the car park, turn right then left, and, after 200m you will arrive back at **Dash Crossing ❹** where you were earlier. Turn right onto the cycle track continuing to **Daring Crossing ❸**. At this point ignore the cycle track and take the road called Groenstraat which runs parallel to the track on the left. The road bears left, away from the cycle track and eventually reaches the main N332 Zonnebeke–Broodseinde road. At the T-junction turn right on to Roeselarestraat and cross the road. Take the next road on the left – Wolvestraat – which takes you into a small estate of private houses. Take the next turn right – De Patine – and in 250m you will come to a T-junction. Turn left and keep bearing right until you see a metal gate leading into the chateau grounds which are ahead of you. Pass through the gate and follow the track past the lake to the museum and your vehicle.

Route 11

Geluveld and Zandvoorde

Suitable for ڳ 🚶

Circular route starting at: Geluveld church.

Coordinates: 50°50 03.92 N – 2°59 40.10 E.

Distance: 8km/5 miles.

Grade: Easy.

Maps: NGI 1:20 000 Zonnebeke–Moorslede 28/3–4 and Wervik–
Menen 28/7–8.

General description and context: This route is ideal for both walkers
and cyclists as it traverses the ground between the two villages, visiting
Zantvoorde British Cemetery on the way. The majority of roads are
narrow country lanes and relatively quiet. Although it is possible for car
users to follow the route, it is not recommended as some of the roads
are of the narrow, single-track variety and mainly used by farm vehicles.
To get here you have driven along the notorious **Menin Road** which
features so frequently in descriptions of the fighting in the Salient.
Geluveld (Gheluvelt) was the scene of some intense and bitter fighting
in the final days of October 1914 when the British line in this sector
stretched from **Polygon Wood** in the north to **Zandvoorde** (formerly
Zantvoorde) in the south. On the morning of 30 October 7 Cavalry
Brigade were in possession of the high ground around Zandvoorde
when they were heavily shelled and eventually overwhelmed by
attacking German infantry. Pushed out of the village the line was
reformed further to the west but still in touch with the infantry
battalions at Gheluvelt. The next morning the front line lay across the
Menin Road just east of Gheluvelt where the road drops down to the
crossroads with the N303. At dawn the whole of this line was attacked
in force, and despite a heroic and dogged defence, the British were
gradually pushed back at huge cost in casualties to both sides. North of

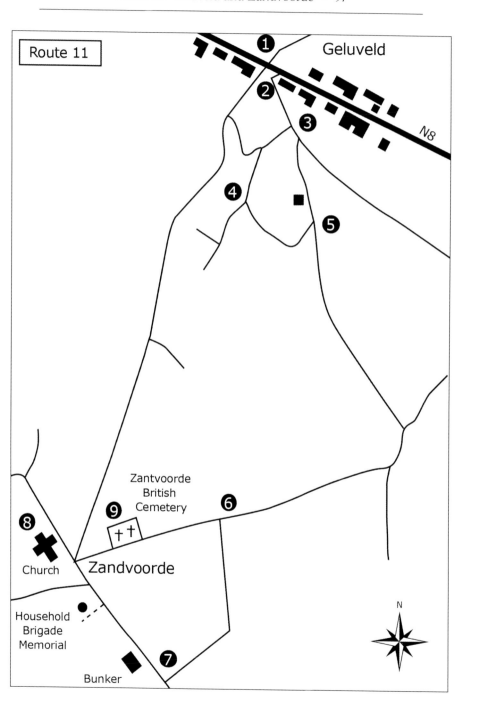

Geluveld Chateau.

the Menin Road what was left of the Scots Guards and South Wales Borderers were forced back into the grounds of **Gheluvelt Chateau** where they were surrounded as the German infantry broke through the line. The situation was critical but the line was recovered at 2.30pm by 2/Worcesters who were ordered to retake the chateau. From their reserve position at **Black Watch Corner** at **Polygon Wood** the 370 men of the battalion led by **Major Edward Hankey** doubled across the kilometre of open ground to drive the German infantry out of the chateau grounds. South of the Menin Road the British infantry were gradually overwhelmed and it is this area which you will visit shortly on the way to Zandvoorde. By the end of the day Gheluvelt was in flames and in German hands and not retaken until September 1918.

Directions to start: Geluveld is best approached from Ieper along the N8 in the direction of Menen (formally Menin). On reaching the village turn left off the main road to leave your vehicle in the village square ❶ where there is plenty of parking.

Route description: In the northeastern corner of the village square a private gated road leads down to **Geluveld Chateau**. This was where the Scots Guards and South Wales Borderers fought their desperate battle before Major Hankey and his Worcesters arrived from across the fields to your left. An information panel here explains the 1914 battle. Directly opposite the church on the other side of the square a cul-de-sac leads to a reproduction of the old windmill and the memorial to the South Wales Borderers. Here also is the memorial to the Worcesters. Return to the square and turn left towards the main road. Cross over the road, which can be busy, and turn left to reach Oude Komenstraat ❷ on the right. Turn right here and after the road bends round to the left, take the first road on the right ❸. Ahead of you in the distance is the church spire of **Sint-Bartholomew** at Zandvoorde. Walk downhill a few metres and stop. For a few moments imagine it is dawn on 31 October 1914. Across to your right in the fields close to the Menin Road are two companies of the King's Royal Rifle Corps (KRRC), to the left of them are another two companies of the Loyal North Lancs. A little behind and to your left is D Company of 1/Queen's Royal West Surreys next to the Welsh who are dug in across the road and beyond. Continue downhill to the Y-junction ❹ and stop again. A Company, 1/Queen's were on your right dug in along the opposite side of the road and facing south and about 150m further to the right were two companies of the Loyal North Lancs. Along the road to your left were the remaining platoons of A Company.

Now take the road to your left and follow it as it curves round to the left to reach a T-junction ❺. Stop here and look across to the farm on your left to from where 1/Queen's commanding officer, **Lieutenant Colonel Beauchamp Pell DSO**, directed operations from battalion HQ. Stretching across to the farm you can see directly ahead of you were the remaining two companies of 1/Queen's with B Company closest to the road and C Company in and around the farm buildings. You are standing in the middle of a battlefield that tragically, in a matter of hours, saw 1/Queen's reduced to 2 officers and 32 men having sustained over 600 casualties, killed, wounded or missing,

The Household Brigade Memorial.

including Colonel Pell who was fatally wounded. One of the many young soldiers killed fighting with 1/Queen's that day was 21-year-old **Private Basil Treffry** from Thornton Heath in Surrey who is commemorated with hundreds of his comrades on the Menin Gate. His younger brother, **Richard Treffry,** aged 19 years was killed two years later at Langemark serving with the Queen's Westminster Rifles. For five hours the defending infantry south of the Menin Road resisted their attackers until, sometime after 9.30am, the Queen's were surrounded and overwhelmed. The remnants of the Loyal North Lancs and the King's Royal Rifle Corps with a handful of Queen's eventually fell back along the Menin Road to **Veldhoek.**

Private Basil Treffry.

From the T-junction turn right following Blockstraat as it descends downhill to meet another T-junction with a large farm to your left. Turn right along the Doornkapellestraat and take the next road on your right by the red-brick house. This is Kruisekestraat. Ignoring the first farm road on the left, turn left at the next road, Komenstraat ❻, which is a narrow, single-track road. The road bends sharply to the right and leads to a T-junction ❼. Turn right towards Zandvoorde and after 150m turn into Gaveratraat which is the next turning on your left. You should be able to see the **Zandvoorde German Command Post bunker** in the field to your right which is accessed through the turnstile. It was built by 3/Company of *Armierungsbattalion* 27 in 1916 and has six rooms. It has been a listed monument since 1999 and there is no charge for entry.

After leaving the bunker turn left at the main road as it climbs up towards Zandvoorde. It was this view that the German 39th Infantry Division had on 30 October 1914 as they advanced towards the British Household Brigade entrenched along the line of high ground you can see in front of you. The tall memorial to the left of the road is the Household Brigade Memorial erected on the site where the grave of **Lieutenant Charles Pelham**, **Lord Worsley, the eldest son and heir of** the 4th Earl of Yarborough, was found after the war. On the fateful morning of 30 October the village was defended by 7 Cavalry Brigade comprising 1st and 2nd Life Guards and Royal Horse Guards (RHG). Charles Pelham commanded the RHG machine guns and, along with two whole squadrons of Life Guards, did not receive the order to retire.

As there were no survivors we can only assume they fought to the last man. This is certainly what occurred a little further to your right when the **Royal Welsh Fusiliers** were outflanked once the cavalry line had been broken. Commanded by **Lieutenant Colonel Henry Cadogan**, the battalion that had numbered over 1,000 officers and men 2 weeks earlier was reduced to 86 men, all the officers having been killed or wounded including Henry Cadogan who is buried at **Hooge Crater Cemetery.** Charles Pelham's remains were transferred to **Ypres Town Cemetery Extension**

Ernst Stadler.

after the war. Amongst the German casualties of 30 October was the poet *Leutnant* **Ernst Stadler**, a reserve officer with the German 80/Field Artillery Regiment. He was educated at Strasbourg and Magdalen College, Oxford and was killed on the southwestern edge of the village. He is buried in Strasbourg. His most important volume of poetry, *Der Aufbruch*, which was published during 1914, is regarded as a major work of early expressionism.

Continue uphill and as you enter the village there is a large farm on your right. Directly opposite is the narrow entrance to the **Household Brigade Memorial** which is marked with the usual green CWGC signpost. Don't forget to add your name to the visitor's book by the entrance. After leaving the memorial continue into Zandvoorde to the church ❽. An information panel explains further the cavalry battle of 30 October, whilst in the churchyard you will find the graves of four 10th Hussars who, as part of 6 Cavalry Brigade, were all killed by shellfire on 26 October in the Zandvoorde trenches. Of these four, **Lieutenant Christopher Turnor** is also remembered inside the church with a rather splendid stained glass window paid for by his mother, Lady Henrietta Turnor.

From the church follow the CWGC signpost along Kruisekestraat to find **Zantvoorde British Cemetery ❾**. Zantvoorde British Cemetery was begun after the Armistice when bodies were brought in from the surrounding battlefields. There are now 1,583 men buried or commemorated in the cemetery of which 70 per cent are unidentified. Special memorials commemorate thirty-two soldiers buried in two of the nearby German cemeteries whose graves could not be located. The

The headstones of four 10th Hussars buried at Zandvoorde Churchyard Cemetery.

cemetery also contains one Second World War burial, **Sergeant Pilot Phillip Grisdale** (I.A.21) who was shot down and killed flying a Spitfire V of 72 Squadron. Two holders of the VC are buried here, **Lieutenant James Anson Brooke** (VI.E.2), who was killed near the Geluveld crossroads serving with the Gordon Highlanders on 29 October 1914, and in the opposite corner of the cemetery, **Sergeant Louis McGuffie** (I.D.12) of 1/5 King's Own Scottish Borderers who was killed on 28 September 1918, six days after he won his cross at **Piccadilly Farm** near Messines. Close by you will find **Colonel Beauchamp Pell** (II.F.1) who died of his wounds on 4 November 1914 whilst in German hands. Find time if you can to visit 23-year-old **Gunner Norman Busby** (I.G.25), who was serving with

Lieutenant James Brooke VC.

156/Howitzer Battery. Norman joined up in November 1915 and was killed in action on 8 October 1918. His battery buried him in an isolated grave on the road between Ten Brielen and Wervik from where his body was exhumed and brought to Zantvoorde after the war. He had served 2 years and 341 days and was killed 33 days before the Armistice was declared. Killed three days after Norman Busby were eleven other gunners of 72/Battery, Royal Field Artillery. They are buried together

(II.H.3) having been killed in the same incident on 11 October 1918. There is a family connection here with the Zillebeke Churchyard Cemetery (see route 14). **Lieutenant Phillip Van Neck** (V.H.14), who was killed fighting with 1/Grenadier Guards on 26 October at Gheluvelt, was a cousin of **Lieutenant John Lee Steere** who is buried at Zillebeke. Tragically Phillip's younger brother, 21-year-old **Lieutenant Charles Van Neck,** was killed a week earlier fighting at Souchez with 1/Northumberland Fusiliers.

Leave the cemetery and retrace your steps back towards the village to take the first turning on the right, signposted Geluveld. From this vantage point the strategic importance of Geluveld at the highest point on the ridge can be appreciated. The church tower soon comes into view as you begin the short climb back up to the village. On reaching the main road stop and look down the Menin Road to your left. At around 3.00pm on 31 October a German artillery piece began firing along the road from a position close to the point where you are standing. It was answered by a single 18-pounder belonging to 54/Battery under the command of **Lieutenant Ralph Blewitt** which was in position on the right-hand side of the road just east of Polygonestraat. With their second round they destroyed the enemy gun and Blewitt was awarded the DSO. It was also along this road that **Captain Robert Rising** of 1/Gloucesters, who won the DSO at Langemark (see Route 4), fought desperately to hold back the tide of advancing German infantry on the same day. They were eventually forced back to the Veldhoek crossroads where the shattered remains of the 1st Division managed to establish a firing line and hold the German forces. Rising was killed on 7 November 1914 and is buried at Zillebeke Churchyard Cemetery (see Route 14). Cross the road with care and return to the square ❶. Before you leave the square pay a visit to the church to see the memorial plaque to **Lieutenant Wilfred Littleboy** of 16/Royal Warwicks. He was killed near Polderhoek Chateau on 9 October 1917 along with 417 officers and men of the battalion. After the war Wilfred's father, a shipbuilder, donated money to the church at Geluveld and the Saltburns War Memorial and in 1939 gave a large plot of land to Stockton-on-Tees Borough Council which became the present-day Littleboy Park at Thornaby-on-Tees. Wilfred is buried at **Hooge Crater Cemetery**, which is visited in Route 12.

Route 12

Bellewaarde Ridge and Hooge

Suitable for 👤
Circular route starting at: Hooge Crater Museum.
Coordinates: 50°50 47.21 – 2°56 36.32 E.
Distance: 4.8km/3 miles.
Grade: Moderate.
Toilets: Hooge Crater Museum.
Maps: NGI 1:20 000 Poperinge–Ieper 28/1–2.
Link this with: Route 13 – Sanctuary Wood and Hill 62.

General description and context: This route uses footpaths designated for walkers only. The first half follows almost exactly the British trench line as it existed on 15 June 1915, whilst the second half follows the German line as it stood in late September 1915. The area was the scene of several vicious and bloody struggles during the summer and autumn of 1915 as both sides wrestled for overall control of the area to secure the higher ground. The first British attack on 16 June 1915 advanced the line some 300m further up the ridge at a very heavy price. Early on 30 July 1915 the Germans unleashed an attack on the British trenches just north of the Menin Road which was notable for the first use of 'liquid fire' using flame projectors. The British were driven back and counter-attacks involving the Rifle Brigade and 9/King's Royal Rifle Corps proved extremely costly. On 9 August the British responded with an attack designed to retake the ground lost and heaved themselves back into Hooge. Late September saw the British again trying to break the German stranglehold on the Bellewaarde Ridge which included the blowing of several mines and although there had been early successes, determined German counter-attacks pushed the British back to where they had started. The Germans took Hooge again on 6 June 1916 and pressed the Allies back, roughly to the line from which they had attacked almost a year earlier. After this, the line on the ridge remained more or less static until the British launched their attack and captured the Bellewaarde Ridge and Hooge during the **Battle of Pilckem** on 31 July 1917. They were to remain in Allied hands apart from a brief period of five months in 1918 after the German offensive.

Directions to start: From Ieper take the N8 along the Menin Road. Continue past Birr Crossroads Cemetery – on your right – until you see Hooge Crater Cemetery on your right. Directly opposite is the Hooge Crater Museum where there is car parking on the hard shoulder of the road.

Route description: We suggest you visit the museum and cafe Ⓐ (see route map on p. 113) when you return to your vehicle. The chapel, in which the museum is located, was built after the war to commemorate those who died in the fighting here. The school building, now the museum cafe, was reconstructed at the same time. Cross the road to the entrance to **Hooge Crater Cemetery**. This large cemetery was begun in early October 1917 and originally contained seventy-six graves. After the Armistice, when graves were brought in from the battlefields of Zillebeke, Zantvoorde and Gheluvelt, it expanded to its present-day size and now contains 5,923 Commonwealth graves, 3,579 of which are unidentified. Buried here is **Private Patrick Bugden** (VIII.C.5) who won his Victoria Cross at Polygon Wood on 28 September 1917 serving with 31/Battalion AIF. Military Medal recipient **Private Joseph Moss** (XII.B.8) was one of thirty-nine men from the Suffolk village of Stoke Ash who fought in the Great War. Killed on 31 July 1917, Joseph was the only man not to return home. **Second Lieutenant Harry Rawlinson** (VIA.G.3) was killed in action on 26 September 1917 aged 23. Harry was on the staff at Lloyd's Bank in Birmingham when war broke out, and

Second Lieutenant Harry Rawlinson.

after enlisting in 1914 was commissioned in April 1917 into the Machine Gun Corps. On 20 September 1917 19-year-old **Francis Chown** (XVI.H.15) flying with 1 Squadron was shot down and killed over the Menin Road. He joined the RFC straight from school and was killed less than a month after arriving in Belgium. Spare a thought for **Lance Sergeant David Orr** (XX.K.4) of the Cheshire Regiment who enlisted in 1914 and saw action at Loos in 1915, the Somme in 1916 and Messines in June 1917. He was killed by a sniper on 20 September 1917 having just returned from home leave.

On leaving the cemetery turn right to take the footpath that leads down the eastern boundary of the cemetery with the dark mass of Sanctuary Wood to your left. The path – roughly following the route of the Old Bond Street communication trench – bends to the right and follows what was the northern boundary of **Zouave Wood**, now long since gone. Keeping to the field edges, head for the avenue of maple trees directly ahead known as Canadalaan leading to the Canadian Memorial on Hill 62 and Sanctuary Wood Museum. You are now walking across the ground where, on 30 July 1915, the British counter-attacks took place in an attempt to recover the trenches lost during the German liquid-fire attack earlier in the day. The second attack, like the first, was a complete failure. Led by 8/Rifle Brigade from the edge of Zouave Wood with 7/Rifle Brigade and 9/King's Royal Rifle Corps in support, the attacking force was cut down by machine-gun fire in a disastrous frontal attack over the ground you are now standing on. Casualties on 30 July alone amounted to 22 officers and 454 other ranks, whilst over the next few days a further 45 officers and 1,440 other ranks were admitted to No. 10 Casualty Clearing Station at Lijssenthoek. The counter-attack that afternoon was the scene of 19-year-old **Second Lieutenant Sidney Woodroffe's VC** – the first VC to be won by a soldier of the New Army – he died a few yards south of Hooge Crater Cemetery. The Woodroffe family lost two more of their four sons in the war, **Kenneth** on 9 May 1915 and **Leslie** on 4 June 1916.

Second Lieutenant Sidney Woodroffe VC.

On reaching the trees and the metalled road ⓑ you have a choice of route. Turn right to continue on Route 12 and turn left if you wish to join the Sanctuary Wood route which will bring you back to this point on Maple Drive after a 3.5km circuit round Observatory Ridge.

Having turned right along Maple Drive look across to your right and note how the ground rises towards Hooge Crater Cemetery and the Hooge Crater Museum across the Menin Road beyond. In 1915 the remains of **Hooge Chateau** and its stables were situated beyond the present museum. Hooge dominates the ground to the south and the west along the Menin Road towards Ypres and from this vantage point it is clear to see why the ruins of the village, the chateau and a mine crater blown by the British in mid-July 1915 were such key positions and to appreciate why the area was so fiercely contested in the summer of 1915. Almost everywhere in this sector the German line dominated that of the British.

On reaching the Menin Road turn left. Continue. After 220m or so you will notice a turning on the opposite side of the road on your right which was known by the troops as **Cambridge Road**. Pause here ©. You are now standing at what was called **Birr crossroads**, although today the crossroads no longer exist. There were several tunnels under the Menin Road, both German and British, but at Birr crossroads 177/Tunnelling Company built extensive dugouts and a dressing station beneath the surface. Continue for another 175m to reach **Birr Crossroads Cemetery** which took its name from the men of the 1/Leinsters whose regimental depot in Ireland was located at Birr. There are 833 Commonwealth servicemen buried or commemorated here, 336 remain unidentified. Here you will find **Captain Harold Ackroyd** (SM.7) who was the medical officer attached to 6/Royal Berkshires. The 40-year-old doctor had already been decorated with the MC and was killed by a German sniper's bullet in Jargon Trench on the edge of Glencorse Wood on 11 August 1917. His award of the Victoria Cross was announced on 6 September. **Gunner William Janes** (I.H.4) from Southsea was killed on 9 October 1918 whilst serving with 113/Siege Battery. Buried nearby is a young man who is a long way from home, **Private Horomana Kanapu** (I.J.39) of the New Zealand Maori Battalion. He was killed on 30 November 1917 and his presence is a poignant reminder that the war was fought by men and women from all over the Commonwealth. **Second Lieutenant Alan Ventris** (II.D.4) was only 18 years old when he was killed on 14 September 1915 serving with 2/South Lancashires. He was the son of Major General Francis Favil who was GOC British Forces in China until 1921.

Leave the cemetery and cross the road to retrace your steps back to Cambridge Road © – or Begijnenbosstraat as it is called today. Turn left here and after crossing the Bellewaardebeek, the road bends right then left as it begins to rise. Continue until you breast the rise ahead. Across to your right was the site of **Y Wood**, so called by the British because of its characteristic shape, although the Germans thought it looked more like a 'T' than a 'Y' and so called it T Waldchen. After the war it was not replanted and has now disappeared under the plough. A little further up on your left is **Witte Poort Farm**. Stop here Ⓓ. The wood directly ahead is **Railway Wood**, so called as it overlooked the Ypres–Roulers railway line, along which now runs the N37. Due to its shape, Railway Wood was known as Eier Waldchen – Egg Wood – to the Germans. The British forward trenches ran up from here towards Railway Wood in a series of four closely packed lines parallel to the road a little way into the fields to your right with the support trenches – in the same pattern – following the line of the road to your left. These fields were the scene of the **First Battle of Bellewaarde** on 16 June 1915. The task was handed to nine battalions of the 3rd Division, who attacked eastwards, away from you, over the ground to your right between the valley you have just left and the line of the present-day N37 ahead.

Although the first German line was overrun, the attack faltered as inexperienced and overenthusiastic troops pressed on too quickly. Men ran into their own barrage, officers were killed or wounded and units became intermixed. Chaos ensued and German counter-attacks drove the British back to the first German line. The operation was eventually called off at around 6.00pm with what remained of the assault units digging and wiring furiously under a vengeful German bombardment. In twelve hours that day some 3,500 men of the 3rd Division had become casualties – 1,000 of them killed – all in the square kilometre of ground you see before you.

Continue and go straight on past Railway Wood until you reach the junction with the N37. There are good views from here of the spires of Ieper giving some impression of the importance of the ridge to the Germans in terms of observation. Before the war the Ypres–Roulers railway ran along the present-day N37 but by summer 1915 all that remained was the track bed pitted with shell holes. Sandbag and barbed-wire barricades were built up where the support lines crossed the railway here. Cross the road and continue to the memorials Ⓔ to **Captain Geoffrey Bowlby** of the Royal Horse Guards and **Captain Henry Skrine** of 6/Somerset Light Infantry. Both were killed in 1915, Bowlby on 13 May and Skrine on 25 September. Their bodies were never found, although Skrine's battlefield cross was found nearby in 1920. Both are commemorated on the Menin Gate. The small wooden cross in the centre remembers the actions of the Liecestershire Yeomanry on the Frezenberg Ridge on 13 May 1915.

Retrace your steps to the junction and re-cross towards Railway Wood, which was a warren of dugouts for various headquarters and stores. Turn left onto Oude Kortrijkstraat following the brown sign for the Liverpool Scottish Stone and continue until the road bends left and a track comes in to meet it from the right. Turn right here, following the green CWGC sign for **RE Grave, Railway Wood** and the brown Liverpool Scottish Stone sign. After some 200m Ⓕ you will come to the RE Grave at Railway Wood and the mine crater. The RE Grave marks the spot where eight Royal Engineers of 177/Tunnelling Company and four attached infantrymen were killed in action underground and stands almost exactly on the final line reached during the attack of 16 June 1915 and was the line from which the British launched their assault in their second attack on Bellewaarde on 25 September 1915. By the early hours of 25 September 1915 the tunnellers had driven a gallery 230ft long beneath no-man's-land from the bottom of Shaft No. 4 in Railway Wood and laid a mine directly beneath a German strongpoint which stood almost at the point where the road across the field meets the eastern edge of Railway Wood. The mine was blown at 4.19am, to coincide with the 9/Rifle Brigade attack left to right across the meadow behind the Cross of Sacrifice. Behind you, and down the slope towards the Menin Road, 5/Ox and Bucks Light Infantry and 5/King's Shropshire Light Infantry attacked at the same time to take the German first and second lines and seize the important strongpoint of Bellewaarde Farm; the present-day farm is on the other side of the wood which you can see standing almost next to the memorial. Some of the Rifle Brigade men left their trenches to attack that day from the very spot upon which you are now standing. The attack was a failure and by mid-afternoon the

The Skrine and Bowlby Memorials near Railway Wood.

The Railway Wood RE Memorial.

The Liverpool Scottish Memorial on the Bellewaarde Ridge.

battle was over and the Germans had driven the last few Rifle Brigade men from positions in the freshly blown mine crater and back to their own front line. Inevitably there were heavy casualties and most of them were lost in the meadow just in front of you, between the memorial and the road heading east from Railway Wood.

From the memorial, return to the footpath and turn left and almost immediately you will see the **Liverpool Scottish Memorial** which commemorates that battalion's part in the battle of 16 June 1915. The memorial – almost in the shape of a grave – bears the regimental crest in stone, which was originally sited above the regimental HQ in Liverpool. It was donated to and placed on this spot by the city of Ieper in July 2000. On the left is the track leading to the present site of Bellewaarde Farm which is private property but by picking carefully through the undergrowth behind the memorial one can see several deep mine craters which bear witness to the ferocity of the subterranean

The area as it was in December 1915. German trenches are in red.

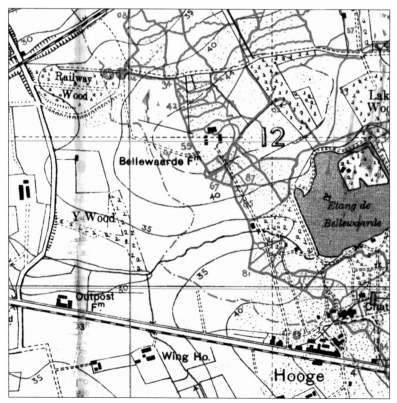

war fought in tunnels and galleries deep below the ground on which you are standing.

Return to the main footpath and turn left skirting the edge of the woods. You are now heading south towards the Menin Road and walking parallel to the British front line at the end of 1915. A glance into the woods to your left will reveal still more mine craters. Follow the footpath as it takes a sharp 90 degree bend to the left. You are now leaving the British front line and stepping into no-man's-land as it was between the end of 1915 and up to the end of July 1917. As you pass the house on the slope to the left you are just few metres below the site of the German front line trench of September 1915 as it curved along the line of contours towards the metalled track you can see ahead. Look down into the valley to appreciate the advantages of the dominance of the line held by the Germans and the fields of fire enjoyed by their machine gunners looking down on the Menin Road and the British trenches. Walk towards the track and turn right ⑥. Bellewaarde Farm is off to the left. Continue downhill. The German front line swung south here and ran in the fields to your right parallel to the track you are on. After crossing the Bellewaardebeek the track begins to rise. Roughly halfway up the rise between the stream and the Menin Road up ahead the German line cut back sharply east across the road and ran through the trees to your left towards the site of Hooge Chateau. It was from these trenches – on either side of the road here – that the Germans launched their liquid-fire attack on 30 July 1915. Continue up to the Menin Road, crossing the British lines once more just before returning to your vehicle at the Hooge Crater Museum. Take this opportunity to visit the **Hooge Craters** in the nearby Hotel Kasteelhof grounds, details can be found in the Museums section.

A German soldier stands in one of the craters made by a mine during the heavy fighting for Hooge.

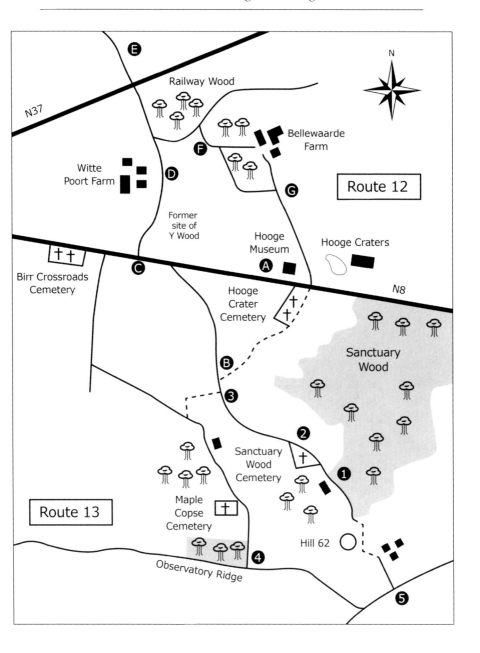

Route 13
Sanctuary Wood and Hill 62

Suitable for 🚴 🚶

Circular route starting at: Sanctuary Wood Museum.
Coordinates: 50°50 14.62 N – 2°56 44.04 E.
Distance: 3.5km/2 miles.
Grade: Easy.
Toilets: Sanctuary Wood Museum.
Maps: NGI 1:20 000 Poperinge–Ieper 28/1–2.

General description and context: This is a short excursion along Observatory Ridge to Hill 62 visiting Sanctuary Wood and Maple Copse Cemeteries using traffic-free pathways and minor roads. The **Battle of Mount Sorrel** took place in this area between 2 and 13 June 1916 and involved units of the British Second Army and the Canadian Corps. It took place along the low ridge that runs between Hooge and Zwarteleen. Much of the ridge was wooded, as it is today, and was topped by two 'hills' – Hill 62, which is at the southern end of Maple Drive, and Mount Sorrel, which lay further to the southwest near Kemphof Farm. Just after 1.00pm on 2 June the Germans advanced on the British and Commonwealth forces defending the area. The main thrust fell against 4th and 1st Canadian Mounted Rifles and PPCLI. The PPCLI held off the attack for some eighteen hours in Sanctuary Wood but elsewhere the Germans captured the heights of **Mount Sorrel** and **Hill 62**. The subsequent Canadian counter-attack was too weak and disorganized to make any serious gains and further plans were set back on 6 June by the German attack on Hooge. However, despite entering the Canadian trenches, the Germans were pushed off Hill 60 which lies to the southwest of Zwarteleen. Finally, on 11 June 1916, Mount Sorrel and Hill 62 were recaptured by the Canadians.

Directions to start: From Ieper leave via the Menin Gate and take the N8 along the Menin Road. Half a mile after the roundabout you will pass Birr Crossroads Cemetery on the right, continue to the next turning on the right, signposted Sanctuary Wood Cemetery – this is Canadalaan. Towards the far end is Sanctuary Wood Museum where there is parking.

Route description: After parking your vehicle ❶ head back towards the N8 to Sanctuary Wood Cemetery. The expanse of Sanctuary Wood on your right has re-grown – albeit to a smaller size than it was in 1914 – and the road you are now walking along would once have been part of the wood. The wood was given its name in 1914 and used mainly to shelter resting troops from enemy observation – hence the name. However, German artillery began shelling the wood in November 1914 and the wood became less of a sanctuary.

The fan-shaped **Sanctuary Wood Cemetery** ❷ is opposite a row of private houses and is the final resting place of 1,989 casualties of whom 1,352 are unidentified. After the Armistice casualties were brought in from the surrounding area. Outside the boundary wall of the cemetery is the memorial to **Lieutenant Keith Rae** which was moved to this spot in 1966 from the place where he was last seen alive near the Hooge

Sanctuary Wood Cemetery.

Crater on 30 July 1915. Another officer who met his death on 30 July 1915 was the son of the Bishop of Winchester, **Lieutenant Gilbert Talbot** (I.G.1), who, like Keith Rae, served with the Rifle Brigade. Talbot died at the head of his men just yards from the edge of **Zouave Wood**. **Talbot House** in Poperinge is named after him. Two brothers from Newcastle-on-Tyne killed on the same day during the First Battle of Ypres on 20 November 1914 were **Lawrence Eade** (III.H.27/34) and his younger brother **Victor**, who lies beside him in the adjacent grave. Both were serving with 51/Howitzer Battery. Killed on the same day in 1915 were two more brothers, **Private Clarence Linnell** (II.M.15) and his younger brother **Percy** (II.M.14). Both boys were serving with 1/4 Lincolnshire Regiment and died on 27 July 1915. Another soldier of the same battalion was 23-year-old **Private George Allen** (II.M.7) from Alexandra Terrace, Lincoln. George enlisted in Lincoln in November 1914 and was serving in the Zillebeke sector trenches when he was killed by shellfire.

Buried close to each other are **Second Lieutenant Charles Ferguson** (III.K.21) of 22 Squadron RFC who was shot down with his observer, **Second Lieutenant Alexander Lennox** (III.K.23), on 18 October 1917 flying in a F2B Bristol Fighter. Charles Ferguson was commissioned on 24 May 1917 and qualified as a pilot thirteen days later, he was 25 years old. Two more aviators who are buried in the same grave (IV.C.7) are **Lieutenant Eric Stroud** and **Captain Cecil White** of 53 Squadron who crashed in their RE8 about 1½km east of Zillebeke on 21 April 1918. Their remains were not discovered until several years after the Armistice and brought to their present location. The headstone of

Second Lieutenant Charles Ferguson.

German aviator **Hans Roser**, who was shot down by **Captain Lanoe Hawker VC**, lies on the inside left wall, he crashed near Zillebeke on 25 July 1915. **Lieutenant Frederick Currie** (II.B.11) was serving with the Shropshire Light Infantry when he was killed on 8 September 1915. The grandson of Sir Frederick Currie, he attended Repton School and joined the Army straight from school. He was 18 years old when he was killed.

From the cemetery continue along Maple Drive for another 450m until you see a concrete pathway ❸ on your left. Stop here and look across the fields to **Hooge Crater Cemetery** on your right. The area in front of the cemetery was the former site of **Zouave Wood**. See Route 12 for details of the British counter-attack which took place here on 30 June 1915. Turn left along the pathway which veers sharp left after 200m. Continue to the T-junction with Schachteweidestraat and turn left, ahead of you is the replanted Maple Copse and **Maple Copse Cemetery**, whilst across to your left is Sanctuary Wood Cemetery and Sanctuary Wood. Maple Copse was the name given to the small copse about 800m east of Zillebeke. The wood, which was then some 300m further northwest, was used by Advanced Dressing Stations and begun in 1915. During the Mount Sorrel battles and those of 1918 the graves were mostly destroyed hence the 230 special memorials commemorating the casualties whose graves had been destroyed. Today 142 graves in this peaceful and tranquil spot are of Canadians, one of whom, 28-year-old **Captain Hon Alfred Thomas Shaughnessy** (SM. D.11) was killed nearby on 31 March 1916. He was the son of Baron Shaughnessy of Montreal and was commissioned into 60/Battalion CEF in September 1915. A stockbroker in civilian life, he left a widow, Sarah, and his brother, William, who acceded the title in 1923.

Two men whose names are also on special memorials are 18-year-old **Private Fred Tyerman** – the spelling on the headstones is incorrect – and his brother, 23-year-old **Private George Tyerman** (S M. 7 & 8). They both enlisted in 4/Yorkshire Regiment before the outbreak of war and served in the same company. Fred was killed by a shell on 27 February 1916 and George was shot through the lung on 2 March 1916.

After leaving the cemetery continue to the T-junction ❹. To your right, marked by two flag poles, is the memorial to the Canadian 15/Battalion and an information board. Turn left at the junction. This minor road – Zandvoordestraat – runs along Observatory Ridge which was crossed by 7 Cavalry Brigade on 6 November 1914 on its way to support 4 Guards Brigade at Zwarteleen. As you head east along the ridge, look across to your left where you will be able to see the Hill 62 Memorial. On the right are Armagh and Zwarteleen Woods and the Brown Road which featured so much in the 1914 defence of this part of the Salient. The road bears right then 90 degrees left. Continue past the next junction until you come to a metalled path on the left ❺ heading

The Hill 62 Memorial with the spires of Ieper in the distance.

towards a group of private houses. This is Pappotstraat and is marked as a cul-de-sac. Turn left here taking the gravelled pathway to the left towards the Canadian Monument. This is a lovely spot and although the monument is rather confusingly inscribed Mount Sorrell, this location is Hill 62 and Mount Sorrel is to the southwest of here, near Kemphof Farm. From this high point the spires of Ieper can be seen on a clear day.

The Canadian line in 1916 ran from Hill 60 near Zwarteleen to Hill 62 where we are now standing and then north to meet the Menin Road. The memorial marks the achievement of the Canadian Corps in recovering most of the ground lost during the Battle of Mount Sorrel. The front line then remained static in this sector until the Third Battle of Ypres began on 31 July 1917. Although the Canadian triumph at Vimy Ridge in 1917 is regarded as the point when Canada established its identity as a nation, Mount Sorrel and the Canadian action at Kitchener's Wood in 1915 must also be counted as part of that process. From the monument follow the path downhill and back to Sanctuary Wood Museum.

Route 14

Zillebeke and the Aristocrats' Cemetery

Suitable for 🚲 🚶
Circular route starting at: Zillebeke church.
Coordinates: 50°50 07.90 N – 2°55 19.92 E.
Distance: 6.4km/4 miles.
Grade: Easy.
Toilets: Hill 60.
Maps: NGI 1:20 000 Poperinge–Ieper 28/1–2.
Link this with: Route 15 – Caterpillar Crater and the Bluff.

General description and context: The area surrounding Zillebeke and Zwarteleen was hotly contested in 1914 when the BEF was fighting the desperate First Battle of Ypres. It was here that 4 Guards Brigade and the units of the 7th Infantry Division fought to maintain the integrity of the front line south of the Menin Road which was so vital in the defence of Ypres. Our route leaves Zillebeke along Observatory Ridge and onto the Brown Road where the Grenadier Guards held the line on Friday, 6 November after the Irish Guards and the French had given way under the German onslaught. Passing through Zwarteleen Woods the route continues to Hill 60 before visiting Larch Wood Cemetery where there are over twenty RFC and RAF aircrew buried. Finally, after your return to Zillebeke we introduce you to the Aristocrats' Cemetery at Zillebeke churchyard. Zillebeke village remained behind the Allied front line for most of the war and many well-known personalities, including the poet **Edmund Blunden**, served in the sector. During the German 1918 offensive the village was briefly taken before it was finally liberated.

Directions to start: From Ieper leave via the Menin Gate and turn right onto the N8. After passing Menin Road South Cemetery on your right turn right again at the roundabout and follow the road to Zillebeke. Park near the church.

Route description: We suggest you visit the Zillebeke Churchyard Cemetery when you return to Zillebeke. With the churchyard on your left ❶ continue along Zillebeke-Dorp to the T-junction ahead. Turn left and keep left round the bend to take the first road on the left, signposted Maple Copse Cemetery. Continue out of the village until you reach the top of the rise just after the last house on the left. Stop here ❷. Looking straight ahead is the replanted **Maple Copse** which is nearer to the road than the original and over to your right are Zwarteleen Woods and Armagh Wood. The road continues to rise past Maple Copse until you find a tarmac track on your left with a green CWGC signpost. This is the path to **Maple Copse Cemetery** which is described in greater detail in Route 13. Just before the entrance to Maple Copse you will find the recently erected memorial to the Canadian 15/Battalion complete with information panel.

After leaving the cemetery return to the road and turn left. Continue until the road rises to the highest point of Observatory Ridge and stop ❸. On your left is Sanctuary Wood and it was approximately here on 6 November 1914 that 7 Cavalry Brigade left the shelter of the wood in response to an urgent call from the Guards Brigade at Zwarteleen which was trying to stem the flood of German infantry advancing through the broken Allied line. It was a desperate moment in the First Battle of Ypres and the ensuing dismounted cavalry counter-attack from 7 Cavalry Brigade succeeded in pushing the Germans back. The sight of the 600-strong brigade galloping hell-for-leather across the ridge must have been something to behold! Also visible to your left is the **Hill 62 Canadian Memorial** which is visited in Route 13. The memorial commemorates the Canadian fight to regain ground lost during the Battle of Mount Sorrell.

As the road bends sharply to the left, take the small single-track road – Pappotstraat – on the right ❹. After passing a large farm on your left stop for a moment at the farm entrance. This is where the German front line crossed the road before the Third Battle of Ypres in 1917. Across to the right you can see the high ground of Mount Sorrel. From this point the German line followed the road south until just before Kemphof Farm up ahead, before it skirted **Armagh Wood** and swung southwest to Zwarteleen and Hill 60. Continue down the road to a point just before **Kemphof Farm,** where you will find a track running across the road ❺ in front of you. A turnstile gate allows access on each side of the road. This is the **Brown Road** which can be a little muddy in wet weather. Go through the turnstile gate on your right. You are now looking along the track defended by 2/Grenadier Guards on 6 November 1914 when the Germans broke thought the line held by the Irish Guards further west. Together with 7 Cavalry Brigade, the Grenadiers held fast and saved the day.

If you are on foot continue along the path to meet the main road at ❼. (Cyclists should continue straight ahead past Kemphof Farm to a T-junction ❻ with the main road. Turn right using the cycle path to rejoin the route at the opposite end of the Brown Road.)

Walk through the trees to emerge at the main road, almost directly opposite is a track ❼ leading through the woods to a residential road. Take this track and turn right past private houses, continuing to bear left along Zwarteleenstraat. Very soon you will be at Hill 60 ❽ which is the open area on your left. Hill 60 is open to the public and accessed through the small gate. Directly opposite the gate is the Hill 60 Bar and Restaurant but unless you are a customer, there is a small charge for the toilets. See Route 15 for more detailed information about Hill 60.

You are now at the starting point for **Route 15.** *Should you wish to extend the route to include the Caterpillar Crater and the Bluff walk across the railway bridge turn left at* ❾ *down the grassy track towards Battle Wood and follow the directions for Route 15.*

To remain on the Zillebeke and Aristocrats' Cemetery route, cross over the railway bridge and continue straight ahead to the T-junction with the main road. Turn right here towards Verbrande Molen – cyclists should use the marked cycle track. After 700m, turn right keeping a sharp look out for the CWGC signpost to **Larch Wood Cemetery** next to a private house on the right. After crossing over the road ❿ with care take the track to the cemetery which is just across the railway line on the right. The cemetery was begun in April 1915 near a small plantation of larches. There are 321 unidentified burials and special memorials to 82 casualties known or believed to be buried in the cemetery. The cemetery was enlarged after the Armistice when graves were brought in

The Brown Road.

from the surrounding battlefields which accounts for the large number of aircrew buried here. On 11 September 1917 **Second Lieutenant Henry Batson** (I.B.2) was flying as air gunner with **Sergeant William Roebuck** in a F2B Bristol Fighter of 48 Squadron when they were shot down and killed. Whilst only Batson has a named grave, Roebuck is now presumed to be the unnamed aviator buried at Boverkerke churchyard, north east of Vladslo. **Flight Sub-Lieutenant Norman Black** (I.B.17) was only 19 years old when he joined 9 RNAS Squadron in September 1917. On 11 October he was shot down over Zarren and died of his wounds the next day. Also 19 years old was **Lieutenant Bryant Lindley** (IV.F.23), a South African pilot of

Flight Sub-Lieutenant Norman Black.

25 Squadron who died of wounds after being shot down on 29 June 1918. Fellow South African **Second Lieutenant Gordon Forbes** (I.A.20) of 65 Squadron was killed in action flying a DH5 on 19 October 1917. Canadian pilot **Lieutenant James Sorley** (I.B.18) was commissioned in 1916 but lost his life flying a Sopwith Camel with 213 Squadron on 25 September 1918 near Ostende. Another Camel pilot, **Flight Sub-Lieutenant Edward Kendall** (I.B.10), of 6 RNAS Squadron was shot down and killed near Slype on 12 July 1917, whilst eight months previously **Second Lieutenant Frederick Gibbs** (I.B.2) lost his life on 13 September flying a Sopwith Pup, one of four machines of 54 Squadron lost that morning. **Lieutenant Ross Cornford** (I.A.14) and **Second Lieutenant Sydney Raper** (I.A.15) were both killed in action flying a 22 Squadron F2B near Handzaeme on 17 August 1917. One more F2B pilot, **Second Lieutenant R. Dutton** (I.B.20), of 48 Squadron was shot down on 19 August 1917 after a clash with Jasta 17, his observer was taken prisoner. Victims of inclement weather on 28 September 1918 were **Lieutenant Ronald Ringrose** (V.F.27) and his pilot **Second Lieutenant Hubert Hollins** (IV.F.28) of 202 Squadron who crashed their DH4 during a storm. **Lieutenant Ambrose Hutchinson** (IV.A.7) and **Second Lieutenant Baron Starfield** (IV.A.6) of 20 Squadron were both killed in action over Wijtschate flying a F2B

The F2B Bristol Fighter.

on 19 January 1918. Two 88 Squadron aircrew, **Lieutenant Prout West** (IV.A.2) from Vermont and **Private Alfred Loton** (IV.A.1), were killed in action flying a F2B on 28 June 1918 by a pilot from *Marinefeldjasta* II. Flying a DH9 of 98 Squadron, **Captain Gifford Horton** and **Lieutenant Harold McConnell** (I.B.15) were shot down by anti-aircraft fire over Brugge docks on 31 May 1918. Horton is buried at Bedford House Cemetery. Buried here are the crew of a 214 Squadron Handly Page bomber, one of four aircraft sent to bomb Brugge on 16 May 1918. Here you will find **Major James Harrison** (IV.F.22), **Captain Cecil Rushton** (IV.F.21) and **Lieutenant Wilfred King** (IV.F.20). Flying a much smaller aircraft was Camel pilot **Second Lieutenant J.E. Harrison** (IV.F.26) of 210 Squadron who fell to the guns of Gerhard Hubrich of Marinefeldjasta IV on 17 September 1918. Before you leave, spend a minute with 22-year-old **Private W. Chadwick** (III.F.9) from Bradford. A trooper with 10/Hussars, he was killed on 23 October at Zandvoorde. Initially listed as wounded and missing, his remains were found at Zantvoorde German Cemetery and brought here in 1919. You might also wish to visit **Lieutenant John Eden** (IV.D.6) of 12/Lancers, he was the brother of Anthony Eden, a future British Prime Minister.

After leaving the cemetery head north to rejoin the track and continue towards Zillebeke village bearing sharp right then left through the housing estate to a T-junction. Turn left past the children's playground to arrive at the main road. Turn right and after 175m turn left to return to the church and your vehicle. The **Aristocrats' Cemetery** is to the north of the church and is so called because of the large number of the aristocracy and landed gentry who are buried here.

The cemetery contains thirty-two burials, seventeen are casualties of the First Battle of Ypres in 1914. Six of the burials are unidentified and special memorials commemorate two casualties whose graves were destroyed by shellfire. One of these was the grave of **Lieutenant Hon William Reginald Wyndham** (SM1), a son of Lord Leconfield who was killed in 7 Cavalry Brigade's counter-attack of 6 November 1914 at Zwarteleen and would have been amongst the horsemen galloping across Observatory Ridge. You will find a further five headstones with the same date, all killed in the same attack. **Lieutenant Colonel Gordon Wilson** (B.2), commanding the Royal Horse Guards, **Second Lieutenant Alexis de Gunzburg** (B.1.), attached to the Horse Guards, **Second Lieutenant William Petersen** (C.3), 2/Life Guards, Brigade

Major, **Captain Norman Neill** (A.4), and **Lieutenant Carleton Tufnell,** 2/Grenadier Guards. Note the inscription on the headstone of Gordon Wilson, 'Life is a city of crooked streets, death is the market place where all men meet.' These lines, written by James Handley, were found in Gordon Wilson's effects by his wife, Lady Sarah Wilson née Churchill. The inscription on Tufnell's headstone, 'Floreat Etona', reminds us that ten of the officers buried here attended Eton School. Killed the next day on 7 November was **Major Robert Rising** (E.5) who died with 1/Gloucesters at Zwarteleen. His award of the DSO is described in the Langemark Area car tour.

Two of the headstones here are non-standard. That of Alexis de Gunzburg was provided by his mother the Baroness Henrietta de Gunzburg, who also funded and donated the new bells for the church. The rather grand headstone of 19-year-old **Lieutenant John Lee Steere** (F.1), 2/Grenadier Guards, was erected by his family before the standardization of CWGC headstones was introduced. Both headstones were allowed to remain in place by the CWGC, making this small cemetery rather unique. Lee Steere was killed on 17 November 1914, the same day his cousin and company commander, **Captain Cholmeley Symes Thompson** (F.2). John Lee Steere's previous company commander, **Major Lord Bernard Gordon Lennox** (E.3), was killed near Bodmin Copse

Lieutenant John Lee Steere.

on 10 November. Another member of the House of Lords and 2/Grenadier Guards was **Henry Parnell the 5th Baron Congleton** (E.2), who died on the same day as Bernard Gordon Lennox and **Lieutenant Michael Stocks** (E.1) during the bitter fighting around the wooded area at Zwarteleen. In the church porch you will find a photograph of 19-year-old **Second Lieutenant Avenel St George** (A.2) who was killed by a sniper returning to 1/Life Guards' trenches at Zwarteleen on 15 November 1914. Here also is a plaque commemorating **Lieutenant Alfred Schuster**, 4/Queen's Own Hussars, who was killed at Hooge on 20 November 1914, the same day that **Captain Richard Dawson** (E.6) of 3/Coldstream Guards died. Amongst this illustrious group lie **Private Walter Siewertsen** (E.4), a Grenadier Guardsman from the East End of London, **Lance Corporal James Whitfield** (A.1) and **Private William Gibson** (A.3), who died

The Aristocrats' Cemetery at Zillebeke, John Lee Steere's headstone can be seen in the front row.

with the London Scottish, a Territorial battalion which was brought into the 1914 fighting on 31 October. The churchyard also contains the grave of **Lieutenant Colonel Arthur de Courcy Scott** (H.3), who was killed on Hill 60 whilst commanding 1/Cheshires on 6 May 1915. He had taken up his command in late November 1914 and died at the head of his battalion. He left a wife, Phyllis, and two children, Rosalind and Herbert.

A victim of the 1916 Mount Sorrel fighting was **Lieutenant Frederick Watson** (F.3), who as a graduate of St Andrews emigrated to Canada in 1912. He was killed on 10 June 1916 near Maple Copse with the Canadian

Lieutenant Frederick Watson.

43/Battalion. Two Canadians who served in B Company, 24/Battalion, were amongst the men of 5 Platoon who were hit by a shell whilst walking along the road in front of the church on the evening of 7 June 1915. Twelve were killed outright and eleven others were wounded.

Private William Croft (B.3) and **Private John Sime** (D.4) were buried in the churchyard. Spare a moment for 24-year-old **Sapper Charles Ilsley** (H.2), an American by birth who joined 6/Canadian Field Company in Montreal after graduating from McGill University in 1915. Arriving in France in September 1915, his company moved to Zillebeke in March 1916 and 'Red' Ilsley was killed by a sniper near Maple Copse on 23 March. He left a widow, Adelia Blanche.

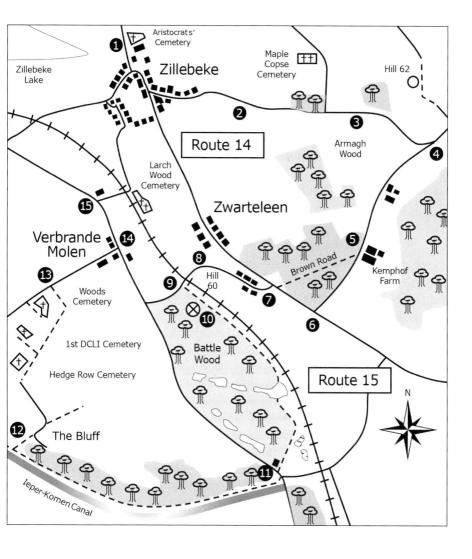

Route 15

Caterpillar Crater and the Bluff

Suitable for 👤
Circular route starting at: Hill 60 car park.
Coordinates: 50°49 26.70 N – 2°55 40.78 E.
Distance: 6.7km/4 miles.
Grade: Moderate.
Toilets: Hill 60 and the Komen Canal.
Maps: NGI 1:20 000 Poperinge–Ieper 28/1–2 and Heuvelland–
  Mesen (Messines) 28/5–6.
Link this with: Route 14 – Zillebeke and the Aristocrats'
  Cemetery.

General description and context: This route takes the walker from
Hill 60 through Battle Wood past the Caterpillar Crater to the
Ieper–Komen Canal and then on to the Bluff. Along with Hooge, the
area became associated with military mining and tunnelling as the
profusion of mine craters bears witness today. The route can be extended
by joining the Zillebeke and Aristocrats' Cemetery route to make a varied
outing of 13.4km in length. However, it should be remembered that the
route through Battle Wood is for walkers only. **Hill 60** was one of the
most fought over pieces of ground in the Salient. An artificial mound,
60m above sea level, it was created by the spoil from the railway cutting.
Before the war it attracted courting couples and was known as 'Lover's
Knoll', after 1914 it became notorious for entirely different reasons. In
December 1914, the Germans took the crest of the hill, the lower
elevations being first occupied by the French and then by the British in
February 1915. On 17 April 1915, mines were blown here in support of
the 5th Division's attack on the hill, an attack that saw four VCs being
awarded and the hill passing into British hands. But success was short-

lived. By 5 May 1915 the hill was reclaimed by the Germans during the Second Battle of Ypres and they remained in possession until June 1917. On 7 June 1917, nineteen mines were detonated along the Messines Ridge – including one under Hill 60 and another beneath the **Caterpillar** on the other side of the railway cutting – as the 'shock and awe' curtain raiser to the **Battle of Messines**. In 1917 the fifth VC was won on the hill, this time by **Second Lieutenant Frederick Youens**. The hill was again in the possession of the Germans after their April 1918 offensive and only finally passed into Allied hands six months later. **The Bluff** was created by spoil from the canal and captured by the Germans in the 1918 April offensive after a particularly desperate last stand by men of 13/Royal Sussex.

Directions to start: From Ieper leave via the Menin Gate and turn right onto the N8. After passing Menin Road South Cemetery on your right, turn right again at the roundabout and follow the road to Zillebeke. At Zillebeke follow signs for Hill 60.

Route description: We suggest you explore Hill 60 after you have completed the walk. Park in the Hill 60 car park ❽ and cross the railway bridge over the cutting. Directly opposite the information board take the grass track ❾ on your left and enter the wood in front of you. This is **Battle Wood** and contains the remains of the huge **Caterpillar Crater** ❿ which you will find on your right. The Caterpillar was sometimes referred to as Hill 59 which, along with Hill 60, soon became one of the most hated and feared sectors on the front line. As at Hill 60, the Caterpillar was formed from spoil dug from the railway cutting and deposited in an 'S'-shaped feature – hence the name. On 7 June 1917 the southern end of the Caterpillar was almost completely destroyed, and along with it the German trenches that sat astride it, by 70,000lb of explosive.

With the crater on your right bear left and follow the track southeast until it emerges on the edge of the wood running alongside the railway line. The path soon takes you past several water-filled features before continuing along a tree-lined avenue to reach a wooden barrier. Turn left here to follow a pathway to join a minor road. Turn right to reach the main road and go straight across ⓫. Ahead is a useful information board and convenient public toilets. Begun in the 1880s and finished in 1913, the canal was destined never to see traffic but the spoil heaps created by

Peaceful now – the Caterpillar Crater as it is today. Note the two figures on the far rim, illustrating the size of the crater.

The path alongside the Ieper–Komen Canal.

the digging of the waterway still form the steep banks on either side. Take the path on the right – north bank – of the canal, noting the numerous shell holes along the way. You will pass two signposted pathways and a flight of steps on your right before you eventually come to a steep path on the right leading up through the woods marked by an information board and a wooden marker post. The path doubles back at an angle to take you up over the Bluff ⓬. Known by the Germans as *Die Grosse Bastion*, the Bluff was the highest mound on the north bank and the British 28th Division took responsibility for the sector on 1 February 1915. The area was notorious for mining operations carried out by both sides and was the scene of numerous trench raids. One of these resulted in the trenches of the 14th (Light) Division being captured by the Germans in February 1916, and retaken by the 3rd Division on 2 March. In the following July the Germans blew a mine under it, but failed to capture the ground.

Once on top of the Bluff, continue on the path round to the right and take the first path on the left which leads down to a gravel track ahead. Once on the track follow it as it turns left into the woods. As the track bends sharply left again continue straight ahead on a grass path which will take you directly to **Hedge Row Trench Cemetery**. Occasionally referred to as Ravine Wood Cemetery, it is named after a

Hedge Row Trench Cemetery.

trench that ran through this area. Burials began here in March 1915 and continued until August 1917 Because of the severe fighting in this area the graves were continually being disturbed by shellfire, so much so that after the Armistice it was impossible to locate individual graves. Consequently the graves are arranged in a circle around the Cross of Sacrifice and although it was known who had been buried here, the headstones were placed in the pattern you can see today. Over half the identified burials here are from the fighting of 1915, and one of these is **Lieutenant Edward Cordeux** (G.8) who was killed on 1 October 1915, his promotion to lieutenant being announced eight days later in the *London Gazette*. The 19-year-old was serving with 7/Notts and Derbys Regiment and was the only son of Robert and Ethel Cordeux of Bunny Hall, Nottingham. After his death his mother had the organ in St Mary's Church, Bunny, enlarged and placed on the south side of the chancel in memory of her son and husband who died in the same year. Four other soldiers of 7/Notts and Derbys who were killed on the same day as Edward Cordeux lie close by. The youngest soldier buried here is 17-year-old **Rifleman Walter Stokes** (E.3) of 3/Rifle Brigade. Probably the furthest from home is **Sapper Charles Polwart** (H.6) of 5/Canadian Field Company who was wounded by a shell splinter whilst wiring the support lines and later died of his wounds. Originally from Glasgow, he emigrated to Canada and worked in the Vancouver area as a surveyor before enlisting in July 1915.

With the cemetery on your left, continue along the grass track and after 130m you will find the track to the **First DCLI Cemetery** on the left. Stop. The views of Ieper and Zillebeke Lake are exceptionally good from here. The DCLI Cemetery contains the graves of sixty-three identified officers and men, fifty-one of whom were serving with 1/Duke of Cornwall's Light Infantry. On both sides of the Cross of Sacrifice you will find Row D which was added after the Armistice when graves were brought in from the battlefield bringing the total number of burials to seventy-six, of which thirteen are unidentified. In May and June 1915, 1/DCLI were in the trenches in this sector of the line and although they made no specific attack, they had 46 other ranks killed and 251 wounded. Many of those men now lie in this cemetery. The only DCLI officer killed in this period was 40-year-old **Captain Charles Woodham** (C.1) who was shot by a sniper on 15 May 1915. A South African War veteran, he was commissioned in 1895 and promoted to captain in 1901. His award of the DSO was announced in the *London Gazette* in February 1915. **Second Lieutenant Arthur Lynes** (A.18) was formally a sergeant with the DCLI and had only just been commissioned into 1/Royal Berkshires when he died of wounds on 10 July 1915. Birmingham-born **Private Albert Clarke** (D.4) of 2/Duke of Wellington's Regiment was killed on 18 April 1915. Albert fought at Mons in 1914 and was subsequently wounded and captured. Escaping from hospital with Captain Ernie Taylor of the same battalion, both men succeeded in reaching the safety of British lines. Like Taylor, Albert was killed on Hill 60.

Return to the track and turn left, continuing down the tree-lined avenue past a water-filled feature on the right to a T-junction. Turn right ❸ here to join a metalled road – Verbrandemolenstraat. To reach the **Woods Cemetery** turn left to find the access path 200m or so further down on the left. Woods Cemetery was begun in April 1915 and used until September 1917 by units holding this sector. The graves of the 2nd, 3rd and 10th Canadian Battalions and the London Regiment are particularly numerous here. The irregular shape of the cemetery is due to the conditions of burial at the time when the front line was just beyond the wood. Here you will find 42-year-old **Lieutenant Bernard Gough** (I.C.3), the medical officer attached to 8/South Staffords who was killed on 17 February 1916. Before he volunteered for service he was a GP in the Mendip village of Compton Martin; his death left his wife Annie a widow. Amongst the Canadian dead is **Private Leonard Endicott** (II.G.2) who served with 2/Canadian Infantry Battalion. He emigrated to Ottowa from his home in Devon and joined the city fire service. He enlisted in February 1915 leaving behind his wife Etta. He was killed by shellfire on 25 April 1916; the day after the battalion moved into the trenches at Railway Cutting near Hill 60.

After returning to Verbrandemolenstraat continue towards the farm buildings ahead of you with woods on the right to reach the junction ❹ with the main road. This is the tiny hamlet of Verbrande Molen (formerly Verbrandenmolen) where 7 Cavalry Brigade was often billeted at the farm on your left during the First Battle of Ypres. After the trench lines became established in this area the road you have just walked along was part of the support line and bore the name **Sunken Road Trench** which continued across the road into **Verbrandenmolen Trench**. This area was very much part of the front line up until June/July 1917 and the Third Battle of Ypres.

Hill 60 bunker.

> *You now have the option of joining* **Route 14**, *the Zillebeke and Aristocrats' Cemetery route. To do this turn left and walk up the road to* ⓯ *and follow the track past Larch Wood Cemetery and into Zillebeke. The directions for Route 14 will guide you from there and return you to the Hill 60 car park.*

To continue on Route 15 – Caterpillar Crater and the Bluff – turn right and walk down the road until the Hill 60 signpost points to the turning on the left that will take you back to the Hill 60 car park. Hill 60 remains a monument to the desperate nature of the fighting that took place in the Salient. By the car park is the memorial to the 14th (Light) Division which was moved to this spot from Railway Wood in 1978. Close by is the memorial to the **1st Australian Tunnelling Company**. From the access gate you can see the restored monument to the **Queen Victoria's Rifles** – 9/London Regiment – which was badly damaged in the Second World War. The battalion was in action here in April 1915. Elsewhere on the hill are several German concrete bunkers and numerous mine craters but as you explore bear in mind the hill is in reality a cemetery without headstones as beneath the surface lie the remains of German and Allied soldiers who fought to retain this tiny patch of ground.

Route 16

Ieper South

Suitable for ⑤ ♁

Circular route starting at: Sint-Maarten's Cathedral, Ieper.

Coordinates: 50°51 06.03 N – 2°53 02.12 E.

Distance: 12.8km/8 miles.

Grade: Moderate.

Toilets: Spoilbank Cemetery.

Maps: NGI 1:20 000 Poperinge–Ieper 28/1–2.

General description and context: This route begins in the centre of Ieper and after leaving the Ypres Reservoir Cemetery continues south along the Ieper–Komen Canal before skirting the Palingbeek to return to Ieper via Zillebeke Lake and the Menin Gate. On the way visits are made to five of the many cemeteries that characterize the area. Whilst we have described each of the cemeteries on the route in detail, it is your choice whether you visit them all.

Directions to start: Sint-Maarten's Cathedral is behind the Cloth Hall where there is ample parking.

Route description: Begin outside the grandeur of Sint-Maarten's Cathedral ❶. With the cathedral on your right continue to the T-junction ahead and turn left past St George's Memorial Church – signposted Veurne, De Panne and Poperinge. Continue along Elverdingsestraat for approximately 300m to take the right turn immediately before the prison – Minneplein – which will take you to **Ypres Reservoir Cemetery**. Once known as the Cemetery North of the Prison, it later became Ypres Reservoir North Cemetery until the name was shortened further to assume its present form. The cemetery was begun in October 1915 and located next to an advanced dressing station and used by field ambulance units until after the Armistice when it contained 1,099

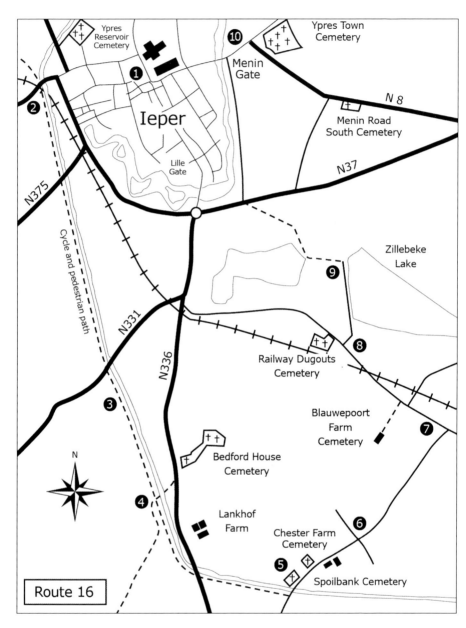

graves. There are now more than double that number of burials, 1,034 of which are unidentified. Here you will find the graves of sixteen officers and men of 6/Duke of Cornwall's Light Infantry, who were billeted in the vaults of the cathedral and killed on 12 August 1915 by shelling from the 'Ypres Express' firing from Houthulst Forest. Many of the survivors were rescued by men of 11/King's Liverpool Regiment but some of the dead were not recovered until after the Armistice. Several sets of brothers lie side by side here. **Lance Corporal James Tinnock Bulkeley Gavin** (VII.B.3) and **Private Gavin Gordon Bulkeley Gavin** (VII.B.12) were killed within hours of each other serving with 26/Australian Battalion on 4 October 1917. A tale of influence surrounds the two Knott brothers, **Captain Henry Knott** (V.B.16) of 9/Northumberland Fusiliers, who died on 7 September 1915, and **Major James Knott** (V.B.15) of 10/West Yorkshire Regiment, who was killed on 1 July 1916, the first day of the Battle of the Somme. The boys' father was Sir James Knott who undoubtedly had something to do with the remains of his eldest son being moved to Ieper from the Somme to rest alongside those of his younger son. Sir James funded the building of the tower of St George's Memorial Church on the corner of Elverdingsestraat. Interestingly, Henry Knott was originally buried at Poperinghe New Cemetery. Was the interment of his two sons at Ieper part of the arrangement? The casualty returns of 1/Grenadier Guards for March 1916 included the two Styles brothers who were both killed on 20 March 1916. **Sydney Styles** (I.C.72) and **William Styles** (I.C.71) were two of six men of the battalion killed by shellfire. Their brother, **Henry Styles**, was killed less than a month later on the Somme. **Lieutenant Colonel Augustus David Geddes** (IV.C.4) was commanding 2/East Kent Regiment when he was placed in temporary command of seven composite battalions of the so-called 'Geddes Detachment' at Sint-Jan in the aftermath of the German gas attack during the Second Battle of Ypres. He was killed by a shell on 28 April 1915 at Sint-Jan and was 48 years old. **Brigadier General Francis Aylmer Maxwell** (I.A.37) VC, CSI, DSO and Bar was commanding 27 Infantry Brigade when he was shot dead by a sniper on 21 September 1917. He won the VC at Sanna's Post in March 1900 during the South African War. Another soldier with the same name was **Lieutenant Colonel John Maxwell** (I.A.31) MC, DSO. Maxwell volunteered for service in 1914 and was one of the few officers of 7/Rifle Brigade who survived the attack made on 30 July 1915 at Hooge which is described in Route 12. He was awarded the MC in June 1916 and in the same month was promoted to major. Having survived the Somme campaign he was given command of 8/KRRC but barely three months later he was wounded by a shell close to Bellevue Farm and died at 101/Field Ambulance Dressing Station on 4 December 1917. Spare a moment to visit **Lance Corporal Clifford Garland** (I.E.56) who, after enlisting in Bristol, was serving with the South Midland 61st Divisional Signal Company, Royal Engineers when he was killed on 28 August 1917. After training at Northampton, Chelmsford and Salisbury Plain, Clifford crossed to France in March 1916 with the division and fought at Fromelles on 19 July 1916 when the division suffered heavy losses. At the time of his death he was in the line around **Schuler Farm** near Kerselaar. **Gunner Wainwright Merril** (I.I.19) from Massachusetts, USA, was serving with 6/Siege Battery of the Canadian Garrison Artillery when he was killed on 6 November 1917 at the age of 19. In 1916 he was selected for Harvard University in what would have been the class of 1918, but instead of continuing his studies he crossed the border into Canada to enlist under the alias Arthur Stanley. Given a temporary grave near the old gun pits on the Bellevue Spur near Passendale, his body was brought here after the Armistice.

After leaving the cemetery turn left and follow the one-way system to the main road junction. Cross straight over to the cycle and pedestrian path which runs south alongside the canal ❷. Cyclists should use the pink cycle lanes. Continue to the next junction, turn right over the level crossing and then turn left into Tulpenlaan. The canal should now be on your left. As you head towards the next junction with the N375 continue straight ahead and over the next junction with the N331 ❸. At this point you should be clear of the built-up area and able to look across to the right to see the church spire at Voormezeele in the near distance and on the ridge in the far distance ahead, that of Sint-Eloi.

Continue for another 900m or so and at the obvious junction ❹ of paths stop. Across to your right the hill in the distance is Kemmelberg and the track running off to the right goes to Voormezeele and its two military cemeteries. You are now going to take the path on your left leading to the N336. Cross the road with care to the path on the opposite side, **Bedford House Cemetery** is 100m back up the road on the right. Bedford House, sometimes known as Woodcote House, were the names given by the Army to the Chateau Rosendal, a country house in a small wooded park with moats. Although it never fell into German hands, the house and the trees were gradually destroyed by shellfire. It

Bedford House Cemetery.

The Lankhof Farm bunkers.

was used by field ambulances and as the headquarters of brigades and other fighting units. This is one of the largest cemeteries in the area and by the Armistice covered much of the grounds of the chateau, all of which is described on the two information boards near the entrance. At the rear of the cemetery the wind turbines stand in stark contrast to the towers and spires of Ieper which you can see in the distance and serve to remind us that the texture of the battlefields of almost 100 years ago are being slowly changed by progress. Today there are 5,139 soldiers from both world wars buried here and 3,011 are unidentified. Such is the appalling price of war.

One young German airman who paid the price was **Walter Rode** (I.F.33), a pilot with *Fliegerabteilung* 3 who was shot down by Lieutenant Gordon Taylor of 66 Squadron on 20 August 1917. Rode's grave is in Enclosure 2 but his observer, Wilhelm Donner, is buried 50 miles away at Fraznoy. Commissioned in 1911, **Captain Thomas Frost** (Enclosure 2. IV.A.41) was killed by a sniper on 28 March 1915 He was the last surviving officer of 1/Cheshires who had served at Mons and Audregnies in 1914. Side by side in

Captain Thomas Frost.

Enclosure 2 are **Lance Corporal Albert Tidy** (IV.A.25) killed on 1 June 1915 and **Private Thomas Peaceful** (IV.A.26) killed three days later. A sad reminder of the frailty of man is **Private Frederick Turner** (Enclosure 4. IV.A.18) who was sentenced to death and shot at dawn on 23 October 1917 after deserting from 6/Northumberland Fusiliers. Also in Enclosure 4 is **Second Lieutenant Rupert Hallowes** (XIV.B.36) VC, MC of 4/Middlesex. His citation reads: 'For most conspicuous bravery and devotion to duty during the fighting at Hooge between 25th September and 1st October, 1915'. He died of his wounds on 30 September 1915 and is also commemorated at Brookwood Cemetery on the Family Plot. Another set of brothers are buried here. **Private George Hamilton** (Enclosure 4. I.P.3) and **Private Sydney Hamilton** (Enclosure 4. I.K.12) were both serving with 21/Canadian Infantry Battalion near Mount Sorrel when they were killed on 14 June 1916. It is difficult not to spend a long time in this cemetery just wandering amongst the headstones but before you leave find time to visit 41-year-old **Sepoy Akka** (Enclosure 4. B.4) from South Waziristan. It is all too easy to forget that considerable numbers of Indian troops fought in the Salient and suffered terribly in the dreadful winter weather. Akka was serving in 129/Duke of Connaught's Own Baluchis when he was killed on 26 April 1915.

Retrace your route and return to the canal cycle path then turn left to continue alongside the canal. At the next junction with the N336 cross over to take the cycle path on the opposite side. Looking across to your left you will see a cluster of British bunkers at **Lankhof Farm**. The farm was originally surrounded by a moat, the remains of which you can still see today, and the bunkers were started by 153/Field Company, RE, in 1917 and completed by the Australian 4/Field Company. The German offensive of 1918 reached Lankhof Farm and there is a demarcation stone on the main N336 which you can see on the left as you cross over. Once across the road you will still be following the line of the canal but this time it will be on your right and if you look carefully you will find the remains of more bunkers about halfway along the canal path to your right. Ahead of you ❺, in front of farm buildings, is the Cross of Sacrifice at **Chester Farm Cemetery**, a little further on **Spoilbank Cemetery** soon reveals itself as you reach the road junction. Ahead of you the canal continues through the wooded area known as the Palingbeek which we describe in Route 15. There are public toilets just inside the wood. Spoilbank Cemetery, also known as Chester Farm Lower Cemetery or Gordon Terrace Cemetery, was begun in February 1915. It is particularly associated with the casualties of 2/Suffolks on the Bluff early in 1916. It was enlarged after the Armistice when graves were brought in from the battlefields. The cemetery contains 520 graves, 125 of which are unknown. One of the earliest casualties of the war was **Private F.W. Johnston** (I.S.21) serving with 1/Bedfordshire Regiment, who was killed on 7 November 1914 during the First Battle of Ypres. Just to the right of the entrance are the graves of three senior officers of 10/Royal Welsh Fusiliers (RWF) all killed on 3 March 1916 when a shell hit the battalion HQ dugout. **Lieutenant Colonel Stewart Binny** (I.M.4) was commissioned into 19/Hussars in 1894 and was awarded the DSO in South Africa in July 1901. On 5 February 1916 he was given command of 10/RWF, a month later he was dead. His second-in-command, **Major Edward Freeman**, is buried next to him as is the battalion adjutant, **Captain William Lyons**. There are two young 17-year-old private soldiers buried here, **Private Alfred Austrin** (I.C.6), who was killed on

23 May 1915 serving with 1/Lincolnshires, and **Private William Armstrong** (I.D.26) of 8/ King's Own, who joined him on 29 November 1915. Whilst 2/Suffolks were on the south bank of the canal during July and August 1915 they buried eight of their casualties here. In January 1916 the battalion was back on the Bluff until March, during which time they suffered 250 casualties, including **Lieutenant Robert Locke** (I.M.2) and the 21 other ranks of the battalion that are now resting here. Buried side by side to the right of the Cross of Sacrifice in Plot I are **Second Lieutenant George Keating** (I.H.3) and his brother, **Lieutenant John Keating** (I.H.4) of 2/Cheshires, who were killed on 17 February 1915. Both were senior NCOs and had been commissioned in 1914 when the battalion arrived back in England from India.

Chester Farm Cemetery takes its name from the farm that you can see up the hill on the right. The cemetery was begun in March 1915 and used until November 1917 and of the 420 burials here, 7 are unidentified. Plot I contains the graves of ninety-two officers and men of 2/Manchesters, who died in April to July 1915 and there are seventy-two London Regiment burials elsewhere in the cemetery. Of the men whose ages are recorded, eighteen were still in their teens when they died. Of these, the youngest is 16-year-old **Private Alfred Bootham** (I.A.5) from Manchester, closely followed by two 17-year-old boys, **Rifleman Ernest Miles** (I.K.33), who was killed on 12 June 1917, and **Private Hugh Bagshaw** (I.B.5) from Buxton, who was killed on 21 September 1915. **Lieutenant Ernest Stafford Carlos** (I.K.36) was a member of the Royal Academy and well known for such works as *Rejected and Dejected* and *The Pathfinder.* He enlisted as a private in the Queen's Westminster Rifles and was commissioned soon after. He was killed on 14 June 1917 leading his platoon in an attack. Another youngster was 21-year-old **Captain Harold Jackson** (I.K.36) from Coventry. He died of wounds on 7 June 1917 sustained whilst flying over German lines. His name also appears on the family grave at St Michael's Cemetery in Coventry.

After signing the visitor's book leave the cemetery and turn left to go past the farm to the small crossroads ➏ 150m up the hill. On the right a CWGC signpost points to Woods, Hedge Row Trench and 1st DCLI Cemeteries. These three cemeteries are a little over 1,500m away to the right should you wish to visit them. However, they are visited and described in Route 15.

As you continue along the gently rising road towards a cluster of private houses at the junction with the Hollebeke road, Blauwepoort Farm is visible to your left and in the distance you should be able to make out the tall spire of Sint-Maarten's Cathedral. At the T-junction ❼ turn left, cyclists should use the cycle path on the left of the road. Ahead on the left is a CWGC signpost to **Blauwepoort Farm Cemetery.** Turn left down the track to the cemetery. Begun by a French battalion of Chasseurs Alpins in November 1914, the cemetery was then used by Commonwealth troops from February 1915 to February 1916. The French graves were removed after the Armistice. Of the eighty burials here all are from the fighting of 1915 except **Sergeant John Heron** (E.2) and **Private William Clish** (E.3), both of whom were killed on 15 February 1916.

Retrace your route to the main road, ahead of you is Zillebeke Lake. Turn right and as you pass the turning to Zillebeke on the right notice

Zillebeke Lake.

the demarcation stone on the central reservation, another reminder of how close the Germans came to Ieper in the spring of 1918. Continue over the railway line to **Railway Dugouts Burial Ground (Transport Farm)**. The cemetery took its name from the Advanced Dressing Station dugouts that had been excavated into the railway embankment and a small farm, known by the troops as Transport Farm. In the summer of 1917 a considerable number of graves were obliterated by shellfire before they could be marked. The cemetery now contains 2,459 burials, of which 430 are unidentified and 261 are represented by special memorials. Other special memorials record the names of seventy-two casualties buried in Valley Cottages and Transport Farm Annexe Cemeteries whose graves were destroyed in later fighting. Amongst the large number of Canadian troops buried here are two brothers, originally from Worcester and who are commemorated on the Valley Cottages Special Memorial. **Private Frederick Wild** and his younger brother, **Private Reginald Wild**, were both killed on 21 August 1916 serving with 43/Canadian Infantry Battalion. Another Canadian who was killed on Hill 60 on 18 August 1916 was **Lieutenant Albert Service** (VI.J.1), the brother of the Canadian poet Robert Service well known for his *Rhymes of a Red Cross Man*. Accidently killed on 5 January 1918 was **Second Lieutenant Charles Benford** (VII.V.4) of 7/DCLI. The battalion war diary gives no detail of his death but it was probably the result of a premature explosion. Benford was one of 650 officers and men of 7/Battalion who were killed in the Great War. Commanding 9/York and Lancaster Regiment when he met his death on 7 June 1917 was **Lieutenant Colonel John Bowes-Wilson** (VII.M.10). A veteran of the South African War who had been commissioned in 1899, he left a wife and two children. His brother, **Captain George Bowes-Wilson**, died of wounds received at Sanctuary Wood on 17 June 1915. Victoria Cross recipient **Second Lieutenant Frederick Youens** (I.Q.3) of 13/DLI was brought here after being severely wounded whilst defending his trench on Hill 60. Sadly his award, which was announced in the *London Gazette* on 31 July 1917, was posthumous as Youens died on 7 July. Killed in action near Mount Sorrel on 17 June 1917 was 39-year-old **Major Arthur Conway** (VII.R.1) who was serving with 1/North Staffords. Wounded in 1914 during the First Battle of Ypres, he won his DSO in 1916. **Private Percy Fulford** (VI.M.23) is amongst several veterans of the Gallipoli campaign who are buried here. He enlisted at Perth on 17

September 1914 and by March 1915 was fighting on the Gallipoli Peninsula with the 11th Australian Infantry Battalion. Evacuated with severe dysentery, he eventually landed in France with his battalion in April 1916. He was killed on 28 September 1916 and amongst his personal effects, which he left to his father, was the fly net he had brought with him from Gallipoli.

On leaving the cemetery turn right to return along the road for 100m until the cycle track ❽ to Zillebeke Lake appears on your left. Cross over and take the track to the lake ahead of you. At the junction by the lake you have the choice of turning right to go round the lake – about 400m down the path on the right you will see a British bunker – or continuing straight ahead. The lake embankment provided cover for numerous dugouts on its western side but much of it was overlooked by the Germans positioned on the high ground to the east. The extreme eastern corner of the lake in particular was notorious for being targeted by German gunners and soon became known as **Hellblast Corner**. Should you decide not to go all the way round the lake carry on past the restaurant to a set of steps on the left ❾ leading down to the pumping station. If you are cycling, continue to the end of the lake and at the parking area find a tarmac track on the left that leads back downhill to the pumping station. Follow the tarmac track towards the N37 ahead of you and take the subway under the road. On the other side keep left, keeping the sports stadium on your right and follow signs for the Rijselsepoort. Continue alongside the road and take the first right – signposted Sport Centrum – keep a look out for the small tarmac path on the left that will take you to the cycle and pedestrian path that runs opposite the rampart walls. Once on this path continue past the large footbridge to reach the Menin Gate ❿ which is described in Route 17. Turn left to pass underneath the arch and, flanked by the thousands of names of the missing to right and left, go straight through and in another 200m enter the Grote Markt.

Route 17

Ieper Town and Ramparts

Suitable for 🚶

Circular route starting at: the Grote Markt.

Coordinates: 50°51 03.82 N – 2°53 09.39 E.

Distance: 3.2km/2 miles.

Grade: Easy.

Maps: NGI 1:20 000 Poperinge–Ieper 28/1–2. The tourist map of Ieper obtainable from the tourist office is also useful.

General description and context: This short walk begins in the centre of Ieper and visits the ramparts, Ypres Ramparts Cemetery, the Menin Gate, Sint-Maarten's Cathedral and the St George's Memorial Church. Details of a longer 2.6km walk – 'The Ramparts Route' – can be obtained from the tourist office free of charge. Public toilets are located behind the Cloth Hall on the cathedral side.

Route description: We begin outside the magnificently reconstructed Cloth Hall – the Lakenhallen – which was only finally completed in 1962. To the right of the central archway – the Donkerpoort – is the tourist office where you can find further details about the history and reconstruction of Ieper. The Grote Markt is almost exactly as it was in 1914 when British troops first entered the town. If you intend visiting the In Flanders Fields Museum you can do so at this point or on your return. With the Cloth Hall on your right walk straight ahead along Boterstraat for 150m and turn left down Patersstraat. Continue and in approximately 300m you will see a tree-lined pathway on the right which will take you to the moat. Take the first path on the left which runs along the eastern edge of the moat. You are now on the inner

The ruins of the Cloth Hall in 1917.

ramparts path along which you will find numerous information boards detailing the history of the town and the building of the outer defences and the occasional machine-gun cupola of Great War vintage. The formidable strength of the rampart walls – designed by the renowned French military engineer Vauban in the late seventeenth century – provided the Commonwealth troops with shelter in what was an almost completely devastated town. Follow the path and in slightly less than 1km you will see the **Ramparts Cemetery** on your right. The cemetery is on top of the old rampart, over what had once been dugouts. It was begun by the French in November 1914 and used by Commonwealth units at intervals from February 1915 to April 1918. The cemetery contains 198 burials. The most senior officer here is **Major George Walford** (F.1) who was Brigade Major to 84 Infantry Brigade. He was killed near Zonnebeke on 19 April 1915. At Sandhurst he graduated top of his intake to win the Anson Memorial Sword, an honour also won by Sir Douglas Haig in 1884. Haig of course would go on to become commander-in-chief of British and Commonwealth forces in December 1915. **Lieutenant Derwent Turnbull** (D.26) was the medical officer attached to 1/Cheshires. The 24-year-old doctor was wounded whilst attempting to bring a man to safety under heavy fire on 10 March 1915; sadly he died of his wounds four days later. In the next grave is another Cheshires officer, **Second Lieutenant Charles Vance**, who was killed on 9 March 1915. Educated at Campbell College, Belfast, Vance was an Irish public schools shooting champion and the son of the Archdeacon of Limerick. The two officers must have known each other and Turnbull may even have treated Charles Vance after he was hit. A number of the Cheshires killed in the Hill 60 area during February and March are also buried here, some probably succumbing to their wounds after arriving at one of the field ambulance units in the town. **Lance Corporal Arthur Ockelford** (J.26) has a rather touching inscription on his headstone, 'Gone but not forgotten from his loving wife and baby Peggy'. Arthur was killed on 21 April 1918 whilst serving with 12/Field Company, RE. Also serving with the RE was **Sapper William Scholz** (F.17). He was just 17 years old when he was killed on 15 March 1915. The inscription on **Private Albert Pacey's** (B.17) headstone reads, 'Some may think that we forget him when at times we are apt to smile'. Leave the cemetery, turn right and follow the path to cross over the **Lille Gate** or **Rijselpoort**. This gate dates from 1384 and was the main entrance and exit from Ypres during the war, the Menin Gate being far more exposed to enemy shellfire. The doorway on the eastern bastion leads to vaulted chambers which once housed a museum and was probably an HQ signals centre during the war. Entry is only by arrangement with the tourist office.

Continue along the ramparts path which now turns north to run along the eastern edge of Ieper. Across to the left is Sint-Pieterskerk and further ahead, the tall spire of Sint-Jacobskerk. It is between these two churches that the casements, constructed below the ramparts, were used as dugouts and shelters. They can be viewed from street level and it is said that it was in one of these shelters on Houten Paard that **Captain Fred Roberts** and men of 12/Sherwood Foresters printed and edited the famous *Wipers Times* after discovering an old printing press in 1916.

With the **Menin Gate** ahead of you stay on the ramparts passing the **Indian Memorial** with its four lions to reach the upper tier of the gate. You can descend to the road down the steps in front of you. Designed by Sir Reginald Blomfield and inaugurated on 24 July 1927, this huge memorial commemorates the names of more than 54,000 men of the Commonwealth who lost their lives serving in the Ypres Salient on or before 15 August 1917 and who have no known grave. Those who died after that date have their names inscribed on the memorial at Tyne Cot. Many who have their names here are amongst the unknown you will find in almost all cemeteries in the area, others were quite simply lost and are amongst the estimated 300,000 who still lie beneath the battlefields of Belgium. You will find names are arranged on panels by regiment – in order of regimental seniority – and rank, the exact location is indicated in the cemetery registers which are to be found on each side of the memorial. Each evening at 8.00pm buglers of the Last Post Committee sound the Last Post, a ceremony that has continued since 2 July 1928. The only period when this did not take place was during the occupation by the Germans in the Second World War when the daily ceremony was conducted at Brookwood Military Cemetery in England. On the very evening that Polish forces liberated the town on 6 September 1944 the ceremony was resumed at the Menin Gate at 6.00pm by a single bugler – Joseph 'Fred' Arfeuille, whom, it was reported, got roaring drunk and played it six times – despite the fact that the retreating Germans were just 2km away!

There are over twenty sets of brothers commemorated on the Menin Gate and you will also find seven of the VC holders listed at the back of the guidebook. The most senior officer, and a VC winner himself in 1899 during the South African War, is **Brigadier General Charles FitzClarence**, the commander who was instrumental in ordering the charge of the Worcesters at Geluveld in October 1914. See Route 11 for details. FitzClarence was killed on 12 November 1914.

To regain the ramparts path take the steps on the north side and continue until the path descends to the roadway and a small roundabout. Cross over the road to walk alongside the canal – the canal should be on your right. At the next crossroads turn left along Diksmuidestraat, turning right at the next crossroads into Surmont de Volsberghestraat. Just after the first turning on the left is the entrance to **Astrid Park**. Astrid (1905–1935), who was married to King Leopold III, was killed in a car accident in Switzerland aged only 29. The statue of her holding her son Baudouin is in the centre of the park.

The Menin Gate Memorial to the Missing.

Walk through keeping to the left, ahead is the imposing edifice of the cathedral. On reaching the road look across to a small green; there you will see the Celtic Cross of the **Munster Fusiliers Memorial** tucked away in the northeastern corner of the cathedral precinct. Turn right and walk through the **Kloosterpoort**, ahead of you to the Vandenpeereboomplein. Across to the right, on the corner of Elverdingsestraat, is **St George's Memorial Church.** The church is another Blomfield design and once supported the spiritual needs of a large British community which settled here after the war – many working for the war graves commission – and remained until forced to leave in 1940. Today the church still holds regular services but has become almost a memorial museum in its own right. Built initially through donations, it still relies on the generosity of the public for its upkeep. The church hosts a vast number of memorial plates commemorating individuals of all ranks, and one of these is **Captain William Megaw**, the adjutant of 1/Norfolks who was killed on 31 March 1915. He is buried at the Ramparts Cemetery which you visited earlier.

The magnificent **Sint-Maarten's Cathedral** was almost entirely destroyed and, like the Cloth Hall, has been rebuilt almost exactly as it was in 1914. Entry is free and amongst the memorials to French and Belgian soldiers you will find the memorial to the Commonwealth dead on the wall of the north transept. The cathedral was often used by troops overnight in the early part of the war thinking they were safe from shellfire. Tragically on 12 August 1915 a direct hit brought down the western end of the building and buried a number of men of 6/Duke of Cornwall's Light Infantry. Many of the men who went to assist the injured were themselves buried as the shellfire continued, and two of these men, **Major Carew Barnett** and **Lieutenant Richard Blagrove**,

The Kloosterpoort.

were killed by a 17in shell. Both men were buried at **Ypres Reservoir Cemetery** and lie side by side in Plot X, Row D, graves 20 and 21. Altogether twenty-one officers and men were wounded and twenty killed, illustrating the dangers that were apparent even when troops were not in the front-line trenches. During the cathedral's reconstruction after the war several more of the battalion were found amongst the ruins. Leave the cathedral and look across to the southern edge of the Vandenpeereboomplein where the Ieper Town War Memorial with its four bronze statues of Belgian soldiers standing on guard. To the left of these sentinels is a plaque commemorating the 13/Belgian Field Artillery Regiment. All that remains now is to conclude your walk with a well-deserved coffee or beer whilst watching the world go by in one of the many hostelries around the Grote Markt.

The ruined Sint-Maarten's Cathedral.

Route 18

A Day in the Salient Car Tour

Suitable for 🚗
Circular route starting at: Grote Markt, Ieper.
Coordinates: 50°51 03.82 N – 2°53 09.39 E.
Distance: 49.8km/30 miles.
Toilets: Passchendaele Memorial Museum, Hill 60, Langemark German Cemetery, Tyne Cot Cemetery, Sanctuary Wood Museum and Hooge Crater Museum.
Maps: NGI 1:50 000 series – Ieper 27–28–36 and Roeselare 19–20.

General description and context: This route includes a number of the more popular features of the more immediate area around Ieper and a few that are possibly not so well known. It is intended for those who have only a day to spare and wish to see as much as possible. To assist you in navigating around the area you will find the NGI 1:50 000 series maps very useful. Where places of interest have already been covered in the guidebook we refer you to those descriptions and details of museums and their opening hours can be found at the back of the guide. We have also included opportunities for short walks to enable you to stretch your legs.

Route description: The tour begins at the Grote Markt outside the magnificent **Cloth Hall** with the tourist information office and entrance to **In Flanders Field Museum**. Behind Cloth Hall you will find **Sint-Maartens Cathedral**. There is plenty of parking around here but you will need to purchase a ticket. After visiting the cathedral you may wish to walk across to the corner of Elverdingsestraat to **St George's Memorial Church**. Details and descriptions of all these visits can be found in **Route 17**.

The interior of St George's Memorial Church.

The concrete dugouts at Essex Farm.

Return to your vehicle and drive down Elverdingsestraat past the prison, which is on your right, to reach a roundabout. Turn right here and continue to the next roundabout where you turn right again. Continue to the next roundabout and take the N369 in the direction of Boezinge and Diksmuide. Just after the road passes under the N38 you will come to **Essex Farm Cemetery** on the right. Park outside the cemetery. Named after a cottage that stood close by and possibly connected with 2/Essex Regiment which arrived in this area in the summer of 1915, this site is probably one of the most visited cemeteries in the Ieper area and is on the itinerary of practically every school group and guided tour. The site today consists of the cemetery, a complex of concrete bunkers built into the earth bank of the canal in 1916 and used as an advanced dressing station and the imposing grey, granite obelisk in memory of the 49th (West Riding) Division, which was unveiled in June 1924.

The western bank of the Yser Canal and the ground north of the present-day cemetery was used as a dressing station and the cemetery, which was begun in April 1915, was used until August 1917. The bunkers, with an interpretation panel outside, have been restored and it is possible to enter the numerous rooms which were used as an operating theatre, wards with dressing cubicles, officers' mess and latrines. A path leads on to the 49th Division Memorial on the canal bank, immediately behind the cemetery and marks the service of the twelve Territorial Force battalions from the West Riding of Yorkshire which arrived in the area in the summer of 1915.

The original burials were made without a definite plan and some of the divisions that occupied this sector of the front line may be traced in almost every part of the cemetery, but the 49th Division buried their dead of 1915 in Plot I, whilst the 38th (Welsh) Division used Plot III in 1916. Today there are 1,200 soldiers buried or commem-orated in this cemetery, 103 of which are unidentified but special memorials commemorate 19 casualties known or believed to be buried amongst them.

It was whilst he was serving in this area attached to a Canadian unit that Ontario-born **Lieutenant Colonel John McCrae** of the Canadian Army Medical Corps wrote the poem 'In Flanders Fields' in early May 1915. He had recently officiated at the

Lieutenant Colonel John McCrae.

burial of **Lieutenant Alexis Helmer**, a young Canadian artilleryman and friend. Inspired by the poppies growing between the ever increasing number of crosses in the cemetery, McCrae had returned to his post and had scribbled down the first few words of the poem on a signal pad. The poem was published in *Punch* in December 1915 and gripped the nation's imagination. Helmer is today commemorated on the Menin Gate Memorial.

Inside the cemetery, the worn ground in front of **Rifleman Valentine Joe Strudwick's** grave (I.U.8) is testament to the huge numbers of visitors this 15-year-old soldier receives, many of them being young people of a similar age. In Plot I.Z.8 lies **Private Thomas Barratt** of 7/South Staffs, a 1917 recipient of the VC, who won the award for covering the withdrawal of his party after a fighting patrol. He was killed by a shell returning to the British lines. In plot I.A.1 lies **Lieutenant Frederick Leopold Pusch** of 1/Irish Guards who was killed, aged 20, on 27 June 1916. He received the DSO for his leadership during house-to-house fighting in the village of Loos in late 1915.

A little further along the path to the north of the bunker complex is another concrete construction built by the Royal Engineers of which only the front wall survives. After the Armistice such was the scale of destruction of the housing stock that returning locals often used these shelters as homes well into the 1920s. Another interpretation board close by has a photograph of a family outside this very bunker.

Return to your vehicle and continue on N369 towards Boezinge turning right over the canal to follow signs for Pilkem and Langemark. In less than a kilometre you will come to the **Carrefour de Roses crossroads** with the **Breton Memorial** on the left. Turn left here to visit **Artillery Wood Cemetery** and the **Francis Ledwidge Memorial**. Details can be found in **Route 6**.

Return to the Pilkem road, turn left and continue towards Langemark passing **Cement House Cemetery**, which you will see on the right. There is parking by the entrance should you wish to visit and details are in **Route 4**.

Continue into Langemark, passing the **Memorial to the 20th Light Division** on the left, and head towards the church where you should pick up signposts for the **Langemark German Military Cemetery**, which is to the north of the town on the Koekuit–Madonna road. The cemetery is signposted 'Soldatenfriedhof'. There is parking and toilets here. Details of the cemetery are in **Route 4** where you will also find the location of the **34th Division Memorial** and another German bunker which are just a short walk away.

Return to Langemark stopping briefly at the church where there are information boards. Follow signs for Zonnebeke towards the junction with the N313 where you will see the tall column of the **Canadian Memorial Park**. There is parking on the far side of the crossroads. Continue towards Zonnebeke, passing **Dochy Farm Cemetery** on your right. Just after entering the town take the minor road on the left – Albertstraat – to the T-junction with Schipstraat. Turn left then almost immediately right to **Tyne Cot Cemetery**. Parking is to the rear of the cemetery where there is a visitor's centre and toilets. Details of the cemetery and surrounding area are in **Route 10**.

From Tyne Cot head towards the junction with the N303. Before the junction you will have first crossed over the former Ypres–Roulers railway track which is now a cycle and pedestrian path. Details in **Route 10**. Turn right at the N303 junction and then right again at the roundabout onto the N332 which will take you back into Zonnebeke. Continue into Zonnebeke, over the roundabout and then take the next turning on the left – Berten Pilstraat. About 100m on the left is the entrance to the **Passchendaele Memorial Museum** where there is plenty of parking. Toilets here. This museum is well worth a visit.

Leave the museum car park and turn left and then next right along Grotemolenstraat. After 200m turn left onto Citernestraat which will take you along a minor road to **Polygon Wood**. Follow the sharp bend round to the right and park outside **Polygon Wood Cemetery**. You may wish to visit this small cemetery before crossing the road to the magnificent **Buttes New British Cemetery.** Full details of these visits are in **Route 9**.

Continue along Lange Dreve and turn left at the junction and right at the crossroads to cross over the A19 motorway. The next left – Polygonestraat – will take you down to the N8 – the notorious **Menin Road**. Turn left to Geluveld and park by the church, which will be on your left. You are now in the area covered by **Route 11** which gives full details of the events of 1914 and the location of the memorials to the South Wales Borderers and the Worcesters. At this point it may be useful to read the account of the events of 31 October 1914 as you will shortly be driving through that battlefield on your way to Zandvoorde. After returning to the N8 cross straight over – with care here – to the Zandvoorde road. The 1/Queen's positions were in the fields across to your left.

Continue into Zandvoorde and park by the church. **Route 11** gives details of the interior of the church and the four 10/Hussars graves in the churchyard. Here there is an opportunity to stretch your legs, leave your vehicle at the church and walk down Komenstraat continuing for 300m to the farm on the left, almost directly opposite is the narrow pathway to the imposing **Household Brigade Memorial**. This marks the spot where 7 Cavalry Brigade fought in vain to hold the high ground in 1914 and where some of them fought to the last man. (See **Route 11**). Don't forget to sign the visitor's book which is by the road.

Return to your car and follow signs for Zillebeke. You will soon see signs for **Hill 60**, turn off left and park in the small car park opposite the restaurant. Toilets here. Hill 60 is described in **Route 15** and there is another opportunity to stretch your legs here. Hill 60 has a number of mine craters and remnants of German bunkers after which you can visit the **Caterpillar Crater**. Walk across the bridge to the information panel on the right-hand side of the road and directly opposite there is a path that leads towards the woods. Follow this path for 200m to the crater.

From the Hill 60 car park drive over the bridge and turn right at the T-junction. You will pass signs for **Larch Wood Cemetery** where there are a large number of RFC aircrew buried, and after 600m you will come to a turning on the right to Zillebeke. Enter the village and park by the church to visit the **Aristocrats' Cemetery**. You will find full details in **Route 14**.

Continue north towards Ieper and take the second turning on the right, once clear of the residential housing bear right along Schacteweidestraat and take the first turning on the left 250m after the farm. After a sharp right-hand bend you will reach the junction with Canadalaan. Turn right, passing **Sanctuary Wood Cemetery,** and park near **Sanctuary Wood Museum**. Walk on past the museum to the Canadian Memorial at **Hill 62**. Full details of this area are in **Route 13**. Refreshments are available at Sanctuary Wood Museum or at **Hooge Crater Museum**, which you can see on the N8 opposite **Hooge Crater Cemetery**.

Turn round and drive up to the junction with the N8. If you are not going to visit Hooge Crater Museum and the **Hooge Crater,** which is a short distance up the hill to your right, then turn left and take the next right towards the Bellewaarde Ridge. This area is covered in **Route 12**. Just before you pass **Railway Wood** there is a minor road on the right which will take you round towards the tall cross of sacrifice at the **RE Grave**, which will come into view across to your right. It may be better to park your vehicle carefully here and walk from the junction to the RE Memorial which is up a track. A little further on from the RE Memorial the **Liverpool Scottish Memorial** can be found.

Continue over the N37 past the **Skrine and Bowlby Memorials** to the junction with the N332. **St Charles de Potyze French Cemetery** is immediately on the right. Created in 1920 as a concentration cemetery for the numerous French dead scattered around the area, there are now over 3,700 graves here and a mass grave containing 600 unknown soldiers. At the entrance is the Calvaire Breton sculpture commemorating the Breton soldiers killed on the Ijzer in 1914, a stark reminder that the northern sector of the of the Western Front in Belgium was held by French and Belgian troops. If you have a moment, visit **Francis le Roux** (Grave 3410), a 20-year-old who was killed at Diksmuide on 24 October 1914. In Grave 323 is **Lieutenant Pierre Ginisty**, the son of Paul Ginisty, author, collaborator of the famous French writer Guy de Mauppasant and the

Potijze Chateau and grounds taken after the Armistice.

Director of the Théâtre de L'Odéon in Paris from 1896–1906. Pierre Ginisty, an author like his father, was killed on Christmas Eve 1914 and his name is commemorated in the Pantheon in Paris. Just over 400m further east on the N332 is **Aeroplane Cemetery** where you will find the graves of three of the five 3/Worcersters who were shot at dawn on 26 July 1915 for deserting their posts. **Privates Bert Hartells**, **John Robinson** and **Alfred Thompson** lie together in Plot II, Row A, Graves 6, 7 and 8.

Continue towards Ieper and into Potijze. The group of cemeteries on your right were once the site of **Potijze Chateau** – known as the White Chateau – which was destroyed by shellfire and used as an advanced dressing station by the British. On 13 May 1915 the dismounted cavalrymen of 10/Hussars received orders to recapture a trench line on the Frezenberg Ridge from their trenches east of the chateau. Together with the Essex Yeomanry the two regiments charged up the slope and expelled the Germans from the trench. Of the four officers who remained standing, **Lieutenant William Murland**, related to one of the authors, was one. He survived the war with the rank of captain and was decorated with the Military Cross in 1918.

At the roundabout turn left along the N345. After 150m you will come to **Hussar Farm** on the left, where there is one of the best remaining examples of an observation post which you should still be able to see from the road. In another 600m you will come to a farm on the right – **Cork Cots Farm** – here partially hidden behind a hedge is a British bunker now apparently used as a summerhouse! Continue to the large roundabout ahead. This junction was known as **Hell Fire Corner** during the war as it was a constant target for German artillery. At the roundabout take the first right on to the N8 towards Ieper but not too quickly as just after the turn you will see an example of the many demarcation stones that record the furthest advance of the Germans in 1918. Reflect here on how close the Germans came to taking the town. Driving on you will pass **Menin Road South Cemetery** on the left before you reach a traffic-signal-controlled junction. Turn left towards the **Menin Gate**, details of which you will find in **Route 17**. Return to the Grote Markt after passing beneath the Menin Gate.

Route 19

Messines Ridge – Wijtschate

Suitable for 🚲 🚶

Circular route starting at: Sint-Medard Church in Wijtschate.

Coordinates: 50°47 55.09 N – 2°52 55.09 E.

Distance: 5.9km/3.7 miles.

Grade: Moderate with two hills.

Toilets: Maedelstede Farm.

Maps: NGI 1:20 000 Heuvelland–Mesen (Messines) 28/5–6.

Link this with: Route 20 – Messines Ridge – Craters and Mines.

General description and context: Formerly Wytschaete, the modern town of Wijtschate was known to the British Tommy as 'Whitesheet', a name that appears to have been adopted by many British battlefield visitors today. Wijtschate sits on the ridge of high ground that was the focus of the **Battle of Messines** which began on 7 June 1917 as precursor to the **Third Battle of Ypres**. The objective was to remove the Germans from their strong positions on the ridge which they had held since the fighting of late 1914. The German front-line system traced the arc of a salient – not unlike the westward-looking face of a woman when seen on trench maps – including several key strongpoints, many reinforced with concrete pill boxes, specifically sited to enfilade no-man's-land and all heavily wired. The second position, known as the **Oosttaverne Line**, ran like a chord across the neck of the German salient on the rear slopes of the ridge and was the final objective of General Plumer's Messines operation. As part of the planning for the operation it was decided to adopt a hitherto unique approach to the problem of eliminating key points of resistance. The blowing of mines beneath tactically significant points had been practised by both sides for several years but for the Messines battle it

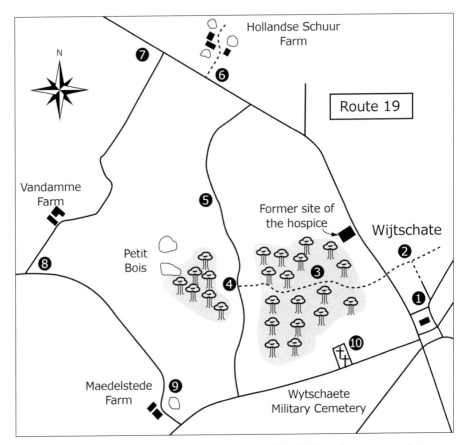

was decided that twenty-four mines would be laid under strongpoints at intervals around the arc of the German salient. On 6 June Major General Sir Charles 'Tim' Harrington, General Plumer's Second Army Chief of Staff, made his famous remark at a press briefing, 'Gentlemen, I do not know whether we shall change history tomorrow, but we shall certainly alter the geography'. In the event nineteen mines at eleven sites, which together were loaded with over 933,000lb of explosives, were actually fired at 3.10am the following day. The violent changes made to the geography of the ridge is today evident in the many large, water-filled craters that still punctuate the landscape on this route and mark out the German salient. This is the first of three routes which focuses on the Messines Ridge and begins in the centre of Wijtschate covering the ground over which the 16th (Irish) Division advanced on

7 June 1917. We visit the mine craters at Hollandse Schuur and Maedelstede Farms and from the high ground northwest of Wijtschate Woods get good views of the Petit Bois craters. The route also visits Wytschaete Military Cemetery and the 16th (Irish) Division Memorial. The route would appear to be only suitable for walkers as the path through Wytschaete Woods has a barrier at each end, however, at the time of writing, there is currently no indication that cycles are not allowed through the woods.

The 16th Irish Division Memorial, Wijtschate.

Directions to start: From Ieper take the N336 to Sint-Elooi where you join the N365 to Wijtschate and Mesen. On entering the town take the first right – Hospicestraat – and continue past the communal cemetery to the town square. Park in the square opposite the church.

Route description: With the rear of the church ❶ on your left head up Kapellerie past the Sint-Medard Health Centre. Keep a sharp lookout for a narrow pathway on the left – Bassevilleweg – which eventually becomes a grass track as it leaves the built-up area. Continue to the T-junction of tracks ❷ where you will find an information board relating to the St Joseph Catholic Orphanage which stood on the site of the modern-day sports centre you can see ahead of you. **The Hospice**, as it was known then, gave the attacking divisions some difficulties before it was finally overcome. From this point you can see the spires of Ieper and the wind farm over the top of the woods ahead. There is a well-known painting of the Hospice by war artist **Paul Nash** entitled *Sunrise, Ruins of a Hospice, Northwest of Wytschaete* which is now held in a private collection.

Cross the main road and go straight across to the track ahead which goes into the woods. Continue along the obvious woodland path and at the point of a bend to your left ❸ look to your right. You should be able to see the remains of a German bunker now being put to use as a bat shelter. You are now walking exactly along the line of **Nancy Communication Trench**. Continue to the junction of tracks, turn right and bear left. Just before the track reaches a wooden barrier a pathway leads off to the right to the remains of a German shaft system. This was operated by German tunnellers attempting to detect their British counterparts by digging galleries designed to intercept and destroy British tunnelling activity with the use of camouflet charges. Retrace your steps to the track and continue to reach the minor road ❹ ahead. Stop here. Straight ahead of you is **Petit Bois Wood** and to the right of the wood, hidden from view, are the two **Petit Bois Craters**, marked as water-filled ponds on the map. Behind you, between the edge of the wood and the road, ran a German trench known as **Nancy Support Trench**, in front of you on the southwestern edge of Petit Bois Wood ran **Nancy Trench** which was part of the German first-line trench system. On the night of 4/5 June 1917 these 2 trenches were raided by a party of 11 officers and 280 men from 6/Connaught Rangers. The attack was in two waves, the first taking Nancy Support Trench and the second overpowering the German garrison in Nancy Switch. There were seven prisoners taken and an estimated sixty of the enemy killed with forty-four of the Connaught Rangers being killed, wounded or missing. Amongst the dead was 19-year-old **Second Lieutenant Dermot MacSherry** from Birmingham and **Second Lieutenant William Hamilton** from Banbridge, Co. Down. Both are buried at La Laiterie Military Cemetery which is described in Route 22. The majority of the casualties would probably have been from the first wave which attacked across the ground in front of you as this is where the defending German garrison put up the greatest resistance.

Turn right and continue up the road to the top of the rise ❺ where you will find an information panel. You are now standing on the German first-line trench system looking across the valley to the line of farms that included Vandenberghe Farm on the right and Vandamme Farm further round to the left. All of these were just behind the British lines. In the distance you can see Kemmelberg on the left and further round to the right is the Vierstraat crossroads where Route 22 begins. In the foreground are the two Petit Bois craters, the first is visible and marked by the two deciduous trees and the second marked by the line of poplars. Both are on private ground. 250 Tunnelling Company began work on the Petit Bois mines in late 1915 with the entrance at Vandamme Farm. Here there was a single gallery some 488m long which forked at that point and led to two chambers each of which would eventually be packed with 30,000lb of explosive. The Germans heard the British at work and on 10 June 1916 blew a camouflet mine causing extensive damage to the British gallery and trapping twelve tunnellers. **Sapper William 'Geordie' Bedson** had watched his comrades succumb one by one until after almost seven days of effort and a frantic recovery operation in which a new tunnel was dug only Bedson was found and brought to the surface with the immortal words, 'Its been a long shift. For God's sake give me a drink.' This mine was also the scene of an unsuccessful attempt to use an underground tunnelling machine which was finally abandoned after it proved too difficult to maintain. It is still in place some 25m below the surface.

From your position you can appreciate the view the Germans must have had from their lines over those of the British. It was across the ground in front of you on the morning of 7 June 1917 that the Leinsters

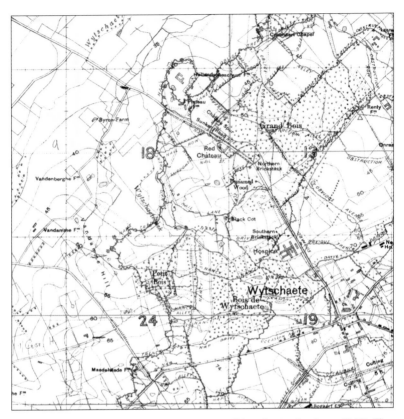

The opposing front-line systems opposite Wytschaete in June 1917. The German trenches are marked in red and the British line in blue. The extent and depth of the German line here, and all along the Messines Ridge, was extensive and previous frontal assaults had been costly failures in terms of casualties. The three mines at Petit Bois, Maedelstede and Hollandse Schuur Farms effectively destroyed the German line at those points and left the defenders weakened and disorientated. It was a relatively straightforward task for the attacking troops to overcome the German first-line trenches. Compare this trench map with the sketch plan of Route 19 and you will see that very little has changed in the intervening years.

and Royal Irish Fusiliers attacked after the two mines at Petit Bois had been exploded at 3.10am. The leading companies of the battalions reached the point where you are standing some twenty minutes later. The 16th (Irish) Division was in the centre of the IX Corps attack with the 19th Division on the left and the 36th (Ulster) division on the right, attacking south of Wytschaete. The significance of these two Irish divisions – drawn from opposite ends of the political divide in the argument over Irish Home Rule – attacking a common enemy together was seen by **Major William Redmond**, the Irish Nationalist MP then serving as a major with the division, as the beginnings of a peace process that could be built upon. Redmond dreamed of building a new united Ireland that would be at peace with itself and its neighbours. On 7 June the two infantry divisions that had been raised in Ireland fought side by side and for a while the old disagreements were forgotten.

Continue to the T-junction with Vierstraat and turn left. After 300m you will come to the farm road on the right leading to ❻ **Hollandse Schuur Farm**. There are three mine craters here, all dug by 250 Tunnelling Company which placed a combined charge of 67,600lb in the three chambers. The largest is almost visible from the road on the left of the farm track up towards the farm building; the other two are behind the farm. This is private property and permission to view the craters must be sought from the landowner.

The Hollandse Schuur Farm craters.

Take the next road ❼ on the left – Mandestraat – looking across to the left is the tree-lined N331 running down to Kemmel. Looking back you can appreciate the observation the Germans at Hollandse Schuur Farm would have had over the British lines. This road runs along the old British lines, ignoring the first private house on the right, the first farm on the right is on the site of Byron Farm and where the road bends sharply to the left is Vandenberghe Farm and 300m further on is the site of **Vandamme Farm**. Here the 19th Division had its HQ and close by, at Lunette dugouts, was the battalion HQ of 7/Leinsters. Shortly after zero hour on 7 June 1917 a German shell landed at the entrance to the battalion HQ killing and wounding the commanding officer and a number of others who were observing the attack. **Lieutenant Colonel Thomas Stannus** DSO, died of his wounds at Etaples ten days later. He was the father of Dame Ninette de Valois. Born Edris Stannus in 1898, she established the Birmingham Royal Ballet and Royal Ballet School. She is widely regarded as the Godmother of English ballet and one of the most influential figures in the entire history of that art form.

Continue to the T-junction with Oosthoekstraat and turn left ❽. This is Vandamme Hill which rises gently to **Maedelstede Farm**. The single crater here ❾, found on the left of the bend by the farm, is the result of the second largest charge – 94,000lb – fired on the day of the attack. Permission from the farm is required to visit the site. The farm has a very welcome cafe and restaurant where there are also some interesting photographs and artefacts. It was close to this farm that Major William Redmond was injured whilst advancing with 6/Royal Irish Rifles. He was taken off the battlefield by stretcher bearers from 36th Division but later died of his wounds at Loker Hospice. See Route 24 for further details. Continue to the T-junction and turn right to find the two obelisks sited on either side of the road commemorating the 16th and 36th Divisions. In a touch of symmetry if you stand behind the 16th Division obelisk there is a direct line of sight with that of the 36th Division on the opposite side of the road and the tower of the **Island of Ireland Peace Park** – described in Route 2 – on the skyline beyond.

Retrace your steps to the road junction and continue to **Wytschaete Military Cemetery** ❿ and the 16th (Irish) Division Memorial. The cemetery was begun after the Armistice when graves were brought in from isolated positions surrounding Wijtschate and there are now 1,002 individuals buried or commemorated in the cemetery. Of these 673 of the burials are unidentified, but there are special memorials to 16 casualties known or believed to be buried amongst them. Here you will find numerous casualties of the opening day of the Battle of Messines, one of whom was **Sergeant Michael Dixon** (I.A.9), serving with 6/Connaught Rangers. Michael was a native of Longwood, Co. Meath. Previously buried at Beaver Farm is 38-year-old **Sapper Cornelius Airley** (III.D.20) who was a stonemason and builder before he was killed on 3 May 1915 serving with 56/Field Company. **Private Evelyn Wood** (IA.B.8) was killed on 3 September 1918 with 12/East Surrey Regiment. He was born in Raunds in Northamptonshire and left a widow and four children. His brother **Ernest Wood** was a regular soldier killed with the Northamptonshires on 24 October 1914 and is commemorated on the Menin Gate. On 7 July 1917, 20-year-old **Second Lieutenant John Gleed** (IV.C.33) was shot down with his pilot, **Lieutenant John Beveridge**, near Houthem. Both were flying a Sopwith 1½ Strutter from 45 Squadron RFC. The inscription on his headstone reads: 'Underneath is peace in thine everlasting arms'. Beveridge is commemorated on the Arras Flying Service Memorial. With some forty days left until the Armistice was declared **Private William McGinty** (III.D.10) was killed on 28 September 1918. An Irishman serving in 1/5 Argyll and Sutherland Highlanders, the inscription on his headstone is understandably a little more wistful: 'Tis only those who have loved and lost can understand the bitter cost'. A victim of the fighting around the Mound at Sint-Elooi in 1915 was **Lieutenant Alfred Batson** (VI.E.3). His date of death is given as 12 March 1915 but the regimental history of the DCLI records his death, along with six officers and seventy other ranks of the 2nd Battalion, as 14 March. The Mound was an artificial earth bank which overlooked the British lines and was the scene of continuous mine warfare.

Sapper Cornelius Airley.

After leaving the cemetery follow the road back to the square and your vehicle.

Route 20

Messines Ridge – Craters and Mines

Suitable for 🚲 🚶

Circular route starting at: Sint-Niklaas Church, Messines (Mesen).

Coordinates: 50°45 50.46 N – 2°53 55.96 E.

Distance: 9.9km/6.2 miles.

Grade: Moderate with some hills.

Maps: NGI 1:20 000 Heuvelland–Mesen (Messines) 28/5–6.

Link this with: Route 21 – Messines Ridge – the Peace Park.

General description and context: This is the second of the Messines routes and takes in the sites south of Wijtschate associated with the Battle of Messines which began on 7 June 1917. We visit Messines Ridge, Lone Tree and Spanbroekmolen British Cemeteries and the mine craters at Kruisstraat, Spanbroekmolen and Peckham. Of the twenty-four mines laid on the Messines Ridge, a mine beneath Petit Douve Farm was abandoned in August 1916 in the face of German counter-mining, and four of the southernmost ones at a German position known as 'The Birdcage' were not used on the opening day of the battle. One of these was triggered on 17 July 1955 probably when lightning struck a nearby pylon, leaving three more – each of 30,000lb of explosive – lying menacingly dormant beneath farmland east of Ploegsteert Wood – for the moment at least!

Directions to start: Take the N336 to Sint-Elooi and then the N365 to Mesen. At Mesen go straight across the first crossroads to take the second road on the left – Kerkstraat – where the main road bends sharp right. Park outside the church.

Route description: With your back to the church entrance ❶ head towards the road junction ahead and turn right onto the main N365. Continue to the crossroads and turn left onto N314, signposted Nieuwkerke and Wulvergem, you will also see a green CWGC sign for **Messines Ridge British Cemetery**. Continue past the buildings of the Peace Village on your left at which point the Cross of Sacrifice of the cemetery will come into view ahead. The cemetery ❷ stands on ground that belonged to the Institution Royale,

The church at Mesen.

the Cross of Sacrifice standing on the site of a former windmill – the Moulin de l'Hospice. Within the cemetery is the **New Zealand Memorial** commemorating over 800 New Zealanders who died around Messines in 1917 and 1918 and who have no known grave. The

The New Zealand Memorial at Messines British Cemetery.

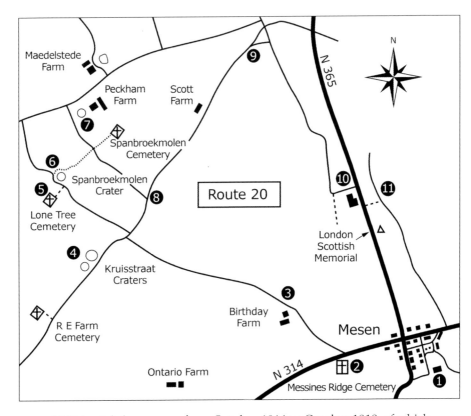

1,531 burials here range from October 1914 to October 1918, of which 954 are unidentified. **Lieutenant Jonathan Becker** (SM. B.2) was killed on 12 March 1915 during an unsuccessful attack on Spanbroekmolen when British artillery shells fell short on his battalion's position near Lindenhoek. His body is believed to lie in the cemetery along with two other officers of the same battalion killed on the same day whose special memorials flank his: **Second Lieutenant Leonard Crabb** (B.1), who was only 18 years old when he was killed, and **Second Lieutenant John Kirtland** (B.3). Former coal miner 21-year-old **Private Arthur Percy Cooper** (I.A.52) was born in Scholes, West Yorkshire. Married to Hilda, he was father to five children before he enlisted in 13/York and Lancaster Regiment – the 1st Barnsley Pals. He was killed on 1 October 1918. **Company Sergeant Major Arthur Collie** (IV.E.19) was 23 years old when he was killed with 4 Company, 2/ Otago Regiment on 7 June 1917, the opening day of the Battle of

Messines. A keen cricketer, he survived the Gallipoli Campaign arriving with the New Zealand Brigade on the Western Front in 1916. Just before his death he had been recommended for a commission.

On leaving the cemetery take the road almost immediately opposite – Kruisstraat – which descends into the valley of the Steenbeek below. This was **Birthday Road** which ran parallel with the German front-line trench system of early June 1917. The German support trench – Oyster Support – ran just to the left of the road and the front-line Oyster Trench was out in the fields to your left. At Birthday Farm ❸, which you can see 300m ahead on the left,

Company Sergeant Major Arthur Collie.

the front line swung almost 90 degrees to the west and towards **Ontario Farm** across to your left. This was one of the key strongpoints chosen to be undermined and obliterated in the pre-assault plan for the Messines operation. Begun by 171 Tunnelling Company at Boyle's Farm, just south of the N314, the mine ran into considerable difficulties with flooding. A new gallery was started and with a day to spare the chamber was packed with 60,000lb of ammonal explosive 32m below the surface. There was no crater when this mine went up and when units of the 25th Division captured the position all they found was a large circular patch of ground bubbling like hot porridge.

As the road begins to rise you pass a farm on your left to reach a crossroads, go straight across here and at the next staggered crossroads ahead – marked as Kruisstraathoek on modern maps but known as Kruisstraat Cabaret during the war – turn left on to Wulvergemstraat. Continue past farm buildings on your left and in the fields on your right you will notice raised and uneven ground which marks the lip of the first of two mine craters known as the **Kruisstraat Craters** ❹. 200m past the buildings of a second farm you will see a track off to the right which gives access to the craters. The craters are now on private property but a few paces along the track will provide a clear view of both water-filled features. There was already an elliptically shaped pond on the site but on 7 June 1917 a three-mine cluster was sprung here using a 2,160ft-long gallery under a protruding section of the German line called **Nathan Trench**. One of the craters – sited on the same side of the road further back towards the crossroads – was actually under the third German trench but has been infilled leaving just two circular ponds to replace the original. When units of the 36th Ulster Division arrived minutes after the three mines exploded they found little, if any, resistance to prevent their advance.

One can appreciate the value of positions like this to the Germans for on a clear day from here – with your back to the craters – Lille can be seen in the distance to the southeast, beyond the grey needle-like tower of the Irish Peace Park and the distinctive dome of the church at Mesen in the middle distance. Look also for the traffic moving on the N365 marking out the crest line of the ridge. Now turn and look in the opposite direction across the craters to the farm on the slope beyond. To the left of the farm buildings one can just pick out the Cross of Sacrifice of Lone Tree Cemetery and beyond the farm the trees that surround the Spanbroekmolen crater. That point marks the very apex of the German salient on the Messines Ridge.

Retrace your route to the Kruisstraat crossroads and turn left. The road climbs gently and passes large farm buildings on your left. The distinct clump of trees ahead and slightly to the right are those that surround the Spanbroekmolen mine crater which you saw earlier. Continue round a left-hand bend. The track off to the left across the fields leads to the irregularly shaped **Lone Tree Cemetery ❺** situated almost on the Allied front line. Nearly all the eighty-eight graves in the cemetery are men from the three infantry brigades of the 36th Division who were killed on the first day of the Messines battle. Aged 31, **Captain Henry Gallaugher** DSO (I.D.2) of 11/Royal Inniskilling Fusiliers was wounded in the right arm after leaving the British line but continued to lead the men of B Company until he was relieved and taken back to an aid post. He was killed by a shell whilst waiting for treatment. His DSO was won on 1 July 1916 when he went over the top with his battalion on the Somme. The inscription on his headstone reads: 'Greater love hath no man than this'. **Rifleman Henry Scott** (II.A.2), serving with 11/Royal Irish Rifles, hailed from Magheragil in Co. Antrim. He died on 8 June, probably from wounds received the previous day. His headstone simply states: 'Ever remembered by his

Uncle David'. **Rifleman Frank Boulding** (II.B.8), from Kingsnorth in Kent, was killed aged 27 on 7 June and was mourned by his parents, Edward and Harriet, and younger sister, Edith. He was two years younger than **Second Lieutenant William Ferris** (II.A.4) who served during the German South West African campaign as a private in 2/Transvaal Scottish. After returning home he was commissioned on 4 August 1916 into 12/Royal Irish Rifles.

Leave the cemetery and turn left, almost directly ahead is the **Spanbroekmolen crater ❻** encircled by trees. Continue along the road to find the main entrance on the right where there is an information panel and access to the water-filled crater. This was the highest point on the German front line – occasionally referred to as Hill 76 – where before the war stood a working windmill. The British lines here ran parallel with the road about 125m to the west and were completely overlooked. Around the ruins of the mill the Germans created a strongly fortified salient, a feature that 171 Tunnelling Company began mining towards in December 1915. German counter-measures were particularly

Pool of Peace – the Spanbroekmolen crater.

effective and troublesome here but failed to prevent the 91,000lb of explosive from detonating on 7 June forming a crater 130m across. After the war the site was bought on behalf of Toc H in Poperinge to ensure its preservation. It is now known as the 'Pool of Peace'. From the crater there is a fine view towards Wijtschate on the left and Mesen, with its distinctive church tower, to the right. On a peaceful summer's afternoon it is hard to imagine the violence and the fury of the 'pillar of fire' which erupted on this spot just before dawn on 7 June 1917.

After visiting the pool cyclists will have to take a short detour to rejoin the tour on Scheerstraat, opposite the path leading to Spanbroekmolen British Cemetery. To do so continue past the crater for 500m and turn right at the T-junction. Continue along the main road for 350m and turn right down Scheerstraat where you will see the water-filled **Peckham Farm** crater ❼ on the left.

Walkers can continue along the path that skirts the northern rim of the crater – note the battered remains of the German pillbox low down on your right – to go through a wooden gate and bear left to follow the footpath across the field. Head towards the white Cross of Sacrifice of **Spanbroekmolen Military Cemetery ❽**. The pointed spire of Wijtschate church is visible almost directly above the cross. Cross the road and take the grass track down to the cemetery. You are now walking roughly along the line of a German communication trench called Naples Row which linked the German support line to the front line at Spanbroekmolen. The cemetery takes its name from the Spanbroekmolen windmill and contains the graves of fifty-eight men killed in action on the first and second days of the Battle of Messines. Special memorials commemorate six men who were known to have been buried in the cemetery but whose graves were later destroyed. Very much a small piece of Ulster in a 'foreign field', there are casualties here from all three infantry brigades of the 36th Division, many of whom would have been killed nearby. One casualty of 7 June was **Rifleman William Kennedy** (C.1) who was born in Lanark but enlisted in Belfast into 14/Royal Irish Rifles. Before his death in action he had been awarded a divisional certificate for gallantry in the field. Tragically his brother, **Second Lieutenant James Kennedy** serving with 1/Royal Irish Rifles, was killed on 21 March 1918

Rifleman William Kennedy.

on the opening day of the German 'Michael' offensive and is buried at Grand-Seraucourt British Cemetery near St Quentin. **Second Lieutenant Sydney Downey** (A.10) was another Belfast man and was 21 years old when he was killed on 7 June. A former employee of the Northern Assurance Company, he was commissioned in January 1916. Before you go spare a moment for 22-year-old **Rifleman Hugh Rock** (A.9) of 11/Royal Irish Rifles who was the postman at Cloughmills in Co. Antrim, a job that was taken on by his sister after he enlisted. Employed as a battalion runner, he was killed on 8 June delivering battalion orders.

After leaving the cemetery retrace your steps to Scheerstraat. Walkers who wish to view the Peckham crater will need to turn right and continue for 300m until the crater comes into view in the field to your right. This is the crater made by the mine which was detonated beneath the German strongpoint at **Peckham Farm ❼**. The German line ran along the road on which you are now standing and turned east at the T-junction to follow the line of the road up to Maedelstede Farm (see Route 19). Mining towards the Peckham strongpoint was started in December 1915 by 250 Tunnelling Company. Two mines were dug here; the crater visible today is the only mine that was blown on 7 June, the second gallery was eventually abandoned in the face of severe flooding.

Turn and retrace your route passing the track to Spanbroekmolen Cemetery on your left. At the next junction ❽ turn left onto Wulvergemstraat. Up ahead is the pointed spire of Wijtschate church and a distinctive red and white transmitter mast. As the road begins to rise you will see **Scott Farm** on the left of the road; don't miss the German bunker in the field on the right. The bunker marks the position of a roughly rectangular field redoubt or strongpoint, straddling the road here, in what the British called a cutting. There were four more of these mini-field forts – constructed for all-round defence to protect the approaches to Wijtschate from the southwest – situated between the second and third German support lines. The information panel here identifies this as '**Skip Point**', although it is clearly marked on 1917 trench maps as 'Hop Point'; 'Skip Point' being on the crest of the rise further along the road on the right. Others were named 'Bone Point', east of the Kruisstraat crossroads, 'Rag Point', in the fields to your left, and 'Ocean Point'.

It was across this ground on the morning of 7 June that 14/Royal Irish Rifles attacked from their assembly trenches opposite

Spanbroekmolen. Opposition was light to begin with but soon stiffened as the Belfast men closed on the Wijtschate–Wulvergem road where you are standing. Fierce fighting developed around the heavily fortified 'Jump' and 'Skip Point' redoubts and it was here that the majority of the battalion's casualties occurred. One casualty was 19-year-old **Second Lieutenant Brian Boyd** who was leading his men in an attack on one of these positions. Boyd was evacuated to No. 2 Casualty Clearing Station but died of his wounds. It was also in this area that **Second Lieutenant Sydney Downey** was killed in command of a 14th Battalion mopping-up platoon near Scott Farm, you will have already visited his grave at Spanbroekmolen. The 14/Battalion lost 44 men killed on 7 June but by nightfall the 36th Division had advanced over 2 miles at a cost of 61 Officers and over 1,000 men killed or wounded.

In April 1918 it was a different story. The German offensive here pushed the Allied forces back at an alarming rate and on the ridge in front of you a desperate stand by the officers and men of 1/Lincolnshire Regiment took place. The battalion held the line from Bogaert Farm on the right to Stanyzer Cabaret crossroads on the left which was extended on the night of 15/16 April to Scott Farm. On 16 April a terrific German bombardment began at 4.30am which enabled the German infantry of IR 162 to break the line at Peckham Farm and the crossroads at Stanyzer, aided by the dense morning mist. With both flanks of the line under attack the battalion stood firm and fought defiantly for the next two hours breaking up the full force of the enemy assault. Finally a handful of men withdrew slowly through Wijtschate Woods at 7.00am to establish a defensive line between Vandamme Farm and Lagache Farm (see Route 19). On 17 April only eight officers and eighty-two men answered their names at roll call. One of the missing was **Private George Cross**, father-in-law of the sister of one of the authors. Cross had enlisted in the Royal Marine Light Infantry in March 1916 aged just 17 but had been discharged as 'underage'. Called up 'deemed to have enlisted' in June 1917, he joined 1/Lincs in a draft of sixty-five men on 17 February 1918 two months before his capture on 16 April. He was eventually repatriated on 11 January 1919 after nine months in captivity.

Continue towards Wijtschate and bear right at the first fork in the road ❾ on to Guido Gezellestraat then turn right at the next T-junction onto Schoolstraat, and head for the red and white transmitter mast which you will pass on your left. Mesen church can be seen up ahead and again good views as far away as Lille can be had on a clear day. You are now heading due south away from Wijtschate almost exactly along the line of a German trench called **Ochre Avenue**. This was part of the defensive system that protected the crest of the Messines–Wytschaete Ridge and on either side of you would have been extensive barbed-wire entanglements!

Bear right at the Y-junction ahead and continue to reach a T-junction. Turn left staying on Schoolstraat. Follow the road which, after 500m, takes a 90 degree bend to the left towards the junction ❿ with the N365 ahead. Turn right along the main road and after 180m turn left onto a farm track opposite farm buildings. At the end of the track ⓫ turn right to join a metalled road. You are now looking east, down the reverse slope of the Messines Ridge towards the main German second-line position of June 1917 which was known as the **Oosttaverne Line**, described in Route 19. After 100m stop and look across the fields to the road to your right. You will see a small clump of conifers framing the cross of the memorial to the **London Scottish** which counter-attacked during the First Battle of Ypres from right to left across the fields in front of where you are standing. The desperate situation on the Messines Ridge and the chronic shortage of troops on the ground was the deciding factor in bringing the 14th Battalion (London Scottish) County of London Regiment into action on 31 October 1914 during the closing stages of the fight to hold the ridge. With some 50 per cent of the battalion's rifles ineffective owing to faulty magazines, the territorials were eventually outflanked and forced to retire back across the Steenbeek valley towards Wulvergem.

Continue towards Messines and at the T-junction at the end of the lane turn right on to Komenstraat, taking the second left on to the one-way street (Kieketelstraat) with the church and the Stadhuis – clearly signposted – ahead at the far end. At the crossroads where the streets open out, go straight across, keeping the band stand to your left and an open, green space to your right which on 7 June 1917, was filled with machine-gun bullets. Note the Ross Bastiaan bas relief, which is easy to miss as it is at fairly low, on the green on the right. This tells the story of the Australian role in the battle of 1917. The church ❶ is ahead of you on the left.

Route 21

Messines Ridge –
The Peace Park

Suitable for 🚶
Circular route starting at: Sint-Niklaas Church, Mesen.
Coordinates: 50°45 50.46 N – 2°53 55.96 E.
Distance: 2.7km/1.7 miles.
Grade: Easy.
Maps: NGI 1:20 000 Heuvelland–Mesen (Messines) 28/5–6.

General description and context: This is the final route on the
Messines Ridge which visits the church at Mesen, the Island of Ireland
Peace Park, the New Zealand Memorial Park and Messines Ridge
British Cemetery and covers the ground taken by 3/New Zealand Rifles
in their advance on 7 June 1917. If you wish to include a visit to the
Sint-Niklaas church tower and crypt you will need to arrange that visit
beforehand by contacting the Stadhuis well in advance either by phone
or email: +32 (0)57 44 50 41 or info@mesen.be. Mesen is the smallest
city in Belgium with a population below 1,000.

Directions to start: Take the N336 to Sint-Elooi and then the N365 to
Mesen. At Mesen go straight across the first crossroads to take the
second road on the left – Kerkstraat. Park outside the church.

Route description: We suggest you begin with a visit to the church as
the views across to the Island of Ireland Peace Park from the bell tower
are superb. The church was completely destroyed during the war but
the crypt survived and was used by the Germans as a field hospital. A
brave German company runner corporal by the name of **Adolf Hitler**
was familiar with the church – he painted it – and perhaps its crypt and
may even have been treated here after being wounded in the arm

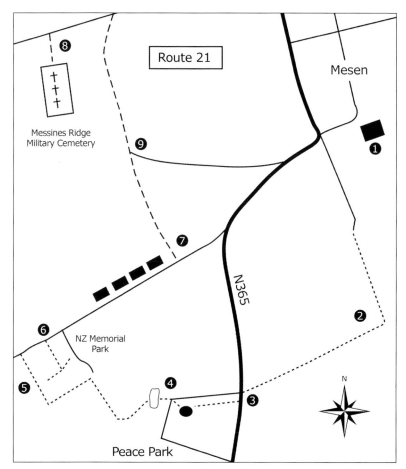

whilst serving with the 16th Bavarian Reserve Infantry Regiment. Buried in the crypt is the Countess Adela, the wife of Baldwin V of Flanders, their union would produce Mathilde who became the wife of William the Conqueror. The church tower boasts some sixty-one bells, each one inscribed with the name of a benefactor, but make sure you are not climbing the ladder to the top just as the bells begin to ring! Outside the church to the left of the entrance is a memorial to **Lance Corporal Samuel Frickleton** of 3/New Zealand Rifles who won the Victoria Cross on 7 June 1917 for rushing and

Lance Corporal Samuel Frickleton VC.

Inside the bell tower of Mesen church.

The Island of Ireland Peace Park.

destroying two German machine guns as his unit entered Messines. Born in Scotland in 1891, Frickleton had been a coalminer before joining the New Zealand Expeditionary Force with his four brothers in 1914. He was wounded just prior to his VC exploit and again afterwards, this time more severely. He stayed in the Army after the war and retired in 1927 as a captain. He died in 1971.

With the church entrance behind you ❶ walk down to the crossroads ahead and turn left down Daalstraat. Continue straight on and take the grass pathway which will lead you into open fields, at this point you will see the tall structure of the Irish Peace Tower across to the right. Walk on and stop at the end of the path ❷ by the picnic benches. On a clear day the views from here are terrific. Looking from left to right, in the far distance is Lille, and slightly further round is the squat church tower of Warneton. A little further across to the right you should be able to pick out the two spires at Armentières. Ahead in the near distance is Ploegsteert Wood. Before you continue turn round for a good view of Mesen church. Follow the path to reach the main road and cross with care to the gates of the **Island of Ireland Peace Park** ❸.

Bunker in the New Zealand Memorial Park.

The idea of the tower was conceived by the Irish Nationalist MP Paddy Harte and the Unionist MP Glen Barr, who, in 1996, visited the area in which the men of the 16th Irish and the 36th Ulster Divisions fought side by side during the Battle of Messines. Although the site of the memorial is not on the actual ground where the two Irish divisions fought in June 1917, it was built as a symbol of reconciliation and commemorates Irish soldiers of all political and religious beliefs who died, were wounded or went missing in the Great War. The 34m high tower is a replica of the structures built in Ireland in the eighth century as a defence against sea-borne invaders. The design of this tower is unique in that it allows the sun to light the interior only on the 11th hour of the 11th day of the 11th month. The building of the tower was marked by differences over who would contribute to construction costs, which were eventually met by the British and Irish governments and other sponsors and today it is tended by the CWGC. However, despite the initial difficulties, the Peace Park was officially opened on 11 November 1998 by the then President of Ireland, Mary McAleese, in the presence of HM Queen Elizabeth II and King Albert II of Belgium. Each year a commemorative Remembrance Day service is held at the Tower at 11.00am on 11 November.

Inside the tower are three brass doors which open to reveal the memorial records of the Irish dead of the Great War. The symbols on the doors denote the 11th Hour. At the entrance to the park is the 'peace pledge' on a bronze tablet and alongside the pathway leading to the tower are nine stone tablets inscribed with prose, poems and letters written by Irish soldiers. A little further on are three memorial stones, one each for the three Irish infantry divisions that fought in the Great War. The landscaped area surrounding the tower also contains an upright tablet listing the Irish counties which are merged together forming one long continuous line of text, suggesting unity in death, and another giving an overview of the Battle of Messines.

Before you leave take a moment to look south towards Ploegsteert, the farm you can see in the Douve valley to the right of the road is **La Petit Douve Farm** (La Basse-Cour Farm) where German counter-mining discovered the work of 171 Tunnelling Company which resulted in the mine being abandoned. The 35 tons of explosive are still in place. Further on, beyond the village of Le Rossignol, the sharp eyed will just be able to make out the raised bump of **Hill 63**, which we visit in Route

25, under which Australian tunnellers constructed a vast series of catacombs.

From the park descend on a grass pathway ❹ through four wooden gates to a decked walkway. Across to the left are the remains of a post-Messines British infantry shelter. At the end of the walkway climb the steps and continue to find a grass track on the left just before a long wooden building. This path will take you behind the **New Zealand Memorial** Park past the two bunkers to an information panel ❺ overlooking the Messines Ridge. It was up this steep rise that the New Zealand troops advanced from their assembly trenches in the valley below you. On reaching the road turn right to the entrance ❻ of the Memorial Park. Picture if you will a dark and misty morning just before 3.10am on 7 June 1917 with the first streaks of dawn appearing and as the British barrage fell silent for a few moments nightingales were heard singing behind the British lines. The New Zealand attack began after the detonation of the huge mine under the German positions at **Ontario Farm**, which, when combined with the mines to left and right, caused the ground to shake and rock. The nineteen explosions killed thousands of German defenders and disorientated those who survived. Seconds after the mines went up the air was torn by the roar of artillery and machine-gun barrages and the dark hillside under Messines was illuminated by the white SOS rockets and flares from the German positions on the ridge. The New Zealand Division was responsible for taking Messines and pushing through to the 'Black Line' behind it. On the southern edge of the New Zealand attack where you are now standing, 3/New Zealand Rifles was detailed to take La Petite Douve Farm where the battalion met some resistance from isolated groups in the ruins before pushing on up the Douve valley, on their left 1/New Zealand Rifles quickly gained the ridge and dealt with the line of strongholds, including those in the New Zealand Memorial Park. By 5.00am that morning Messines had been taken but not without cost – the division suffered 3,660 casualties in the attack, with 700 killed. The memorial park lies parallel with the German outer-ring defences which were garrisoned at this point by the 18th Bavarian Infantry Regiment and whilst you are here reflect for a moment on the young lives that had come 'from the uttermost ends of the earth' and were lost in the fighting here. To quote a phrase used by Alexander Turner, 'Those Kiwis had come a long way to die for Britain'.

From the park turn right up the hill passing a row of private houses at the end of which you will find a pathway on the left ❼ leading to **Messines Ridge British Cemetery**, which is a little over 500m away. Here you will find the **Messines Ridge New Zealand Memorial** ❽ commemorating over 800 Kiwis who died in or near Messines in 1917 and 1918 and have no known grave. For details about the cemetery see Route 20. After leaving the cemetery retrace your route across the fields to find Wulvergemstraat ❾ on the left. This residential road will take you back to your vehicle outside the church.

Route 22

Kemmel Area Car Tour

Suitable for 🚕
Circular route starting at: the Goudezeune Prefab Factory on N331.
Coordinates: 50°48 03.74 N – 2°51 06.58 E.
Distance: 22.4km/13.7 miles.
Maps: NGI 1:50 000 Ieper 27–28–36 and 1:20 000
   Heuvelland–Mesen (Messines) 28/5–6.

General description and context: This tour is designed for those who wish to visit the area by car but it can be undertaken by cyclists who enjoy a longer outing as it generally avoids the busier main roads. Cyclists may find it more practical to leave their vehicle by the Kemmel village green and begin their tour from Kemmel church on Reningelststraat. For a more complete picture of the area we advise reading this together with the Route 23 and 24 route descriptions.

Directions to start: The tour begins just south of the Vierstraat crossroads on the N331 which runs between Ieper and Kemmel. There is ample parking on the roadside next to the factory buildings. From this vantage point there is an excellent view across to the Messines Ridge.

Route description: The Goudezeune Prefab Factory is the large factory building on the Vierstraat crossroads. Although a rather ugly blot on the landscape, it does provide a useful lay-by in which to park. From the lay-by look over to your left towards the east and the Messines Ridge. You will see a road rising gently away from you up the ridge, to the left is a cluster of red-roofed farm buildings that is Hollandse Schuur Farm. There are three craters at the farm all blown by 250 Tunnelling Company on 7 June 1917. Permission from the landowner is required to visit. Further left in the middle of a field is Croonaert Chapel Cemetery and beyond is Croonaert Wood (Kroonaard on the maps) where the reconstructed Bayernwald trenches are to be found (see museums section). The church spire you can see in the distance is the church at Wijtschate. In 1917 the German line ran along the base of the ridge and can be traced today by the line of mine craters that were detonated on 7 June as a prelude to the very successful Battle of Messines.

Return to your vehicle and continue towards Kemmel, after 250m the American Memorial to the 27th and 30th United States Divisions will appear on your left. These two infantry divisions were fighting in the area from 18 August until 2 September 1918. Further on you reach a CWGC signpost to **La Laiterie Military Cemetery** which is on the right. Stop here.

The cemetery, named after a local dairy farm, was begun in November 1914 and used until October 1918 by units holding this sector of the front. The different plots were, to a great extent, treated as regimental burial grounds; the majority of the graves in Plots II, III and X, for instance, were those of the 26th, 25th and 24th Canadian Infantry Battalions, respectively, and all but one of the graves in plot VIII are those of men of 5/Northumberland Fusiliers. Buried here is pilot **Lieutenant Henry Eric Dolan** (II.D.8) who was credited with seven aerial victories. Dolan was born in England and later emigrated to Canada, where, on the outbreak of war, he enlisted in the Canadian Expeditionary Force. He originally served in the artillery as an officer and was awarded the Military Cross on

Lieutenant Henry Dolan.

29 December 1916. After transfer to the Royal Flying Corps, in early 1918, he was posted to No. 74 Squadron. He was assigned to 'A' Flight, under the leadership of Mick Mannock and scored his first victory when he shot down an Albatros D.V. on 12 April 1918. He scored steadily throughout the following month, notching his seventh victim on 11 May. The following day Dolan fell to the guns of Raven Freiherr von Barnekow. The cemetery also contains twelve soldiers of 1/5 Yorkshire

Regiment who served in the trenches at Kemmel during June and July 1916. Most of their casualties were the result of random shellfire; two of these, **Second Lieutenant Andrew Turnbull** (VII.D.16) from Scarborough and **Private Tom Woodthorpe** (VII.D.14) from Beverley, were killed on 17 July. Andrew Turnbull was a solicitor in the family firm before the war and enlisted as a private before being commissioned. Three days later **Captain Edward Bagshawe** (VII.D.12), a veteran of the South African War who resigned his commission in 1907 – only to rejoin when war was declared in August 1914, was killed in action on 20 July 1916 aged 36. Finally, one young man who probably passes unnoticed by many battlefield visitors is **Joseph Hickey**, a Canadian infantryman whom, for whatever reason, served in 24/Battalion under the name of **Private J.T. Smyth** (X.C.15). It will only take a minute or two to pay your respects before you go.

After leaving La Laiterie Military Cemetery you will see **Kemmel Chateau Cemetery** across the fields to your right which will be visited later in the tour. In 800m a road to the left will enable you to take a short detour to **Irish House Cemetery**. This cemetery owes its name to a small farmhouse 90m to the west of the cemetery, known to the troops as Irish House. It was begun in June 1917 by the 16th (Irish) Division, and used at intervals until September 1918. In Row A are the graves of thirty-three officers and men of 1/Gordon Highlanders, killed in action in December 1914 in the 3rd Division's attack on Wytschaete, and reburied here in June 1917. The ground was in German hands from April 1918 to the end of the following August.

Return to the main N331 and drive on. On reaching the roundabout ahead go straight across, following signs for Armentières, Nieuwkerke and Wulvergem. At the next crossroads is the turning on the right to **Lindenhoek Chalet Military Cemetery.** If you intend to visit this cemetery be aware that parking a vehicle on the single track road is difficult. The first burials were made in the cemetery in March 1915 and it continued to be used by fighting units and field ambulances until October 1917. It was enlarged after the Armistice when over 100 graves were brought in from the battlefields surrounding Kemmel. There are now 315 servicemen buried or commemorated in the cemetery including 6 special memorials.

Back on the main N331, continue towards Wulvergem and take the next turning right – Kemmelstraat – which joins Kruisabelestraat after

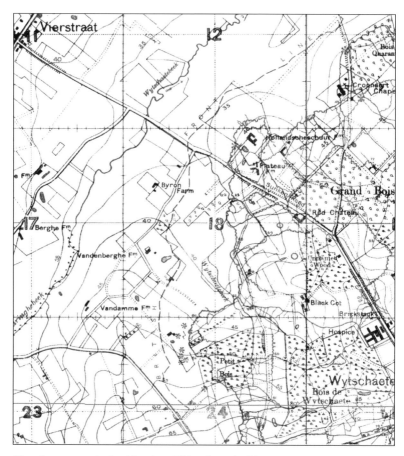

The view across to the Messines Ridge from the Vierstraat crossroads as it was in 1917. The German trench lines are in red and you can make out Hollandse Schuur Farm and Croonaert chapel in the top right-hand corner. The British lines are in blue. From your viewpoint at Vierstraat it is possible to appreciate the advantage the Germans had over the British lines from the high ground of the Messines Ridge and why the ridge was the focus of the June 1917 Battle of Messines.

400m. Keeping the high ground of Kemmelberg on your right, continue for another 2.8km until you enter Dranouter (formerly Dranoutre). At the junction with the N332 continue straight ahead towards the church of Sint-Jan-de-Doper. Park here to visit **Dranoutre Churchyard Cemetery**. Dranouter was occupied by the British 1st Cavalry Division

Dranoutre Military Cemetery.

on 14 October 1914 and was taken by the Germans on 25 April 1918 in spite of the stubborn resistance of the 154th French Division. It remained in German hands until 30 August 1918. Dranouter churchyard was used for Commonwealth burials from October 1914 and July 1915. The churchyard contains seventy-nine Commonwealth burials. The CWGC plots are to the left and right of the church entrance. Here you will find **Private Albert Filer** (VI.A.II), killed on 19 July 1915, who served under the alias of A. Adams and **Captain Robert Otter** (II.B.2) of 1/Norfolks whose epitaph reads: 'A gallant Englishman and a good sportsman'. Another gallant Englishman was **Lieutenant Robert Flint** (II.A.2) who won his DSO during the Battle of the Aisne in September 1914 ferrying troops across the river by raft. Serving with 59/Field Company, this Royal Engineers officer fought at Mons and Le Cateau and was mentioned in despatches. There is also an interesting Second World War memorial in the shape of an aeroplane tail plane dedicated to a Belgian pilot who was killed in action on 5 May 1942.

Leave the churchyard and keeping the church on your right follow signs for Loker. After 200m or so you will see a CWGC sign for **Dranoutre Military Cemetery**, follow the single-track road and park in the parking area behind the large building. You should just be able to see the Cross of Sacrifice on your left on the other side of the hedge.

The cemetery was begun in July 1915 and used by fighting units and field ambulances until March 1918 (Plots I and II), many of the burials being carried out by 72 Brigade (24th Division) in April–June 1916. Plot III was added in September and October 1918. In 1923, nineteen graves were moved from the churchyard when the church was rebuilt. The cemetery now contains 458 Commonwealth burials and 1 German war grave. In this secluded spot you will find **Private Frederick Broadrick** (II.J.24) of 11/Royal Warwicks who was executed for desertion on 1 August 1917. Had he not been under a suspended sentence for a previous desertion he may have been spared the death penalty. Find a moment to visit **Second Lieutenant Thomas Hanson Averill** (II.J.25) of 17/King's Liverpool Regiment. A clerk of works from Great Witley near Worcester, he enlisted in the Army Veterinary Corps in January 1915 and worked his way up to acting sergeant before being commissioned in April 1917. He was killed on 30 August 1917 whilst his company was engaged on working parties in the front line along with his platoon sergeant (II.J.26) who is in the next grave. **Private Fred Hollman** (I.C.19), a 21-year-old former postman from Ightham in Kent, enlisted a month after war was declared in 1914. Having completed his basic training with 9/Queen's Own Royal West Kent Regiment, he was transferred to the 8th Battalion and sent to France in early January 1916. He was killed in action on 23 April 1916 after serving less than five months at the front.

Return to the main N322 road and turn left along Dikkebusstraat for another 450m. On your left is **Locre Number 10 Military Cemetery** with ample parking in the lay-by and great views across the valley beyond. There are more German burials here than there are British, the evidence being the two German mass graves to the left of the entrance. A number of the London Scottish who took part in the attack on the German line at **Locrehof Farm** – a little further up the road on your right – on 21 August 1918 are buried here. The farm was taken and held but the battalion lost two officers and twenty-seven other ranks killed. One of these men, **Private Jack Johns** (B.8), was a professional golfer from Ashford in Middlesex who enlisted in January 1916 and served with 2/14th Battalion at Salonika and in Egypt, where he was sentenced to ten days close confinement for ignoring a battalion march order when he bought oranges from a hawker en route!

Leave the cemetery and continue into Loker, note the demarcation stone on your left just before you enter the village. On your right Locre

Hospice Cemetery is signposted with the usual green CWGC sign, follow the signs turning right onto Dondeyneweg. If you are travelling by car, park at the bottom of the hill near the hospice where there are information panels relating to the hospice and Major William Redmond. A short walk down the hill will bring you to **Locre Hospice Cemetery** with its entrance immediately after the private house on the right. On your way you will also pass the site of the original hospice on your left. Details of the cemetery can be found in the Route 24 description.

Return to the hospice and continue up the hill towards the church and village centre, at the T-junction you will see the church and Locre Churchyard Cemetery ahead of you. There is parking to your left. A description of this cemetery can also be found in Route 24. After returning to your vehicle, keep the church on your right and drive to the junction ahead of you. Turn right onto the N375.

Continue through the village past the junction with the N372 on your left. Just before the road descends towards Klijte (previously La Clytte) you will pass the wooded Scherpenberg Hill on your right. Continue to the roundabout at Klijte, turn left onto the N304 towards Poperinge to visit **La Clytte Military Cemetery** 100m further along the road on the left. The cemetery was started on 1 November 1914 and between that date and April 1918 Plots I, II and III and part of Plot IV were filled. The hamlet of La Clytte was used as Brigade Headquarters and the burials were carried out by infantry, artillery and engineer units (of the 600 graves, 250 are those of artillery personnel and 66 are Royal Engineers). The two Mitchell brothers from Rotherham are buried here. **Gunner William Mitchell** (II.E.1) served with 107 Brigade, Royal Field Artillery and was killed on 9 August 1917, whilst his brother, **Private Leonard Mitchell** (III.A.2), was shot for desertion on 19 September 1917. He was already under sentence of death for a previous desertion.

Retrace your route and return to the roundabout. Go straight over, staying on the N304 towards Wijtschate and Kemmel. The road descends towards Kemmel affording good views over towards Kemmelberg. Note the demarcation stone on your right as the ground begins to rise again. Just before you enter Kemmel village you will arrive at a crossroads. Turn right here onto Pingelarestraat following the signs for Camping Ypra. The road climbs up on the eastern side of Lettenberg Hill past the campsite which is on your right. At the next junction turn right onto Lokerstraat, signposted 'Site Lettenberg'. After 100m, opposite a private house, is a lay-by. Stop here. Looking to the north you will see the **Lettenberg British Bunkers** cut into the hillside down the track on your right, which are described in Route 23. Continue along Lokerstraat until the road descends towards a crossroads ahead. On your right was the approximate position of the **Kemmel Shelters** and just before the last farm on the right, two British bunkers can be seen in the field.

At the crossroads turn left onto Kemmelbergweg and drive up the hill towards the Kemmelberg. Halfway up you will see a cafe/restaurant on the left and immediately opposite is the **French National Ossuary** where there is parking. At this point the road surface changes to cobbles and is quite steep. Ahead are the striking **French Memorial** and the summit of Kemmelberg. Parking is available here. Follow the road round to the Belvedere Brasserie on the right, the views over the Ypres battlefields are now largely obscured by trees.

The road now descends steeply ahead past the Brasserie de Alverman to a T-junction with Bergstraat. Directly ahead is a parking area where good views can be had on a clear day over the Messines/Wijtschate Ridge. Turn left at the junction and continue downhill towards Kemmel returning to the village green and bandstand. This is a good point to visit **Kemmel Churchyard Cemetery**, park by the green and walk across to the church. The cemetery is described in Route 23. Return to the green and with the bandstand behind you continue downhill to a T-junction, turn left here onto Reningelststraat then take the right turning opposite the church onto Nieuwstraat, leading to the large **Kemmel Chateau Military Cemetery** on your right. Stop here to visit the cemetery.

Kemmelberg from the west.

The French National Ossuary on Kemmelberg.

Godezonne Farm Military Cemetery.

The cemetery, which took its name from Kemmel Chateau, was established on the north side of the chateau grounds in December 1914. The chateau was used as an advanced dressing station and the cemetery continued to be used by divisions fighting on the southern sectors of the Belgian front until March 1918, when after fierce fighting the village and cemetery fell into German hands in late April. The cemetery was retaken later in the year, but in the interval it was badly shelled and the old chateau destroyed.

There are now 1,135 burials in the cemetery and 21 from the Second World War which date from the Allied withdrawal ahead of the German advance of May 1940. The graves of two soldiers shot for desertion in 1917 lie here, 21-year-old **Private Stanley Stewart** (G.66) of 2/Royal Scots Fusiliers was executed on 29 August and 26-year-old **Private James Smith** (M.25) of 17/King's Liverpool Regiment on 5 September. Also buried here is an uncle of the novelist Daphne du Maurier, **Lieutenant Colonel Guy du Maurier** (L.4). He was commanding 3/Royal Fusiliers, and was aged 49 when he died on 9 March 1915. Here you will find the graves of three of the Connaught Rangers who were killed by shellfire whilst their

A young Guy du Maurier.

battalion was out of the front line at the Kemmel Shelters. The 17-year-old **Private John O'Donoghue** (L.18), **Private James Bannerman** (L.17) and **Private Owen Treanor** (L.19) lie side by side. Canadian soldier **Private F.L. Reid** (G.1), who served under the name of **Gorman**, was killed on 1 December 1916 serving with 24/Battalion Canadian infantry. An early casualty of the war was **Captain Edward Martin Crawley-Boevey** (B.10) who was the 41-year-old second son of Sir Thomas Hyde Crawley-Boevey of Flaxley Abbey in Gloucestershire. He was serving with 1/Royal Fusiliers and was killed by a sniper in the trenches near Bailleul. He was commissioned in 1895 into the Royal Sussex Regiment and served in South Africa. He was married to Rosalie Winifred Sartorius, the granddaughter of Sir George Rose Sartorius who was appointed Admiral of the Fleet in 1869.

Leave the cemetery and continue along the road out of Kemmel and just after a sharp left-hand bend turn right at the T-junction onto Kriekstraat. On your left is a memorial obelisk to the 32nd French Division and 250m further on is **Godezonne Farm Military Cemetery** on your right. The cemetery was made in the garden of Godezonne Farm between February and May 1915 by 2/Royal Scots and 4/Middlesex. Unusually there are no unidentified burials in this small cemetery. Old Etonian, **Captain Hon Douglas Arthur Kinnaird**, Master of Kinnaird (II.A.1) was killed on 24 October 1914 near Zandvoorde whilst serving as a company commander with 2/ Scots Guards. The 20-year-old **Lieutenant Lachlan Henry Veitch Fraser** (I.A.7) of 4/Middlesex has an entry in *Burke's Landed Gentry*. He was killed by shellfire at Vierstraat on the evening of 24 February 1915 along with three other men, two of whom, **Privates Linton** (I.A.6) and **Albert Willis** (I.B.3), lie close by.

Leave the cemetery and continue carefully as immediately after the last house on the left you will find the narrow entrance to **Suffolk Cemetery**; it is easy to miss. This cemetery was begun in March and April 1915 by 2/Suffolks. Apart from one burial made in November 1917 the cemetery was not used again until October 1918 when the 38th Labour Group buried men killed during the German advance the previous April. At this time, it was called Cheapside Cemetery. Despite the Suffolks' regimental historian writing that this sector in March 1915 was relatively quiet, the war of attrition exacted its daily toll of dead and wounded due to random shellfire and rifle grenades. **Sergeant Thomas Rush** (B.8) was killed on 20 March, followed three days later by **Second Lieutenant Francis Schroder** (B.6) who was hit by a rifle grenade near La Clytte on 23 March (his headstone is incorrectly inscribed 15 March). Next to him is 31-year-old **Private David Page** (B.5) from Ipswich who died six days later on 29 March from shellfire.

Leave the cemetery and at the T-junction ahead either turn left to visit **Kemmel No. 1 French Cemetery** and **Klein Vierstraat British Cemetery** or right to complete the tour at the Goudezeune Prefab Factory. Note the demarcation stone on the right immediately after making a right turn at the crossroads which marks the furthest point reached by the Germans in the spring of 1918. If you are a cyclist and began your tour at Kemmel then continue down the N331 to Kemmel village.

Route 23

Kemmelberg

Suitable for 🚶
Circular route starting at: Kemmel village bandstand.
Coordinates: 50°46 58.97 N – 2°49 53.88 E.
Distance: 4.1km/2.6 miles.
Grade: Strenuous – some steep climbs and descents.
Maps: NGI 1:20 000 Heuvelland–Mesen (Messines) 28/5–6.
Link this with: Route 24 – Loker.

General description and context: Kemmelberg lies just inside the Belgian border and was in Allied territory for most of the war years until it was captured briefly by the Germans during their April 1918 offensive. The hill was initially held by the British during a determined attack on 17 April, but lost on 26 April when the French were subjected to a hurricane artillery bombardment followed by a strong infantry attack which saw the Germans advance almost to Loker where they were finally held. At Loker British and French units finally forced the by now exhausted German units to retire, but Kemmelberg remained in occupation until the end of August 1918 when the American 27th Division and the British 34th Division eventually recaptured the hill.

Directions to start: Leave Ieper via the Rijselpoort – the Lille Gate – and go straight over the roundabout on to the N336 towards Sint-Elooi. After 600m take the right turn onto the N331. The village of Kemmel is 9.5km/5.9 miles from Ieper on the N331.

Route description: Park in the area around the village green in Kemmel ❶. The bandstand was a feature of the green during the war years and frequently played host to military bands entertaining the troops. We suggest you visit the small Kemmel Churchyard Cemetery on Reningelststraat on your return to the village. With the bandstand behind you and the church on your right, locate Lokerstraat almost

Kemmel village bandstand.

The Lettenberg bunkers.

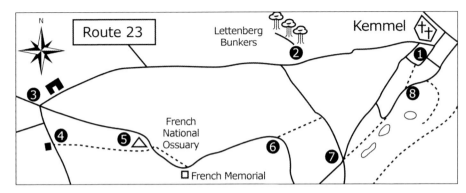

directly ahead of you heading west away from the village green. Continue out of the village keeping the terrace of houses on your right as the road begins to rise gently. As the road levels out slightly after 600m you will come to a turning on the right, almost immediately ahead a set of steps ascends the bank in front of you to a further set of steps on the left leading down to the **Lettenberg British Bunkers ❷**. Built into the side of the Lettenberg Hill, these shelters were constructed by the men of 175 Tunnelling Company during April and May of 1917. The bunkers you see today are the entrances to a much larger, but now collapsed, underground complex which contained a command post. One of the bunkers is still marked by a large red cross and was used as an aid post. The position was captured by the Germans in April 1918 during the Battle of Kemmel. You will notice that one of the existing shelters is now used as a 'bat box'.

Retrace your steps to the main road and turn right onto Lokerstraat with good views behind you to Lettenberg and the bunkers. Continue along Lokerstraat with Kemmelberg on your left and ahead of you views over to Scherpenberg Hill on the right and Rodeberg almost straight ahead. The area is sometimes referred to today as the Belgian Alps. When you reach the third turning on your right leading to a farm, stop. This was the site of the **Kemmel Shelters**, a large hutted rest camp that occupied the low ground to your right. Although the camp was thought to be in a relatively safe position hidden in a wooded depression and well back from the front line, it did suffer from random shellfire. On 8 February 1917 the men of 3/Connaught Rangers were hit by enemy shelling at 10.30am and a direct hit on the hut occupied by men of

C Company resulted in three men killed and eleven wounded. The youngest of the dead was 17-year-old **Private John O'Donoghue** who is buried next to his comrades, **Privates James Bannerman** and **Owen Treanor**, at **Kemmel Chateau Military Cemetery**, which is visited on the Kemmel Area Car Tour – Route 22. A fourth man, Private James Hamilton, died the following day and is buried at Bailleul Military Cemetery.

Continuing past the farm take note of the pair of British concrete bunkers situated in the field on the right before you reach the crossroads ❸. The farm at the crossroads on your right was the former site of Redvers Camp which occupied the low ground behind the farm.

> *The crossroads is also the point at which the route joins **Route 24**. If you wish to do so, turn right and join the Route 24 guidance at ❻.*

Go straight over the crossroads onto Montebergstraat passing a farm on your left and ignoring the road on your right. Ahead of you on the right is a private house and directly opposite is a bridleway ❹ leading uphill towards the summit of Kemmelberg. Take care here as the path is apt to be a little slippery in wet weather. Continue up the track until it meets the junction of Kemmelbergweg and Kleine Kemmelbergweg at the **French National Ossuary**. Opposite the ossuary gates ❺ are three interpretation boards providing information about the ossuary itself. Created in 1922, this mass grave contains the bodies of 5,294 French soldiers most of whom fell in the German attack of 25 April 1918. It is only when you have spent a few minutes here that you realize all but fifty-seven are unidentified. On the obelisk are listed the names of the commanding officers and the units of the French Army involved in the fighting.

Should you feel the need for refreshments the nearby Brasserie 'au Chalet' is perfectly located before you continue uphill taking the cobbled road towards the summit of Kemmelberg. Ahead you will see the imposing French memorial of Nike, the winged goddess of victory which was unveiled in 1932 by Marshal Pétain. At the memorial turn left, continuing on a metalled road (Kemmelbergweg) along the crest of Kemmelberg. Directly opposite the Hostellerie Kemmelberg and the military signal station is the triangulation point marking the summit of Kemmelberg. Continue past the Belvedere Brasserie after which point the road reverts to cobbles and begins to descend. Take care here as the cobbles can be very slippery when wet. Where the road bends to the right, carry straight on and take the well-worn path ❻ into trees. Although steep, it soon reaches a single-track metalled road. Turn right here and continue on to the crossroads ❼ where you will find a sign for the Der Lork Outdoor Centre for Children.

Go straight over the crossroads taking the wide forest track immediately on the left through the turnstile signposted Palingbeek. Continue past a lake on your right and a large chateau on your left; ahead the church tower at Kemmel is visible. Where the track bends to the right, take the narrower track ❽ off to the left, to emerge eventually at Kemmel village green ❶ with the bandstand directly ahead of you. Continue downhill past the bandstand towards the church and **Kemmel Churchyard Cemetery**.

The churchyard contains twenty-five Commonwealth burials of which three are unidentified. The graves of fifteen casualties destroyed by shellfire are represented by special memorials, as is **Private Frank Dallow** (SM.1) who was killed by a sniper at 9.00am on 22 November as he stood up to throw a piece of biscuit to a friend in the next stretch of trench. He died half an hour later. Dallow was mentioned in despatches for his good work whilst in support of 4/Dragoon Guards on the Messines Ridge in early November 1914. The Oxfordshire Hussars was a territorial yeomanry cavalry unit which had the distinction of being one of the first yeomanry units in action with the BEF. Two former international rugby union captains who both served with 10/King's Liverpool Regiment also have their names on special memorials. The 36-year-old former solicitor **Lieutenant Percy Dale 'Toggie' Kendall** (SM.14) captained the England side and played forty-five matches for Cheshire and is commemorated next to **Second Lieutenant Frederick Harding Turner** (SM.13), who captained the Scottish rugby union team in 1913 and held fifteen caps for Scotland. Turner was killed on 10 January 1915 and Kendall on 25 January. **Second Lieutenant Musgrave Cazenove Wroughton** (A.3) was one of the twenty boys whom Robert Baden-Powell took on the first ever Scout camp to Brownsea Island in August 1907. He died on 30 October 1914 aged 23, from wounds received during the German attack on the Messines Ridge serving with 12/Lancers. As a consequence of his part in the action, he was mentioned in despatches. Buried close by is 41-

year-old **Major George Geoffrey Humphries** of 129/ (Duke of Connaught's Own) Baluchi Light Infantry, a regiment of the Indian Army which fought on the Messines Ridge in 1914. He came from a distinguished family, his grandfather served under Nelson at the Battle of Copenhagen and his uncle, William Alexander, was commissioned into 12/Lancers. In 1911 he was appointed ADC to King George V who sent the family a personal note of condolence after Humphries died of wounds on 30 October 1914. He left a widow, Olive, and three children and was mentioned in despatches. Commemorated with a

Second Lieutenant James Mylles.

special memorial is 21-year-old **Second Lieutenant James Mylles** (SM.12) who was studying to be a doctor at Glasgow University when war was declared. Commissioned into the Gordon Highlanders, he was killed after only a few days at the front on 30 December 1914.

Route 24

Loker

Suitable for 🚲 🚶

Circular route starting at: outside the church at Loker.
Coordinates: 50°46 56.12 N – 2°46 17.09 E.
Distance: 4.5km/2.8 miles.
Grade: Easy to moderate.
Maps: NGI 1 20 000 Heuvelland–Mesen (Messines) 28/5–6.
Link this with: Route 23 – Kemmelberg.

General description and context: Loker (formerly Locre) was in Allied territory for the most of the Great War and several field ambulance units were located in the old convent hospice buildings of St Antoine. After the German 1918 spring offensive the village changed hands on several occasions between 25 and 30 April 1918 but was finally recaptured by the French in May. Being behind the lines, the area around Loker was used extensively to house troops being held in reserve or withdrawn from the front line for refit and recuperation. Many of the camps consisted of semi-permanent huts, whilst others were large tented areas. Earlier in the war, before many of the camps were completed, the village itself was used to billet troops and on one occasion in 1915, **Captain Bruce Bairnsfather**, the well-known cartoonist who created the character of 'Old Bill', was billeted in the church overnight with his men occupying the choir stalls.

Directions to start: Leave Ieper via the Rijselpoort – the Lille Gate – and go straight over the roundabout on to the N336 towards Sint-Elooi. After 600m take the right turn onto the N331. Turn right after 2km at the Kruisstraat crossroads then left on to the N375 through Dikkebus and Klijte to Loker which is 10km southwest of Ieper on the N375.

Route description: The tour begins in the centre of Loker where there is ample parking near the church ❶. Before you begin your tour take a

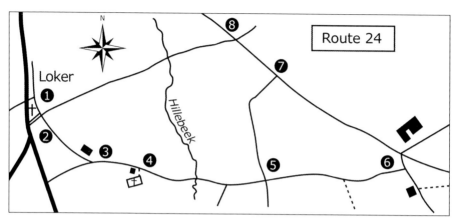

few minutes to visit **Locre Churchyard Cemetery** which is divided into two plots on either side of the church. The churchyard was used by field ambulance units from 1914 up until the Battle of Messines in June 1917. Buried here are three soldiers who were shot at dawn for desertion: 17-year-old **Private Joseph Byers** (Plot I.A.1.) and 16-year-old **Private Andrew Evans** (I.A.2.) were executed together on the morning of 6 February 1915, followed by **George Collins** (I.B.1), aged 20, who was executed on 15 February 1915. Many of the burials here are soldiers who died after being wounded in action elsewhere. **Rifleman Samuel McKee** (Plot 2.A.4), from Lisburn, Northern Ireland, is one such casualty. He died of wounds serving with 'A' Company 2/Royal Irish Rifles on 21 February 1915, he was 19 years old. McKee was fatally wounded whilst attempting to bury two dead Gordon Highlanders who were only yards from the front-line trenches at Maedelstede Farm. **Second Lieutenant Cecil Hawdon** (1.D.6) was killed on 27 June 1916 serving with 4/ Yorkshire Regiment during a trench raid. He died along with **Lance Sergeant Robert Trafford** and **Privates Smith and Bellwood** who are buried close by. Tragically, Hawdon's two brothers were also victims of the conflict, Rupert, on 4 November 1918, whilst serving as a captain with the Royal Garrison Artillery, and the eldest, Noel, who was an Army chaplain and died of influenza five days after the Armistice was declared. Finally, before you leave take a look inside the church and allow your imagination to gaze upon the sight of muddy and tired soldiers spread out before you on the floor with rifles and equipment piled up around the walls. The

Locre Hospice Cemetery.

company commander is probably in earnest conversation with the pastor who is most concerned that the church fittings and holy relics are not disturbed or broken – or worse, stolen. The men are probably too tired to care about anything beyond sleep and getting something to eat. On leaving the church, with the entrance behind you, turn left along Dikkebusstraat, then first left at the Belgian Memorial to the fallen into Kemmelbergweg and finally right at the crossroads into Godtschalkstraat ❷. You are now walking down towards **St Antoine's Hospice** which you should be able to see ahead of you. On your right where the new houses are was Wicklow Lines and at the

Private Joseph Byers, shot at dawn on 6 February 1915.

bottom of the hill was Birr Barracks, reputedly named by the men of the Leinster Regiment whose regimental depot was at Birr, Co. Offaly, Ireland.

As the road bears round to the left pass in front of the hospice ❸ where there are information boards providing detail about Major William Redmond. Continue straight ahead, on your right is **Locre Hospice Cemetery** which is opposite the site where the original hospice stood before it was destroyed by shellfire in 1918. Up until April 1918 the hospice was used not only by field ambulance units but also provided shelter for refugees from Ieper. The entrance to Locre Hospice Cemetery ❹ is immediately after the private house on the right. Follow the grass path to the cemetery. **Major William Redmond's** grave is directly behind the rear wall of the CWGC cemetery and accessible via a path running alongside. The cemetery was begun by field ambulance units in June 1917 and many of the men buried here are casualties of the Battle of Messines. The cemetery contains 244 Commonwealth burials and commemorations of the Great War, of which 12 are unidentified and 10 graves destroyed by shellfire represented by special memorials. The fourteen Second World War burials date from late May 1940 and the withdrawal of the BEF to Dunkirk ahead of the German advance. There are also two German soldiers buried in the cemetery. Apart from **Private A.F. Cameron** (II.C.24) who died in 1915, the remaining burials are all from 1917 and 1918. The cemetery is the last resting place of **Brigadier General Ronald MacLachlan** DSO (III.C.9) who was commanding 112 Brigade when he was killed on 11 August 1917 and **Lieutenant Colonel Richard Chester-Master** DSO and Bar (II.C.8.) who met his death from sniper fire whilst commanding 13/King's Royal Rifle Corps on 30 August 1917. You will find two more soldiers executed for desertion buried here: **Private Denis Blakemore**

Major William Redmond's grave at Loker.

(I.A.2), who faced the firing squad on 9 July 1917, and **Private William Jones** (I.C.4), who was executed on 25 October 1917. A total of 346 men including 3 officers were executed during the war of which 37 were executed for murder – the last of those being in 1920 – but the majority were found guilty of desertion or cowardice. Before you leave take time to visit 23-year-old **Rifleman Thomas Emerson** (I.A.12). He died of his wounds in the old hospice opposite the cemetery on 20 June 1917 serving with 'C' Company 14/Royal Irish Rifles. Originally from Hillsborough, his parents lived in Belfast and chose the inscription 'Peace perfect peace' for their son's headstone.

Major William Redmond's grave is still kept separate from the main CWGC cemetery and he died of wounds received during the 16th (Irish) Division's attack on Wytschaete on 7 June 1917. The 56-year-old Redmond was an Irish Nationalist MP and was allowed to take part in the attack on the understanding he only went as far as the first objective. Originally buried in the hospice grounds, his grave was moved after the war but his insistence that he was not to be buried in a British cemetery is still upheld by his family today. The two pieces of masonry by his grave are from the original hospice building. There is also a separate visitor's book here.

From the cemetery turn right along the road, descending gently into a small valley before rising again to a crossroads at Koenraadstraat ❺ which was the location of Birmingham Camp in the fields to your left. Stop here and look behind you. The church tower you can see on the skyline to the left is at Dranouter and the CWGC cemetery just visible by its Cross of Sacrifice is **Locre No. 10 Military Cemetery**. Carry on straight over the crossroads towards the Kemmelberg which is visible in the distance. The road continues, passing the obvious track on the right leading to a private house, to reach a T-junction ❻.

This is the point at which the route joins Route 23. If you wish to continue over the Kemmelberg turn right at the T-junction and join the route description for Route 23 at ❹. Bear in mind the Kemmelberg route is quite strenuous and only recommended for walkers able to cope with steep ascents and descents.

Turn left at the T-junction to the crossroads and then turn left again into Kemmelbergweg. As you reach the crossroads glance across to the farm ahead of you, this was the site of Redvers Camp. You are now walking towards Loker village and ahead of you on the right is the tree-covered **Scherpenberg Hill** which had a windmill and a farm on its summit and, unlike Kemmelberg, was usually spared random shellfire. It was generally used as an observation point and on a clear day there are views across to Wijtschate, Mesen and Ieper and to the sea beyond. On 15 December 1914, King George V together with numerous other dignitaries, including Sir John French, who was Commander-in-Chief of the BEF at the time, watched the disastrous attack by the Royal Scots and the Gordon Highlanders on **Maedelstede Farm**. It was some of the dead from that attack that young Samuel McKee (see p. 205) was attempting to bury when he was killed two months later. We visit Maedelstede Farm along with Hollandse Schuur Farm in Route 19 from where you can get superb views over the Kemmel area.

Continue past the calvary ❼ and the electricity sub-station. Just beyond the minor road on the left is a demarcation stone. Stop here. You are now at the point where a former light railway ran south across the road to Birmingham Camp with a branch that ran back alongside the road on your left towards Redvers Camp. The line continued north to supply Butterfly Farm Camp some 1,000m to the northeast of you. The area around here positively bristled with camps, ahead of you on the left was Redan and Cyclists Camp and on the right, tucked away in the valley, Buller and Leeds Camp. It was to camps such as these that the popular actress **Miss Lena Ashwell** would bring her concert party to entertain the troops. Lena Ashwell (1872–1957) was the first to organize large-scale entertainment for the troops at the front.

Miss Lena Ashwell.

Continue on up to the crossroads and turn left ❽. The road ahead descends gently into a small valley where on the left and right was situated Alma Lines. The straight road ahead of you was dubbed **Gordon Road** by the troops who would have shared the view of Loker church which you now have in front of you. Continue slightly uphill into the village. Just before you enter the village turn around for a final glimpse of **Kemmelberg** on the right and **Scherpenberg Hill** to your left. The church ❶ is directly ahead.

Route 25

Ploegsteert Wood and Hill 63

Suitable for ⬥

Circular route starting at: Cafe L'Auberge.

Coordinates: 50°44 14.89 N – 2°52 56.54 E.

Distance: 6.9km/4.3 miles (with the option of a further 1.6km/ 1 mile to Hill 63).

Grade: Strenuous if you include Hill 63, otherwise easy.

Toilets: Cafe L'Auberge.

Maps: NGI 1:20 000 Heuvelland–Mesen (Messines) 28/5–6.

General description and context: Ploegsteert Wood, or 'Plugstreet' as it was known to the British troops who fought in the area, was a relatively quiet place in 1914 after it was captured by the British 1st Cavalry Division. Later on the Germans took part of it again and during April 1918 it was totally recaptured by the Germans. Only during September 1918, during their advance, was it in British hands again. Many of the place names used for locations in and around the area – The Strand, Hyde Park Corner, Somerset House, Charing Cross, Regent Street and Oxford Circus – show a strong London connection and can be traced to the London Rifle Brigade's occupancy of the sector in 1914. Trench maps also mark an 'Essex Farm' which should not be confused with the more famous Essex Farm Cemetery on the N369 just to the north of Ieper (see Route 18). Two individuals who served in this sector, **Winston Churchill** and **Anthony Eden**, later went on to become, respectively, Prime Minister and Secretary of State for War in 1940. The wood was also home for a few months to poet and soldier **Lieutenant Roland Leighton**, the fiancé of feminist writer Vera Brittain who worked as a nurse in a Voluntary Aid Detachment. Leighton died of wounds on the Somme on 23 December 1915 aged 20. Brittain was heartbroken by his loss and that of others of her generation – including her brother Edward – but went on to marry in 1925 and to become the mother of the well-known British Labour and Liberal Democrat politician Baroness Shirley Williams.

Directions to start: Leave Ieper via the Rijselpoort – the Lille Gate – and go straight over the roundabout taking the N336 to Sint-Elooi. Follow the N365 through Mesen, past the Irish Peace Park to the Ploegsteert Memorial on the northern edge of the wood. Park at the Cafe L'Auberge with permission from the owner or on the road outside the memorial.

Route description: The route includes seven military cemeteries and whilst we will draw attention to all of them, it is entirely up to you which of them you choose to visit – but we do suggest you visit the Ploegsteert Memorial at the end of your excursion. There are also numerous information panels at strategic points along the route. Leave your vehicle ❶ and head north up the road in the direction of Mesen. You will soon arrive at a road junction on the left, signposted **Underhill Farm Cemetery.** Stop here. You can either extend the route to Hill 63 by turning left or continue to Hyde Park Corner.

Descending the steep track from Hill 63.

To reach Hill 63 walk along the road towards Underhill Farm Cemetery – ignore the first green gate on the right – and after some 500m a second gate opposite a forest track signposted Bois de la Hutte leads to a steep path ❷ climbing up the wooded hillside on your right. Go through the gate at the top to reach the top of the ridge. There are superb views from here to Kemmelberg on the left and Mesen church on the right. Straight ahead is the spire of Wijtschate church. It was under the steep escarpment you are now standing on that Australian engineers dug the huge underground dugout complex called The Catacombs, a little further to the west was the site of Rosenberg Chateau. Retrace your steps to the junction of paths, turn left and walk along the top of the ridge until another pathway ❸ on the right which runs alongside a field edge – signposted 'Euro Circuit 2' – will return you steeply to the roadway. Turn left here and retrace your steps to the road junction and turn left to Hyde Park Corner.

Continue to Hyde Park Corner ❹, turning right onto the obvious track. This track was known as Mud Lane and continues straight ahead past the private house. Ploegsteert Wood is now to your right and in a few metres you will find a panel with information featuring three of the men who served in the locality. Stop here. **Lieutenant Richard Talbot Kelly MC** was a gunner officer serving with 52 Brigade Royal Field Artillery in the area in 1917; his gun pit dug in in a 'verdant thicket of little willows and blackberry bushes' on the edge of the wood near **Hyde Park Corner (Royal Berks) Cemetery**, which is visited later. Grandson of the Dublin-born artist Robert George Kelly and son of artist and Egyptologist Robert George Talbot Kelly, he exhibited at the Royal Academy and the Paris Salon and illustrated several books on bird life. After the war he taught art at Rugby School, served in the Second World War and died in 1971. **Lieutenant Ronald Poulton Palmer** was the England Rugby Union captain and heir to the Reading biscuit empire of Huntley and Palmer. He was killed by a sniper at 12.20am on 5 May 1915 whilst standing on top of a dugout overseeing repairs. His body was carried along Mud Lane on a stretcher to the Field Ambulance in the Convent in Ploegsteert. His death made national headlines and such was the effect on the men of his battalion and beyond, that many, including his father, Edward Bagnall Poulton, felt that he had been specifically targeted by the Germans. Richard Talbot Kelly who, like

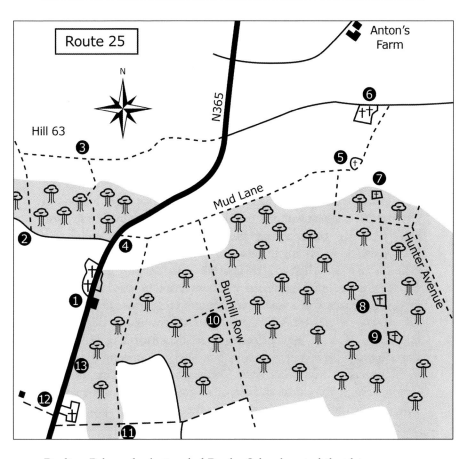

Poulton Palmer, had attended Rugby School, noted that his grave was just yards away from his gun position. 'I felt here was a strange re-union of Rugbeians, dead and living in Arcady', he later wrote. One of a number of very young soldiers buried in and around Ieper is 16-year-old **Rifleman Albert French** who died serving with 18/King's Royal Rifle Corps on 15 April 1916.

At the next junction of tracks continue straight on noting the information board on the left with some interesting detail on the mapping of Ploegsteert Wood during the war. Across to your left the ground slopes up to the crest of the ridge that effectively shielded Mud Lane from enemy observation for much of its length and provided a secure approach to the front-line positions for troops and supplies moving into or out of the line. Continue to the point where a track comes in from the right, you will see a cemetery straight ahead and another on the slope to your left. Stop at the first cemetery ❺. This is **Mud Corner Cemetery,** a true Anzac cemetery as all eighty-five soldiers buried here are Australians and New Zealanders killed in June, July and August 1917, a period when II Anzac Corps were fighting to the north and then holding the line at Ploegsteert.

Leave the cemetery and turn left. The track rises to meet a metalled road and across to the left you will see **Prowse Point Military Cemetery.** At the T-junction, turn left to the cemetery entrance ❻. This cemetery is unique in being named after an individual and is on the site close to the stand by 1/Hampshires and 1/Somerset Light Infantry in October 1914, which featured the heroism of **Major Charles Prowse** DSO who was commanding the Somersets. On 30 October the Hampshires were holding the line from the Le Gheer crossroads to the Petit Douve River when a German artillery and infantry assault broke the line. Prowse and his men were in reserve and he was instrumental in saving the day with a well-timed counter-attack close to where you are now standing. Later as a brigadier general he would be killed on the first day of the Battle of the Somme, whilst commanding 11 Infantry Brigade. Prowse is buried at Louvencourt Military Cemetery. Also killed in the attack on 30 October were **Lieutenant William Trimmer** and **Captain Reginald Harland**, both of whom are buried at the nearby Ploegsteert churchyard along with four other 1/Hants officers and men.

Prowse Point Cemetery was begun by 2/Royal Dublin Fusiliers and 1/Royal Warwicks, and was used from November 1914 to April 1918. Buried here is 29-year-old **Private Harry Wilkinson** (I.A.7) who served with 2/Lancashire Fusiliers. His remains were found in the year 2000 by local historian Patrick Roelens some 800m to the southeast where he was killed during a raid on German trenches on 10 November 1914. Identified by his personal belongings, he was reburied in 2001 with full military honours in the presence of the Duke of Kent and with his family descendants in attendance. His name was the first to be read out at the 25,000 sounding of the Last Post at the Menin Gate the same evening in the presence of the Duke of Edinburgh.

In March 2006, close to where Harry Wilkinson was found, the remains of three more British soldiers were discovered, one of whom was identified as **Private Richard Lancaster** (III.C.113) who, like Harry Wilkinson, served with 2/Lancashire Fusiliers and also died on

10 November 1914. Buried close to each other, in Plot III, Row B, Graves 1, 3 and 4 are Privates **Vivian Main**, **Charles Jennings** and **John McGuire**, all of 27/Battalion (South Australia) and all killed in action on Christmas Day 1917. You might wish to stop at the grave of 22-year-old **Sergeant Arthur Dale** (III.C.4) who won an MM and Bar whilst serving with 2/Rifle Brigade. The Sheffield-born miner was killed on 25 September 1917.

On leaving the cemetery look across the fields to the red tiled roof of the farm opposite. This is the rebuilt Anton's Farm which was used as a sniper's position by men of Ronald Poulton Palmer's 1/4 Royal Berkshire Regiment when they came into the line here in 1915. There was much sniping in the front line hereabouts and the Germans held the upper hand for the most part. On 28 April 1915, 17-year-old **Private Frederick Giles** was hit by a sniper's bullet and fell from the parapet of the trench into the arms of Ronald Poulton Palmer. He died of his wound a short time later and was the first man of 1/4 Royal Berks to be buried at Hyde Park Corner (Royal Berks) Cemetery. Looking further – beyond Anton's Farm – there is a wonderful view of the imposing dome of Messines church as it breaks the skyline on a clear day and rising in the distance to the left is Kemmelberg.

Retrace your route to ❺, turning left at the three CWGC signs and follow the track into the woods signposted Toronto Avenue, Ploegsteert Wood Military and Rifle House cemeteries. Continue to the junction of tracks and turn left, continuing to a cross tracks. Toronto Avenue Cemetery ❼ is down the track 100m to your left. Taking its name from the path of the same name, Toronto Avenue is another small piece of Australia in that it is the last resting place of seventy-eight officers and men of 16 Australian Infantry Brigade who were casualties of the Battle of Messines 1917. Typical of many of these men is the story of 40-year-old **Private Godfrey Allison** (A.28) who enlisted in Australia on 18 May 1916 and arrived in England seven months later in January 1917. On 14 March that year he arrived at Etaples and from there was posted to 33/Battalion. He was wounded in the leg on 7 May which warranted a twelve-day stay in hospital. Rejoining his unit on the 19th in time for the assault on Messines, he was killed in action on 9 June 1917. Like the Kiwis buried at Messines, he had come a very long way to die for the mother country.

Return to the cross tracks and go straight over following signs for

Ploegsteert Wood and Rifle House cemeteries. The ride you are now on did not exist on trench maps and was created when the wood was replanted, but for part of the way it follows roughly along the line of **Fleet Street**, one of several routes that made use of pre-existing tracks or rides in the wood. Off to the left and running parallel to your route was another very important north–south track called **Hunter Avenue** which was protected by a line of British pill boxes. It should be noted, however, that today the woodland to either side is private and this should be respected at all times. The first cemetery you come to on your right ❽ is **Ploegsteert Wood Cemetery**. This is a beautiful and peaceful spot set in a glade in the woods. The cemetery is the result of the enclosure of a number of small regimental cemeteries and contains 164 burials. Plot II was originally named the Somerset Light Infantry Cemetery in December 1914, the thirty-two graves it contains, as well as ten in Plot I, are all from that battalion. Plot IV, the Bucks Cemetery, was made by the Ox and Bucks Light Infantry, in April 1915. Plot III contains graves of 1/5 Gloucesters, the Loyal North Lancs and a number of Canadian graves, casualties of June to October 1915. **Lieutenant George Parr** (II.C.5) was one of five officers of 1/Somerset Light Infantry who died on 19 December 1914 and are buried together. Parr died at the head of his men during an attack on 'The Birdcage' and was the only son of Major General Sir Henry Parr. A fluent French and German speaker, he was employed as a liaison officer to Brigadier General Hunter-Weston during the Battle of the Marne. **Captain Robert Orr** (II.C.3) was another of the battalion's officers killed that day. He was originally from Newcastle, Co. Down where his family's firm of solicitors was based. **Private Reginald Cole** (III.D.13) was killed in action whilst on sentry duty on the morning of 12 May 1915. His parents ran the 'Famous 2, Gentleman's Outfitters' in the High Street, Cheltenham, whilst nearby is **Private Archibald Hawkins** (III.C.7) who served with Reginald Cole in 1/5 Gloucesters. He was killed on 6 June 1915 and also came from Cheltenham, it is likely the two boys knew each other. Tragically, Archie's younger brother, 19-year-old **Lieutenant Reginald Hawkins**, was killed on 29 July 1918 flying with 79 Squadron. Both brothers are commemorated on the grave of their parents at Cheltenham Cemetery.

Leave the cemetery and turn right. Up ahead you will see the entrance to **Rifle House Cemetery** ❾. This is another very calming spot and was named after a timber-built shelter of the same name erected by 1/ Rifle Brigade which was very near to a junction of communication trenches named Piccadilly Circus, Fleet Street and Haymarket. A concrete shelter built by New Zealand Engineers on 6 April 1917 was erected near the same spot.

The earliest graves are of 1/Rifle Brigade in Plot IV and the latest are from June 1916. Of the 230 burials here the youngest is a 15-year-old Jewish boy from Stoke Newington, **Rifleman Robert Barnett** (IV.E.10). Serving with 1/Rifle Brigade, he was killed with twenty-six others from the battalion during the attack on the notorious Birdcage on 19 December 1914. Killed on the same day was 49-year-old **Private Rothwell Lomax** (IV.G.1). The oldest casualty in the cemetery, Lomax was serving with 1/King's Liverpool Regiment. In addition to Robert Barnett there are a further eighteen teenage casualties buried here between the ages of 17 and 19, many of which are amongst the twenty-four casualties from the Rifle Brigade buried here.

On leaving the cemetery retrace your steps all the way back to Mud Lane ❺ and turn left. Continue to the junction of tracks and turn left into the woods. This very straight track was called **Bunhill Row,** named after the street of the same name where the HQ of the Territorial Force unit of the London Rifle Brigade was based. Note the many curly 'pig's tails' screw pickets in the fields which once used to hold up the British barbed-wire entanglements and are, in many cases, still used by the farmers for the same purpose.

Continue through the woods noting the uneven ground to your right and left which still bears the marks of shell craters in places. Approximately halfway along you will notice a track running off to your left at right angles. This was the junction of Bunhill Row with the **Strand ❿** communication trench. The entrance to the Strand is now wired off to prevent unauthorized access and, like the routes to Hunter Avenue further east, should be taken seriously. That said, even by travelling the accessible tracks such as that which you are now on, one can get at least a flavour of what it might have been like to have been in the wood during the war as its texture was much the same then as it is today. The wood escaped the absolute obliteration that was the fate of many other woods sited in sectors that saw heavy and continual fighting. Although still deadly for the rash or unwary, the sector was deemed to be relatively 'safe' and so played host to 'raw' units coming

Rifle House Cemetery.

into the front line for the first time as a nursery sector. It was here – usually attached to experienced battalions – that men could begin to learn the unfamiliar and dark arts of the troglodyte world of trench warfare.

At the end of the track follow through a 90 degree bend to the right and continue to a junction of tracks beside a large information board. You are now travelling along the line of the communication trench that was known as **Regent Street**. Turn right off the main gravel track on to a narrower track between fields which leads towards a copse ahead. At the cross tracks ahead ⓫ continue straight across, over the line of a light railway that ran left to right across your path and which was used to ferry supplies towards the front line. With the copse on your right and a hedge close on your left, continue until you see the enclosures of a cemetery on your right. This is **Strand Military Cemetery**. Turn right at the main road to reach the entrance ⓬. Almost opposite the cemetery entrance a farm road leads down to what was known on trench maps as Cinder Farm.

Charing Cross advanced aid post.

The Ploegsteert Memorial to the Missing.

The cemetery began as a small burial plot in 1914 close to a nearby advanced dressing station called Charing Cross but was not used again until 1917. After the Armistice graves were brought in from some small cemeteries and from the battlefields lying mainly between Wijtschate and Armentières. Today there are over 1,400 graves here of which over 350 are unidentified. Immediately inside the cemetery there are special memorials to nineteen men and a Duhallow block commemorating eleven men whose graves were lost in Ploegsteert Wood New Cemetery. There are also eight graves dating from May 1940. The three earliest burials are **Private Samuel Fletcher** (VI.A.11) 18/Hussars, who died on 15 October 1914, **Private William McCann** (IX.G.8), who died of wounds on 19 October, and **Private Edward Vaux** (X.I.12), who died the next day. Royal Canadian Engineers officer **Lieutenant Duncan Bell-Irving** (X.H.9) was killed by shellfire on 26 February 1915 and is thought to be the first Canadian officer to be killed in the Great War. There is another teenage Rifle Brigade soldier buried here, 17-year-old **Rifleman Albert Collins** (VIII.R.2), who was killed on 11 April 1915, a month described in the 1/Rifle Brigade war diary as a 'relatively quiet' in which the battalion lost forty-nine officers and men killed and eighty-nine wounded!

Turn right after leaving the cemetery and continue towards the large Ploegsteert Memorial to the Missing which will come into view ahead. After the second private house on the right stop at a private drive and turn to look back into the fields over your right shoulder to see a series of three concrete bunkers ⓭ which were part of the **Charing Cross** advanced aid post. Now on private land, permission is required to visit them.

As you approach the Cafe L'Auberge you will find **Hyde Park Corner (Royal Berks) Cemetery** on the right just beyond the cafe building and across the road the larger **Berks Cemetery Extension** and Rosenberg Chateau plots together with the circular **Ploegsteert Memorial to the Missing**. Hyde Park Corner was first used in April 1915 by 1/4 Royal Berkshire Regiment and was used at intervals until November 1917. It contains eighty-three Commonwealth and four German war graves. Here lies **Ronald Poulton Palmer** (B.11), **Frederick Giles** (B.13) and 16-year-old **Albert French** (B.2). On 4 January 1917, 2/Irish Rifles arrived back in the Ploegsteert sector and almost immediately began taking casualties. **Second Lieutenant**

Patrick Jackson (A.2) was a veteran of the Somme campaign and was wounded on 1 July 1916 at Thiepval. He joined 2/Royal Irish Rifles on 9 December 1916 and was killed less than a month later on 4 January 1917. In the same battalion and only appointed acting captain on 16 December 1916, **Ernest Leach** (B.10.) was killed on 2 January 1917. Another member of the battalion, **Rifleman Samuel McBride** (A.17) was shot for desertion at Hope Farm on 7 December 1916. McBride had been sentenced to two years' imprisonment with hard labour in 1915 on a charge of desertion but was released on suspension in January 1916. Whilst the battalion was in the Vimy Ridge sector in May 1916, McBride went absent again and was caught near Boulogne.

England Rugby Union Captain and Royal Berkshire Regiment soldier Ronald Poulton Palmer.

The extension was begun in June 1916 and used continuously until September 1917. Plots II and III were added in 1930 when graves were brought in from the nearby Rosenberg Chateau Military Cemetery and Extension. Of the 876 graves here only 3 are unidentified. **Rifleman Leonard Crossley** (I. E.20) and **William Crossley** (I. E.21) were twin brothers and both served with 21/King's Royal Rifle Corps. Aged 31 years, they were killed on 30 June 1916 by shellfire whilst in reserve billets. Another soldier with two brothers was **Private Leslie Blackman** (I.B.16) from Ballarat, Australia, who served with D Company, 5/Battalion. Leslie, a gas fitter employed by the Melbourne Gas Company, was killed on 29 June 1916. His two brothers were both MC holders and serving with the Australian infantry as were his two cousins who also both won an MC. All survived the war.

Bombadier William Kerr (II.D.17) was a wool sorter at Waingawa Freezing Works in New Zealand. He enlisted in August 1914 and was assigned to the New Zealand Field Artillery, serving in Gallipoli before arriving in France in time for the Somme offensive. He was killed on 16 April 1917, possibly by German counter-battery fire on his battery. He is commemorated at Papanui on the club honours board as one of the seventeen men from Merivale Rugby Club to die in the Great War.

The imposing Ploegsteert Memorial to the Missing commemorates

11,447 Commonwealth soldiers who have no known grave. The memorial serves the area from the line Caestre–Dranoutre–Warneton to the north, to Haverskerque–Estaires–Fournes to the south, including the towns of Hazebrouck, Merville, Bailleul and Armentières, the Forest of Nieppe and Ploegsteert Wood. Those commemorated on the memorial did not die in major offensives, such as those that took place around Ypres to the north or Loos to the south. Most were killed in the course of the day-to-day trench warfare that characterized this part of the line, or in small-scale, set-piece engagements such as the attacks on the Birdcage and at Prowse Point. However, it does not include the names of officers and men of Canadian or Indian regiments who can be found on the Memorials at Vimy and Neuve Chapelle. On the first Friday of each month the Last Post is sounded here at 7.00pm. On Panel 1 are the names of three VC winners, **Private James McKenzie**, of 2/Scots Guards who won his Cross for rescuing a wounded comrade and was killed on 19 December 1914, the 43-year-old Rotherham miner **Sapper William Hackett**, of 254 Tunnelling Company who refused to leave an injured comrade after the tunnel he was working was badly damaged by German counter-mining, and **Captain Thomas Pryce**, 4/Grenadier Guards. Pryce already held an MC and Bar when he held up an enemy battalion with some forty men for over ten hours on 13 April 1918. There are six men originally of the Ulster-based North Irish Horse, a cavalry regiment that the great uncle of one of the authors served in, commemorated on Panel 9. They are **Rifleman Thomas McKillop**, **Rifleman John Smith**, **Private George Mark**, **Private Andrew Pepper**, **Private Samuel Pinkerton** and **Private William Timbey**. The regiment was disbanded in 1918 and its officers and men dispersed to Irish infantry regiments. There are nineteen men commemorated on the memorial who, before they went to war, were bell ringers in their parish churches. One of these is **Second Lieutenant Frank Steward Raikes**, a member of the Cambridge University Guild of Bell Ringers, who was killed in action on 9 May 1915 at Aubers Ridge. Educated at Wellington College and Trinity College, Cambridge, he was commissioned on August 1914 into his father's regiment, 2/Rifle Brigade, and his name can be found on Panel 10.

After leaving the cemetery you may well find a coffee or beer in the cafe the perfect conclusion to your walk.

Appendix 1

Museums and CWGC Cemeteries

MUSEUMS

The Raversijde Domain Atlantic Wall Museum
★ ★ ★

Cafe and toilets

The Atlantic Wall Museum is a large coastal complex in the dunes of the former estate of Prince Karel located near the airport at Ostende on the N318. The site is part of the Second World War Atlantic Wall fortifications but does contain the Aachen Battery which was one of the numerous coastal batteries active during the Great War. The site is open from 2.00pm until 5.00pm from 1 April to 11 November. At weekends and holidays opening hours are 10.30am to 6.00pm. Included in the admission fee of €6.50 is an audio guide.

The Ijzertoren www.ijzertoren.org
★ ★ ★ ★

Cafe and toilets

The 84m high tower dominates the town of Diksmuide with its twenty-two floors of exhibits covering all aspects of the Belgian front. There is a political undertone to much of the display in that it celebrates the Flemish soldier and the Flemish language. Well worth a visit if you are in the area. The site is open all year round except in January. Admission is €7 for adults, €5 if you are 65 or over. Children up to 6 years are free and young people pay only €1. Groups of twenty or more pay €5 per person.

Trenches of Death
★ ★ ★

Cafe and toilets

These preserved trenches are to be found about 1.5km north of

Diksmuide and can easily be reached on foot or by bike from Diksmuide. From the centre of Diksmuide cross the river and turn right along the Ijzerdijk, the trenches are to be found on a bend in the river. The trenches feature galleries, shelters, fire-steps, concrete duckboards and concrete sandbags providing the visitor with a very good impression of Great War trenches in this sector of the Western Front. These trenches were held by the Belgians for over four years during the Battles of the Yser. The trenches are open from 9.00am until 12.30pm and 1.00pm until 5.00pm from 1 April to 30 September. Outside of these dates the site is only open at weekends. There is plenty of parking for vehicles and entrance is free.

Yorkshire Trench
* *
No facilities
The most straightforward route from Ieper is north along the N368 towards Boezinge passing under the N38. At Boezinge turn right over the canal and follow the road (Langemarkseweg) round to the right to take the fourth turning right. Follow this road through the industrial estate until you reach the trenches on your right. There is ample parking. The name Yorkshire Trench was given to the front-line trenches dug by men of the 49th (West Riding) Division at Boezinge during 1915 and 1916. Opened in 2003 after extensive work by local battlefield archaeologists, the reconstructed trench system is at its original depth and features fire-steps and loopholes. The site is permanently open and entrance is free. Information panels in Flemish, English and French provide additional information and the site has the added attraction of several British trench mortars, many of which were found in the area beyond the trench near the canal.

Ramparts Museum
* * *
Toilets and cafe
Located next to the Lille Gate on the Rijselsestraat in Ieper, the museum is at the rear of the Cafe Klein Rijsel. Tickets can be purchased inside at the bar. This is a surprisingly good museum with some excellent authentic exhibits positioned at intervals in a reconstruction of trenches, tunnels and dugouts. The background sounds of battle add to the experience. Non-smokers may not wish to dwell too long in

the bar where there are other exhibits. Open from 10.30am to 8.00pm. Closed on Wednesdays. Admission is €3.

In Flanders Fields Museum   www.inflandersfields.be
★ ★ ★ ★

Toilets and souvenir/book shop
Newly refurbished (2012), the museum is situated in the magnificent reconstructed Cloth Hall which stands on the edge of Grote Markt in the centre of Ieper. There is plenty of car parking available in the square or nearby but be warned, at the height of the tourist season parking can be difficult. You will need to pay except on Sundays and holidays. Each visitor receives a personalised microchip poppy bracelet – (€1) which can be kept or returned on exit for a refund – which allows the discovery of four personal stories of those who served in the Ypres Salient in the Great War via numerous interactive displays/events. The museum is open daily from 1 April to 15 November from 10.00am until 6.00pm. Winter opening is from 16 November to 31 March when it is open every day apart from Monday, from 10.00am until 5.00pm. Admission is adults €8 per person, children and students aged between 7 and 25 €1. There is no charge for children under 7. Concessionary rates of €5.50 per adult are available for groups. The charge for school groups is €1 per person. The €1 bracelet fee is extra and an optional visit to the bell tower is €2. The museum has a Facebook page.

Hooge Crater Museum   www.hoogecrater.com/en/war-museum
★ ★ ★ ★

Cafe, souvenir shop and toilets
The museum is located 4km east of Ieper on the N8. Housed in a former chapel and school built directly opposite the **Hooge Crater Cemetery**, the museum, which is privately owned, has a fascinating collection of Great War memorabilia and artefacts including a full-size German Fokker Triplane. There is ample parking either in front of the museum or in the small side road to the left of the building. The museum is open every day except Monday from 10.00am until 6.00pm. Admission is adults €4.50 per person, children and students €2.00. Concessionary rates of €3.00 per person are available for groups of twenty or more. A guided tour with a historical overview is available through a personal audio set in English and Dutch for which there is no charge.

Hooge Crater Museum from Hooge Crater Cemetery.

The Hooge trenches/craters are in the grounds of the nearby Hotel Kasteelhof and group access can be arranged from there. Admission is €1 per person. Group concessions for a party of twenty or less is €10 and for groups up to a maximum size of fifty, admission is €15. http://www.hotelkasteelhofthooghe.be

Sanctuary Wood Museum Hill 62
★ ★

Cafe, toilets and books, postcards and memorabilia are on sale in the cafe

This museum can be reached by following the N8 (Menin road) out of Ieper until you see the signs for the Canadian Memorial on your right. As you turn onto the access road called Maple Drive, Sanctuary Wood is on your left and the museum is just past **Sanctuary Wood Cemetery** on the right. There is plenty of good parking available. The Sanctuary Wood Museum is privately owned. The museum collection contains a large amount of material gathered from the battlefield, some of which is of Second World War vintage. Unfortunately, little of it is identified leaving the visitor to make their own deductions as to its origin and purpose. The museum does have a remarkable collection of photographs and a large, rare collection of three-dimensional photo images in viewing boxes, some of which are quite lurid in detail. Probably the greatest asset the museum has is the trench system at the rear of the building. The museum is open daily from 10.00am until 6.00pm and has a Facebook page.

CWGC signposts with their distinctive green and white paintwork.

Memorial Museum Passchendaele 1917   www.passchendaele.be
★ ★ ★ ★ ★

Toilets and bookshop

Located in the old Zonnebeke Chateau on the Ieperstraat (N332) in Zonnebeke. The museum reopened in 2004 after an extensive refurbishment and includes an impressive reconstructed trench and dugout system, the access to which is down steep stairs, a lift is available for the less able-bodied. At the time of writing extensive improvements were underway both within the museum itself and in the local area to link the museum with Polygon Wood and Tyne Cot Cemetery by two walking and cycling routes. The museum is open from Monday to Friday 9.00am until 5.00pm. During December and January the museum is closed to visitors. Entrance is €5 for adults and €1 for children and students. Concessionary rates are available for groups of fifteen or more. Entrance for guides and teachers attached to groups is free and there is ample parking. The museum has a Facebook page.

Mesen (Messines) info@mesen.be

The small museum in the Stadhuis at Mesen has been closed for the foreseeable future, although the collection remains *in situ*. However, if you wish to visit the bell tower and crypt of Sint-Niklaas Church you must arrange your visit through the Stadhuis.

Kemmel & Bayernwald Trenches (Croonart Wood)

★ ★ ★

No facilities

Access to these German open-air trenches must be obtained from the tourist information office at Kemmel. The office is situated in the centre of Kemmel on Reningelststraat (N304) and has a small parking area outside. The office is open from 1 April until 31 October from 9.00am until midday and from 1.15pm until 5.00pm. At the weekend and on national holidays opening is from 10.00am until midday and from 2.00pm until 5.00pm. During November through to the end of March the office is closed at the weekend and on national holidays. Tickets are €1.50 each which will give you access to the trenches and the electronic code for the gate and instructions on how to find the trenches. Once you have arrived you will see **Croonaert Chapel Cemetery** across the fields to your left. On your right is a large pond. Park and continue on foot to the main entrance. **Adolf Hitler** served in this area during the Great War and it was for his work as a runner carrying messages that he was awarded the Iron Cross. He later visited the site in 1940. Local battlefield archaeologists have faithfully followed German trench maps in both layout and reconstruction. There are also four bunkers on the site and an entrance to a mine shaft.

VISITING COMMONWEALTH WAR GRAVES COMMISSION CEMETERIES

In the area covered by this guidebook there are over 175 British, Commonwealth and Allied military cemeteries. There are also four German military cemeteries.

CWGC cemeteries are noted for their high standards of horticultural excellence and the image of rows of headstones set amid grass pathways and flowering shrubs is one every battlefield visitor takes away with them. On each headstone is the badge of the regiment or corps or in the case of Commonwealth forces, the national emblem. Below that is the name and rank of the individual together with any decoration they may have received. At the base is often an inscription that has been chosen by the family. Headstones of Victoria Cross winners also have the motif of the decoration on their headstone.

Where there is doubt as to the exact location of a grave a special memorial headstone can be found with the words 'Believed to be buried in this cemetery'. Where graveyards were destroyed by shellfire or lost in the turmoil of the battlefield the words 'Known to be buried in this cemetery' or 'buried near this spot' are used. Typical of these shell-torn burial grounds is **Maple Copse Cemetery** near Zillebeke. The cemetery was largely destroyed in the fighting that took place in the area, so much so that after the Armistice very few of the graves could be positively identified and consequently the visitor today will find 230 special memorials. Graves of the unidentified are marked with the inscription suggested by **Rudyard Kipling**, 'Known Unto God'.

The majority of cemeteries will have a cemetery register and a visitor's book which can usually be found behind the small bronze panel near the entrance. Please make a point of signing the visitor's book before you leave. Any cemetery containing over 40 graves will have a Cross of Sacrifice designed by Sir Reginald Blomfield and those with over 1,000 graves also have a Stone of Remembrance. There are exceptions to this and the **RE Grave at Railway Wood** – seen on Route 12 – is one. In each cemetery mentioned in this guidebook we have attempted to provide the visitor with a little detail about some of the men who lie therein. Some are indeed noteworthy because of their family circumstances or they achieved recognition as poets or writers or were decorated for gallantry. Others we have highlighted because they were very young, have interesting connections or died in particularly tragic circumstances. We have also indicated the location of soldiers who were 'shot at dawn'. However, the vast majority of men buried in CWGC cemeteries simply died doing their job and it is these men, whose names can be lost in the sea of white headstones, which are often passed by unnoticed. Many of these men, particularly in the larger cemeteries and in the more isolated sites, may never have had a visitor pause and read their name, wonder how they died and what their personal circumstances were. Every one of these men has a story, a family and someone who loved them and in an attempt to draw attention to these almost forgotten men we have made a conscious effort to highlight at least one individual – usually an NCO or a private soldier – in each cemetery, whom you can visit and spend a moment with before you leave. Further information and directions to each cemetery can be obtained from the CWGC website at www.cwgc.org.

Appendix 2

Where to Find VC Winners

There were ninety-seven VCs won by serving soldiers and two by airmen in the Ypres area during the four years of the Great War. The following VC holders, not all of whom won their cross in the Ypres theatre of war (indicated by *), are buried in cemeteries or commemorated on memorials within the area covered by this guidebook and are listed chronologically. Those names marked with a † were either killed during the action that resulted in their award or died soon afterwards from wounds received in the action.

Name	Burial/Commemoration	Reference
*Grenfell, Captain Francis 9/Lancers	Vlamertinghe Military Cemetery	II.B.14
*Johnston, Major William 59/Field Company Royal Engineers (RE)	Perth Cemetery (China Wall)	III.C.12
*Brooke, Captain James † 2/Gordon Highlanders	Zantvoorde British Cemetery	VI.E.2
Vallentin, Captain John † 1/South Staffords	Menin Gate Memorial	Panel 35
*Mackenzie, Private James 2/Scots Guards	Ploegsteert Memorial	Panel 1
Morrow, Private Robert † 1/Royal Irish Fusiliers	White House Cemetery	IV.A.44
Fisher, Lance Corporal Frederick † 13/Battalion, Canadian Expeditionary Force (CEF)	Menin Gate Memorial	Panel 24
Hall, Company Sergeant Major Frederick † 8/Battalion CEF	Menin Gate Memorial	Panel 24

Name	Burial/Commemoration	Reference
Warner, Private Edward *1/Bedfordshires*	Menin Gate Memorial	Panel 33
Lynn, Private John † *2/Lancashire Fusiliers*	(Grave lost) Grootebeek British Cemetery	Vlamertinghe Churchyard Memorial
Woodroffe, Second Lieutenant Sidney † *8/Rifle Brigade*	Menin Gate Memorial	Panel 46
Hallowes, Second Lieutenant Rupert *4/Middlesex*	Bedford House Cemetery	XIV.B.36
***Hackett**, Sapper William † *254 Tunnelling Company*	Ploegsteert Memorial	Panel 1
Youens, Second Lieutenant Frederick † *13/Durham Light infantry*	Railway Dugouts Burial Ground	I.O.3
Barratt, Private Thomas † *7/South Staffords*	Essex Farm Cemetery	I.Z.8
Best-Dunkley, Lieutenant Colonel Bertram † *2/5 Lancashire Fusiliers*	Mendinghem Military Cemetery	III.D.I
Colyer-Fergusson, Captain Thomas † *2/Northamptons*	Menin Road South Mil' Cemetery	II.E.I
Davies, Corporal James † *13/Royal Welsh Fusiliers*	Canada Farm Cemetery	II.B.18
Hewitt, Second Lieutenant Denis † *14/Hampshires*	Menin Gate Memorial	Panel 35

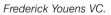

Frederick Youens VC. *John Skinner VC.* *Louis McGuffie VC.*

Name	Burial/Commemoration	Reference
Ackroyd, Captain Harold *RAMC*	Birr Crossroads Cemetery	Special Mem 7
Chavasse, Captain Noel † *RAMC*	Brandhoek New Mil' Cemetery	III.B.15
Skinner, CSM John † *1/KOSB*	Vlamertinghe New Mil' Cemetery	XIII.H.15
Birks, Second Lieutenant Frederick *6/Battalion Australian Imperial Force (AIF)*	Perth Cemetery (China Wall)	I.G.45
Bugden, Private Patrick *31/Battalion AIF*	Hooge Crater Cemetery	VIII.C.5
Bent, Lieutenant Colonel Philip † *9/Leicesters*	Tyne Cot Memorial	Panel 50
McGee, Sergeant Lewis *40/Battalion AIF*	Tyne Cot Cemetery	XX.D.I
Robertson, Captain Clement † *1/Battalion Tank Corps*	Oxford Road Cemetery	III.F.7
Clamp, Corporal William † *6/Yorkshire*	Tyne Cot Memorial	Panel 52
Jeffries, Captain Clarence † *34/Battalion AIF*	Tyne Cot Cemetery	XL.E.I
McKenzie, Lieutenant Hugh † *7/Company Canadian MGC*	Menin Gate Memorial	Panel 5326
Robertson, Private James † *27/Battalion CEF*	Tyne Cot Cemetery	LVIII.D.26
Dougall, Major Eric *LXXXVIII Brigade RFA*	Westoutre British Cemetery	Special Mem 1
***Pryce**, Captain Thomas † *4/Grenadier Guards*	Ploegsteert Memorial	Panel 1
McGuffie, Sergeant Louis *1/5/King's Own Scottish Borderers*	Zantvoorde British Cemetery	I.D.12
Seaman, Lance Corporal Ernest † *2/Royal Inniskilling Fusiliers*	Tyne Cot Memorial	Panel 70

Noel Chavasse VC and Bar.

The only individual to win two Victoria Crosses in the Great War was **Noel Chavasse**. A medical officer with 1/10 King's Liverpool, he won his first cross for actions on 9/10 August 1916 at Guillemont on the Somme, his second for his actions rescuing the wounded between 31 July and 2 August 1917 when his battalion was in action at Wieltje.

Appendix 3
Demarcation Stones

Demarcation stones are the stone monuments to be found along the battle line of the Western Front in Belgium and France. The idea was introduced in 1920 by the French sculptor Paul Moreau-Vauthier to commemorate the line from which the Allies launched their offensive against the German Army in 1918 and consequently correspond with the furthest points reached by the Germans. The original idea was to place a stone monument for every kilometre along the 650km line of the Western Front from Nieuwpoort to Pfetterhouse on the French–Swiss border. Between 1921 and 1930 118 demarcation stones were put in place, 22 in Belgium and 96 in France. During the Second World War 24 of the demarcation stone monuments were destroyed. Today some 93 still exist, although some are in poor condition.

Demarcation Stone near Zillebeke.

Further Reading

There is a vast library of ever-increasing titles covering aspects of the Great War on the Belgian front. The nine **Battleground Europe** titles which focus on the Western Front in Belgium provide a host of supplementary information on some of the most visited parts of the area. Here you will find the personal experiences of soldiers who served in the area, contemporary photographs and trench maps.

Nigel Cave, *Sanctuary Wood & Hooge,* 1997.

Nigel Cave, *Hill 60,* 2004.

Nigel Cave, *Passchendaele,* 2007.

Nigel Cave, *Polygon Wood,* 2007.

Graham Keach, *St Julian,* 2001.

Stephen McGreal, *Boesinghe,* 2010.

Mike O'Connor, *Airfields & Airmen of Ypres,* 2001.

Mike O'Connor, *Airfields & Airmen of the Channel Coast,* 2006.

Peter Oldham, *Messines Ridge,* 2003.

Augmenting the above is *Walking the Salient* (2004) by Paul Reed, which suggests several of the favourite walking routes of the author accompanied by accounts of the actions which took place along them.

The five titles in the **Cameos of the Western Front** series (2004–2009) written by the late Tony Spagnoly and Ted Smith and aptly called *Salient Points One* to *Five*, contain a wealth of detail and research into a wide range of incidents and actions that took place in the Ypres Salient. These highly interesting and informative books are an excellent addition to any battlefield visitor's bookshelf. These, the **Battleground Europe** series and *Walking the Salient* are published by Pen & Sword Books, www.pen-and-sword.co.uk.

There are a number of other battlefield guidebooks available that provide a more detailed overview but are generally written for the tourist who is primarily using a vehicle to explore the area. *Major & Mrs Holt's Battlefield Guide to the Ypres Salient* (Pen & Sword, 2006) is more Ypres Salient specific but the recently updated Rose Coombes Guide, *Before Endeavours Fade* (After the Battle Publications, 2006), which is in A4 format, covers a large portion of the Western Front from Nieuwpoort to the Marne. Both are good value.

Osprey Publishing, www.ospreypublishing.com, publishes a comprehensive Great War series of books, which includes *First Ypres* (1998) by David Lomas, *Messines 1917* (2010) by Alexander Turner, *The British Army on the Western Front 1916* (2007) by Bruce Gudmundsson and *World War 1 Trench Warfare* (2002) by Stephen Bull. There are also some very informative titles about the various expeditionary forces of the Allied armies and a mini-series covering the German Army. Two volumes that are always useful as reference are Gerald Gliddon's *VCs Handbook, The Western Front 1914–1918* (Sutton, 2005) and Martin Middlebrook's excellent guide to British Army infantry divisions, *Your Country Needs You* (Pen & Sword, 2000). For battlefield visitors who wish to expand their knowledge in more depth, the following may be of interest:

Ian Beckett, *Ypres, The First Battle, 1914* Pearson, 2006

Ian Connerty et al., *At the Going Down of the Sun*, Lannoo, 2001
The stories of 365 soldiers of the Great War who died in Flanders Fields

Jon Cooksey (ed.), *Blood and Iron Letters from the Western Front*, Pen & Sword, 2011
Letters written by Hugh Montagu Butterworth who served with 9th Battalion The Rifle Brigade at Hooge and on the Bellewaarde Ridge in 1915

Jon Cooksey, *Flanders 1915*, Pen & Sword, 2005
A photographic record of 1/5th York and Lancaster Regiment in the Ypres Salient in the summer of 1915

Dominiek Dendooven, *Ypres as Holy Ground Menin Gate & Last Post*, de Klaproos, 2000

John Dixon, *Magnificent but not War – The Second Battle of Ypres 1915*, Pen & Sword, 2009

Peter Hart and Nigel Steel, *Passchendaele The Sacrificial Ground*, Cassell, 2000

Jerry Murland, *Aristocrats Go To War – Uncovering the Zillebeke Cemetery*, Pen & Sword, 2010
The stories behind those who lie in the Zillebeke Churchyard Cemetery

Alan Palmer, *The Salient – Ypres 1914–18*, Constable, 2007

Ian Passingham, *Pillars of Fire The Battle of Messines Ridge, June 1917*, Sutton, 2004

Index